# AUSTRALIAN
# BATS

## Sue Churchill

Second edition

JACANA
B O O K S

ALLEN&UNWIN

This edition published in 2008 by Allen & Unwin
First edition published by New Holland Publishers (Australia) Pty Ltd in 1988
Copyright © in text: Sue Churchill 2008
Copyright © in photographs: Sue Churchill 2008, unless otherwise credited
Copyright © in illustrations: Sue Churchill 2008

Jacana Books, an imprint of
Allen & Unwin
83 Alexander Street
Crows Nest NSW 2065
Australia
Phone:    (61 2) 8425 0100
Fax:       (61 2) 9906 2218
Email:     info@allenandunwin.com
Web:      www.allenandunwin.com

National Library of Australia
Cataloguing-in-Publication entry:

    Churchill, Sue.

    Australian bats

    2nd ed.

    978 1 74175 461 2 (pbk.)

    Includes index.
    Bibliography.

    Bats—Australia.
    Bats—Australia—Identification.

    599.40994

Photograph on p. 1: Michael Pennay & Terry Reardon
Design and typesetting by Avril Makula
Additional typesetting by Midland Typesetters, Australia
Printed in China through Colorcraft Ltd, Hong Kong

# Contents

# Acknowledgements

I have been delighted and encouraged by the help I have received from so many people during this revision.

Above all I would like to thank Bruce Thomson for generously providing me with his superb photographs of most of the Australian bats. Others who kindly donated their outstanding photographs include Lindy Lumsden, Glenn Hoye, Michael Pennay, Terry Reardon, Paul Barden, Damian Milne, Bruce Taubert, Chris Tidemann and Al Young. Peter Helman and Paul Zborowski helped me with my own photo collection.

I am particularly grateful to Greg Ford, Brad Law, Damian Milne, Michael Pennay and Melanie Venz for help and support in many ways. Steve Van Dyck and Heather Janetzki at the Queensland Museum have been very hospitable and helpful. A special thank you to Heather Janetzki for feedback about the identification keys.

Taxonomic discussions with Belinda Appleton, Frank Bonaccorso, Les Hall, Kris Helgen, Harry Parnaby and Terry Reardon helped me to decide what species to include. The final taxonomic decisions were my own.

Measurements and distribution records for various species were provided by Belinda Appleton, Kyle Armstrong, Paul Barden, Andrew Breed, Bob Bullen, Anja Divljan, Adam Fawcett, Greg Ford, Sam Fox, Glenn Hoye, David James, Heather Janetzki, Cary Kuiper, Brad Law, Jenny Mclean, Brendan Metcalf, Damian Milne, Steve Murphy, Harry Parnaby, Michael Pennay, Terry Reardon, April Reside, Monika Rhodes, Wes Sechrest, Garry Smith, Melanie Venz and Al Young.

Kyle Armstrong, Andrew Breed, Bob Bullen, Roger Coles, Chris Corben, Greg Ford, Sam Fox, Les Hall, Kristofer Helgen, Brad Law, Lindy Lumsden, David James, Jenny Mclean, Nikki Markus, Norm McKenzie, Brendan Metcalf, Damian Milne, Steve Murphy, Michael Pennay, Terry Reardon, April Reside, Monika Rhodes, Bruce Thomson, Chris Tidemann and Al Young provided references, reprints, reports, unpublished theses and anecdotal notes.

Help with echolocation calls came from long and valuable discussions with Roger Coles and Chris Corben. Other calls were provided by Kyle Armstrong, Paul Barden, Luke Hogan, Lindy Lumsden and Terry Reardon.

Thank you to Louise Egerton, my publisher at Allen & Unwin, who encouraged me to do this revision and I have greatly enjoyed the task. A special thank you to my editor Clara Finlay for all her hard work, enthusiasm and dedication, Avril Makula for layout, Rachel Sullivan for copyediting and Sue Vader for proofreading; their efforts have greatly improved the book.

Rogan, as always, helped with everything!

# Introduction

This book has been written with two aims: it is hoped that the initial chapters will stimulate the interest of the general naturalist who wishes to learn more about bats and that the keys and species accounts will be a valuable resource for bat researchers and people requiring detailed ecological information on particular species. I have attempted to use as few technical terms as possible.

Readers of the previous edition of this book appear to have risen to the challenge of the huge gaps in our knowledge of many Australian bats, and their publications over the past decade have enabled me to provide far more comprehensive species accounts.

Inevitably, there are some name changes. The 1988 first edition incorporated the dramatic changes in the names of bats that had taken place in the previous 20 years, such as the little brown bat, *Eptesicus pumilus*, being recognised as nine species of *Vespadelus*. The changes have continued in the last 10 years and in this edition I have incorporated all the changes that have been reported in the literature. They include species upgraded from subspecies, species found to be invalid and removed, newly described species and many currently waiting to be named. Some of the taxonomy is still unpublished but fortunately the researchers working on these bats have generously provided me with their preliminary results. This has allowed me to include most of the bats likely to be considered valid species in the near future. For details of changes to taxonomy, see the Appendix.

Of course, the more things change the more they remain the same. For example, the names of the long-eared bats, genus *Nyctophilus*, after so many changes, now conform closely to those suggested 80 years ago by Ellis Troughton in the 1926 edition of Le Souef and Burrell's *The Wild Animals of Australasia*!

I hope I have managed to do as well in this book! I also hope the book is useful, that it gives you pleasure and that it stimulates you to learn more about these fascinating animals.

MICHAEL PENNAY & TERRY REARDON

**ABOVE** The lesser long-eared bat, *Nyctophilus geoffroyi*, echolocating in flight.

# How to use this book

This book is divided into two parts. Part I gives a **general introduction** to the lives of these fascinating beasts. Chapters cover bat biology, where bats live, what they eat, how they reproduce and some of the special aspects of being a bat. Practical aspects of studying bats are also addressed: how to catch and handle them and record useful information, and potential problems and dangers of working with bats.

Part II contains the **keys to identification** and the **species accounts**. Unlike birds, which can be identified at a distance by colour and behaviour, most bats need to be in the hand for accurate identification. Even then many bats are difficult to identify and for this reason often quite arcane details (such as penis shape or ratios of wing bone lengths) need to be examined to tell them apart.

The **identification keys** are arranged in two parts. The first key will get you to the family level. The second level of keys appears at the beginning of each family section, and will take you to species level. The evening bats (Vespertilionidae) are identified in three stages; there are so many species of vespertilionids that an intermediate key to genus has been devised with separate keys to species within each genus.

The keys are a series of alternate choices. Diagrams are provided to help with some of the more detailed characters. The keys will help to confirm or refute your identification: use them in conjunction with the species accounts and distribution maps.

The **species accounts** are standardised to allow quick and easy access to areas of interest.

**COMMON NAME** Bats don't always have common names as they are not commonly known creatures. The taxonomy of the freetail and long-eared bats is still being worked out, and there are few names available. In these cases I have suggested some common names that can be used until the taxonomy is published. I have tried to maintain consistency between editions of this book in the use of common names except for a change in the use of hyphens. I have continued to leave out hyphens for wings and tails (e.g. freetail bat and bentwing bat) but have reinstated them for ears and noses (e.g. long-eared bat and

**LEFT** The grey-headed flying-fox, *Pteropus poliocephalus*, is the most southern-ranging fruit bat.

**RIGHT** The bare-rumped sheathtail bat, *Saccolaimus saccolaimus*, is a little-known species from northern Australia.

BRUCE TAUBERT

broad-nosed bat). Most people who work with bats find it more convenient to use the scientific names.

**SCIENTIFIC NAME** Species accounts are arranged in alphabetical order of scientific names within each family. This allows closely related species to be placed near each other. The keys also use scientific names for the same reason, so if you think you have keyed out your bat, do a quick check with the species on adjacent pages. The author and publication date of the species description are included but, unless a recent addition, the references to these publications are not included in the Bibliography. Many bats are still awaiting a scientific name and for these species use of the common name is more appropriate.

**TAXONOMY** The taxonomy of Australian bats is still being worked out, and this section covers only species that have recently changed or are currently undergoing taxonomic revision. For name changes prior to 1995 please refer to the first edition of this book (Churchill 1998).

**DISTRIBUTION** This describes distribution within Australia and should be used in conjunction with the distribution map. The distribution outside Australia (extralimital distribution) is also listed. It is noteworthy that almost every Australian bat found on the tip of Cape York is also known from New Guinea. All bats that do not reach this far north are endemic to Australia.

**DISTRIBUTION MAP** We still have a lot to learn about our bats so distribution maps are changing with time. If you find that the species you have identified is well outside its known distribution then consider keeping a specimen and sending it to your state museum. This will give you confirmation of your identification as well as providing a valuable record for the museum.

**DESCRIPTION** This is aimed at enabling field identification of live bats. Where possible external characters are used and the most distinctive identification characters are highlighted in **bold**. Although I have described fur colour, it can vary widely within a species. Used in conjunction with the measurements and distribution map, these notes help confirm identification made using the keys. In some cases, where identification using external characters is difficult or impossible, skull and teeth characters are also provided.

**ROOST HABITS** Roost type, colony sizes and roosting behaviour; in other words, where the bats spend their daylight hours.

**HABITAT** Vegetation types in which the bat is known to roost or forage.

**DIET AND FORAGING** Food items and information on flight and foraging patterns.

**REPRODUCTION** The timing of the major reproduction events in this species.

**MEASUREMENTS** A series of external measurements, usually from live bats. These assist in field identification, and most of the measurements were taken in the field. There is sometimes considerable geographical size variation within any one species and I have attempted to provide measurements from different areas where possible (bats from cooler climates are generally larger than those from warmer climates). The source of the measurements is given at the bottom of each table. Where several sources are listed the information has been combined. Not all measurements are available for all species. See **Handling, measuring and examining bats** for abbreviations and details of how the measurements are made.

**REFERENCES** An alphabetically arranged list of authors and dates of the source material used for each species account. The list is not comprehensive but provides a useful guide to further information. Full references are provided in the Bibliography. The species accounts also include many of my previously unpublished personal observations.

**ECHOLOCATION CALLS** These small charts are designed to give a *guide only* to the characteristic calls of each bat species. They will *not* be useful for a definitive identification but will perhaps help to show what calls you may encounter in a particular area. For accurate identification it is essential that reference calls from the local area are used (see **How to catch and survey bats**). The charts show a plot of zero-crossing analysis displaying frequency (kilohertz) against time (milliseconds). There are four different scales used, but all species with similar calls have the same scale so that direct comparisons can be made. Some species cannot be identified using this method—for example most species of long-eared bats (*Nyctophilus*)—but they are included so that you will at least know what genus they are.

## A chance to add your bit
Please make note of any errors, omissions, different distribution records or measurements, what keys worked and what didn't, and any suggestions you may have for improvements. I would be very pleased to have your comments and opinions for the next edition. Contact me at australianbats@yahoo.com.au.

# Part I
## All About Bats

# What are bats?

**B**ats live their lives in a dimension so different from ours that we cannot escape a sense of wonder at the precision of even the simplest aspect of their biology.

Bats' uniqueness among mammals—their ability to fly—controls every feature of their bodies: the smallness, the lightness, the exquisite redesign of their hands to become wings, the muscularity of the upper body, and the reduction of the pelvis and legs. Their bodies are an amazing balance of a multitude of specialisations that have enabled them to colonise the night sky.

For at least 50 million years bats have existed, constructed just as perfectly as they are today. They are one of the most successful and abundant orders of mammals in the world and yet we are scarcely aware of their presence and their ways are still mysterious to us.

## Defining bats

Bats are mammals, that is they are warm-blooded, covered in hair and feed their young milk.

There are about 1100 species of bats in the world, in 19 families. In Australia we have 77 species in eight families. Bats are one of the largest groups of mammals, comprising over 20 per cent of the world's total. They range in size from the 2-g bumble-bee bat, *Craseonycteris thonglongyi*, of Thailand, the smallest mammal in the world, to the giant flying-fox, *Pteropus giganteus*, of India with a wingspan of 1.8 m and weighing 1200 g.

Bats are placental mammals, and most species have only a single young each year, although twins do occur. The young is suckled for 1 to 5 months. Females have two teats, one near each armpit. Bats breed slowly but compensate for this by having a very long life for such small animals. It is likely that most bats live for at least 5 to 10 years, but many bats caught in the wild are so old that their teeth are worn down almost to the gum-line. In Australia an eastern bentwing bat was banded as an adult and recaptured 20 years later.

## New classification of bats

Previously bats were classified into two suborders: the Megachiroptera (megabats), containing only the fruit bats of the family Pteropodidae, and the Microchiroptera (microbats), which included all other bats.

The megabats are usually large and live on a diet of fruit, blossom and nectar. They have large, well-developed eyes for seeing in the dark and a strong sense of smell for finding food. They do not use echolocation and so cannot fly in complete darkness.

Most microbats are small with a wingspan of about 30 cm; they eat insects and use echolocation to navigate and find food.

Molecular studies of modern bats have shown that this classification is no longer valid. Surprisingly, bats of the superfamily Rhinolophoidea (including the horseshoe bats, leaf-nosed bats and ghost bats), which all have very sophisticated echolocation and elaborate nose-leafs, have been found to be most closely related to the Pteropodidae (fruit bats) which have no echolocation! These two groups are now placed together into a new suborder, Yinpterochiroptera. All other Australian bats are grouped into three superfamilies and placed together into the suborder Yangochiroptera.

Recently a molecular time scale was used to reconstruct the evolutionary pathways of modern bats. There is now compelling evidence that about 65 million years ago all bats

BRICE THOMSON

**ABOVE** The northern blossom bat, *Macroglossus minimus*, is the smallest Australian fruit bat. Its large eyes give it excellent night vision.

evolved from a common ancestor of the mammal group that diversified to become the carnivores, whales, horses, pigs and pangolins.

The Yinpterochiroptera and the Yangochiroptera diverged very early in their evolutionary history, about 64 million years ago. Within the Yinpterochiroptera, the Pteropodidae and Rhinolophoidea split 58 million years ago so it is not surprising that they are now very different, with the pteropodids discarding echolocation and developing specialised eyesight. The rhinolophoids went on to evolve the most sophisticated echolocation of all the bats.

Within the Yangochiroptera the superfamilies (Emballonuroidea, Vespertilionoidea and the Noctilionoidea) split about 50 to 52 million years ago at a time of global warming and at a peak in plant and insect diversity. There would have been refinement of echolocation and wing morphology during this period.

The fossil record gives us no clues about the evolution of bats. Bat fossils are rare because the small bones do not preserve well and the oldest fossil bats (51 million years old) were already fully-formed bats very little different to modern species.

The ancestors of bats, or proto-bats, were most likely to have been small insectivorous gliding mammals with webbed fingers, and skin between the legs and tail to maximise gliding surfaces. The presence of webbed fingers was an important step towards developing wings and would have aided in gliding manoeuvrability. They probably hung under branches which would have allowed them to forage in the smallest branches in search of insects and positioned them for gliding forays between branches and other trees. It is most likely that the proto-bats could make ultrasonic sounds and perhaps echolocate.

Bat design is very ancient and evidently successful. By 30 million years ago all contemporary families were distinguishable; in fact many fossil taxa from 30 million years ago represent existing genera.

In this book I have chosen to use the terms megabats for the fruit bats (Pteropodidae) and microbats for all other bats as a matter of convenience.

## Bat wings

Look at this photo of a bat being released: every part of the human hand, the forearm, the upturned thumb, the hand and each finger, is present, exquisitely and precisely modified in the bat's left wing. Stretched over this framework is the flight membrane, a remarkable skin that is soft, strong and flexible and will repair itself if punctured. It is stretched between the fingers and along the side of the body to the leg. The skin is extremely elastic and when a bat closes its wings the membranes contract, leaving no loose folds, and yet the wing opens with almost no force required to stretch it. The thumb has been left free of the wing and has a claw on the end that is used for grooming and clinging to roosts. There is usually an extra flight membrane between the hind legs that encloses the tail. It is stiffened and extended by a spur of bone (the calcar) protruding from the ankle.

Bats' wings are covered with tiny touch receptors, small bumps with a tiny hair protruding from the centre. The hairs are particularly sensitive to air flow and allow bats to control their flight by 'feeling' for turbulence. They are particularly important for helping the bat to turn and maintain altitude. There is a second type of receptor cell in the membranous part of bats' wings that responds when the membrane stretches and is used to help catch insects on the wing. The parts of the wing that are most commonly used to catch prey have the highest numbers of receptors.

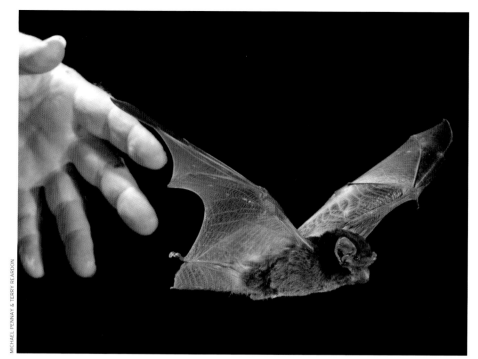

MICHAEL PENNAY & TERRY REARDON

**ABOVE** A Gould's wattled bat, *Chalinolobus gouldii*, being released.

## Why do bats hang upside down?

Bats hang upside down because they fly. When, during the evolution of flight, the arms altered to form wings, the legs changed as well. The hip joints have been rotated to allow the bat to control the shape and size of its wing membranes. This is seen when you hold a bat in your hand and its knees appear to bend the wrong way. The pelvis has also been modified and reduced in size to minimise weight.

These modifications mean that bats can no longer stand on their hind legs, although some can scurry along on their folded wings and hind feet with surprising speed. Bats don't even have to hold on to hang by their hind legs: the tendons in the foot are arranged so the bat clings without effort but has to use its muscles to let go.

Hanging upside down allows bats to launch more quickly for flight. This is important as many have to glide initially to gain speed and lift. It also permits them to roost in safer and more favourable situations such as cave ceilings.

Hanging upside down can also present some difficulties, however, and bats have solved these by turning head up and hanging by their thumb claws to defecate and urinate. Giving birth is also a potentially difficult matter but most bats cling to the roost with their thumbs and feet when giving birth. They use wing and tail membranes to catch the newborn young and support it until it gets a good hold on its mother with its over-large feet and attaches itself to a teat.

## The cost of flight

A large amount of energy is needed to fly and bats need to fly to obtain sources of energy. They eat energy-rich food such as insects or nectar in large quantities. Some species eat almost half their own body weight in insects each night.

To compensate for the expense of flight, the bat lifestyle is designed to conserve energy. Roost sites are chosen that economically maintain body temperature when at rest and minimise water loss. Bats also use daily torpor and much more prolonged periods of hibernation to reduce their metabolic rate. Bats store energy as fat deposits in their body, but cannot store much fat without the increase in weight affecting the energy cost of flight. Hibernation allows many temperate species of bats to survive the winter on their small fat stores. Disturbing bats during hibernation wastes their limited resources and may mean that they do not survive. Hibernating bats should be left alone.

The vast majority of bats are tropical species and it is likely that all bats originated in the tropics as bat design is most suited to warm and humid climates. They have a large surface area to volume ratio, meaning they lose heat from a large area, but have only a small volume to generate it. The large wing membranes are capable of losing vast amounts of heat and moisture. This is an advantage in hot climates or when it is necessary to get rid of the excess heat generated by flight, as the wings act as a radiator. In cold climates this is a disadvantage and only the use of hibernation and torpor has enabled many species to colonise the temperate regions of the world.

# Where do bats live?

**B**ats roost in many places: deep inside caves, exposed on branches of trees, in tree hollows, under bark, in abandoned bird nests and in church belfries. Roosts provide bats with daytime protection from both predators and environmental extremes.

## Cave-dwelling bats

Bats are most commonly thought of as cave dwellers and almost one-third of Australian bats do live in caves. Caves can vary from simple splits in the rock to boulder piles, shallow overhangs or extensive limestone caverns. Each species of bat has a preferred type of cave or mine or area within them. Caves are ideal because their stable climate allows bats to select a roost and rest there throughout the day, expending little energy. Caves also have the advantage of providing protection from predators: few potential predators can enter totally dark caves and find their way back out again, and even if they do, the bats hanging from the ceiling are quite inaccessible.

Cave bats are most vulnerable at a narrow entrance. One study I did required me to sit quietly at night at a 50-cm high cave entrance, for 4 hours at a time, counting 25 000 orange leaf-nosed bats (*Rhinonicteris aurantia*) as they left to forage. It was common to see barn owls and ghost bats (*Macroderma gigas*) swoop past to grab a bat or two. On one occasion an olive python calmly slithered over my shoulder and down along my leg on its way to dinner. Another time I watched two northern quolls walk into the cave mouth at bat exit time. They reappeared 20 minutes later, with the wings of orange leaf-nosed bats still sticking out the sides of their mouths, looking fat and very smug.

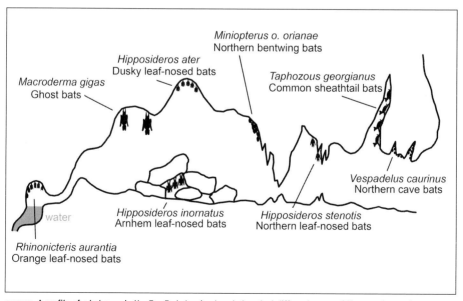

**ABOVE** A profile of a bat cave in the Top End showing how bats select different areas of the cave to roost.

**ABOVE** A cluster of eastern bentwing bats roosting on a cave ceiling.

Most bats that live in the dark part of caves are very fussy about the microclimate at the roost site. The eastern bentwing bat, *Miniopterus orianae oceanensis*, flies long distances, up to 300 km, each spring to find the right cave conditions to give birth to its young. Young bats need to be kept warm and the pregnant females roost in caves with domed ceilings. They gather in very large numbers, usually many thousands, and their body heat causes the cave air to become hot and humid, raising the temperature by up to 15°C. This hot, moist air rises and becomes trapped at the top of the dome and it is here that the bats are born. The young bats congregate into thick clusters to form crèches of up to 3000 per square metre. After a couple of months they become independent and all the bats disperse to other caves.

During temperate winters, when there are few insects available for food, bats have to survive long periods without eating. They rely on their accumulated body fat and go into hibernation, reducing their body temperature to within a couple of degrees of the roost temperature. This allows them to conserve a considerable amount of energy by not having to keep warm. Even their breathing rate and heart beat are reduced to less than one-tenth of normal. To find suitable conditions for hibernating, bats select cave roosts that are cold, but where the temperature and humidity are stable.

Many tropical bats, such as the dusky leaf-nosed bat, *Hipposideros ater*, are incapable of hibernating. These bats leave the cave every night to eat, as there are insects available throughout the year, although there are far fewer insects in the cooler months. To conserve energy during the day, they select caves with very hot and humid roost microclimates, which allow the bats to maintain their normal body temperature and water balance without having to burn up unnecessary energy.

Abandoned mines provide the same opportunities for bats as caves do, although they are less stable and are more prone to human disturbance. However, their presence has provided opportunities for cave bats to expand their range into areas previously inhospitable to them throughout Australia.

## Forest-dwelling bats

In a country like Australia where there are few hilly areas, caves can be hard to find. By roosting in trees and other similar places, bats can survive in all parts of Australia and in all habitats. Forest-dwelling bats are far more tolerant of fluctuations in temperature and humidity at the roost than cave dwellers and so have a broader range of homes available to them.

Flying-foxes have the simplest roosts of all. They congregate in colonies in trees, hanging exposed from a branch with little protection from the weather or predators. These camps are

**ABOVE** A large colony of diadem horseshoe bats, *Hipposideros diadema*, in a mine. Several species of north Australian bats occasionally have a bright orange or red fur colour.

usually in tall trees often within monsoon or rainforest patches, in paperbark swamps or mangroves. Ideally they would be in areas away from human disturbance, but this is not always the case: during the last 15 years there has been an increase in the numbers of flying-foxes living in cities. Brisbane, Darwin, Cairns, Sydney and Melbourne all have large colonies in parks and along waterways. Flying-foxes often have a very strong affinity with one group of trees and will use the same camp year after year. Camp sizes vary greatly depending on season and the amount of food locally available, and at times the number of flying-foxes becomes so great that the weight of their bodies breaks off branches from their favourite roost trees.

A visit to a flying-fox camp is an unforgettable experience. There are usually hundreds or thousands of these large bats hanging from branches. Some are lazily fanning themselves with one wing while others, wrapped up in their wings, are trying to sleep. There is constant noise from flapping wings and bats squabbling and jostling for the best position. Some disturbed bats fly off to another branch only to cause further chaos when they land and upset their new neighbours. Quiet sometimes descends, but only for a few minutes at a time. At dusk the bats rise above the trees with much flapping and noise and slowly spiral upwards, their shapes silhouetted against the evening glow. They peel off towards their chosen foraging area, singly or in groups, radiating out in all directions.

Other fruit bats also roost in trees but in small, quiet groups of one or two animals. Blossom bats rest during the day with their wings furled around them, looking like a cluster of dead leaves. They reinforce this illusion by occasionally swaying their bodies back and forth as if moved by the wind. Unlike flying-foxes, they do not have regular camps. Instead they generally change roosts within a group of favourite trees every day or two to avoid predation.

Other forest bats roost within hollow branches, in tree trunks or under bark. Tree hollows are common in eucalypts and these provide excellent roost sites for bats. The river red gums (*Eucalyptus camaldulensis*) that grow along dry water courses throughout most of inland Australia provide many tree hollows in areas otherwise devoid of trees. In forest areas there is a large choice of roost sites available and most bats use several roosts regularly. The best hollows are used while the females are nursing young and usually several females share the roost at this time. The young are left behind to huddle together when the females go out foraging at night.

Bats also use abandoned birds' nests: notably fairy martin nests in culverts and scrubwren or gerygone nests in rainforests, sometimes moving in while the nest is still occupied by the original builder.

Some bats appear to be opportunistic in their choice of roost and move each day. They find a suitable spot before each dawn and move on again the following night. It is not known whether these bats remain in one area throughout the year or if they wander perpetually.

## House-dwelling bats

Many bats have found that house roofs provide all the right conditions for shelter: protection from the weather, a pleasant microclimate and freedom from predators. Bats can live in roofs in large numbers without the owners being aware of them. They generally cause no problems and the telltale sign of droppings and the associated aroma is often all that can be found on a visit into the roof. However, a close look in the roof's cracks and crevices will reveal the bats. Some species such as the inland freetail bat, *Mormopterus* species 3, roost in incredibly hot

places, tightly squeezed against a metal roof in the summer where the metal is too hot for a human hand to touch. Other species are easy to find hanging from the rafters.

With the continual clearing of trees for agriculture and the removal of old trees in the suburbs, houses are often the only available roost. Bats in your roof don't do any harm and often use the roof for only part of the year anyway.

Bats will roost almost anywhere that offers shelter including drainpipes, chimneys, under the floor and in water tanks. I have found lesser long-eared bats, *Nyctophilus geoffroyi*, roosting inside a rolled-up swag that was stored in a shed and in an old wood stove in a fallen-down house. Even cave bats can be flexible: during a wet season field trip, a group of dusky leaf-nosed bats, *Hipposideros ater*, moved into my Landcruiser for several days.

© JAY SARSON/LOCHMAN TRANSPARENCIES

**LEFT** Flying-foxes often roost in large camps along waterways.

# Bat reproduction

**B**ats are placental mammals, like us, and many of the fundamentals of their reproductive systems are similar to ours. However, among the bats there is about as much variation in regard to the detailed reproductive patterns as there is in all other mammals combined.

Compared with most small mammals, bats have a longer life span, slow development to sexual maturity, longer pregnancies and smaller litter sizes. They usually have only one litter per year.

Tropical bat species have food available and remain active throughout the year. Tropical microbat reproductive patterns are quite straightforward and similar to most other placental mammals.

Typically, reproduction involves the synchronisation of sperm production and ovulation. Mating is followed by immediate fertilisation and pregnancy that continues uninterrupted until the young are born about 3 to 5 months later. Young are suckled by the female for about 4 to 6 weeks before they are weaned. They usually reach adult size by 3 months of age. Births occur during the period of maximum food availability to provide females with enough food for the later stages of pregnancy and during lactation. The young are weaned when there is still plenty of food available for them to grow rapidly while learning to hunt.

Temperate microbat species have a problem. For a large portion of the year, during winter, there is little food available, and bats survive by hibernating. But pregnancies cannot grow during hibernation and sperm cannot be produced at this time. There is not enough time during the summer season for males to produce sperm, for mating to occur and for females to complete pregnancy and lactation in time for the young to be weaned and grow large enough to survive the next period of hibernation.

Instead the reproductive cycles are split over two seasons. Testicular growth and spermatogenesis take place in spring and summer, the months of warmth and abundant food supply. Mating follows soon after sperm production peaks in autumn and may continue during hibernation. Sperm production in the testes ceases during winter in hibernating bats but these bats are able to continue mating through to spring because sperm is stored in the epididymides, even though the testes have regressed.

The pregnancy will not grow at the reduced body temperature of the hibernating female in winter and some temperate bats delay ovulation until spring. This necessitates sperm storage in the female. The sperm heads are lined up in special depressions in the lining cells of the uterus, where they are nourished and protected until spring, when the egg is released and fertilisation occurs. This pattern is found in most vespertilionid bats such as long-eared bats, *Nyctophilus*.

**ABOVE**  A newborn bat beside a 50-cent coin.

**ABOVE** A male grey-headed flying-fox, *Pteropus poliocephalus*, investigating a female prior to mating.

In other bats fertilisation occurs soon after mating in autumn and the fertilised egg develops into an early embryo, called a blastocyst. This is held in the uterus at this stage of development during hibernation, a process known as delayed implantation. In spring when temperatures rise and more food is available, the blastocyst implants and pregnancy resumes. This pattern is found in the eastern bentwing bat, *Miniopterus orianae oceanensis*, which completes its testicular cycle before winter in temperate latitudes. This species occurs from temperate to tropical areas and its reproductive patterns vary according to latitude. At the southern end of their range they mate in April, at latitude 28°S in late May to June, and in the north in September. In each case the young are born in December. For this to be possible the implantation delay must be flexible.

In other temperate bats the blastocyst implants at once but is kept dormant or growing very slowly in a process called embryonic diapause.

Bats produce only one or two young per litter and in temperate summers there is usually not time for a second pregnancy. These bats are seasonally monestrous. In tropical areas second pregnancies in the same year are more common, making the bat seasonally polyestrous. Some bat species appear to produce young throughout the year and do not have defined breeding seasons. They are referred to as aseasonally polyestrous.

Pregnant female bats may congregate into maternity colonies a few weeks before they give birth. Some colonies comprise thousands of bats, others just a few. The young are born huge, often 25 to 30 per cent of their mother's body weight, something no human would relish.

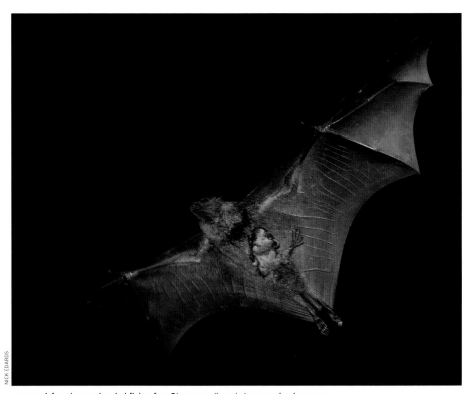

NICK EDARDS

**ABOVE** A female grey-headed flying-fox, *Pteropus poliocephalus*, carrying her young.

The newborn is initially carried everywhere attached to a teat near its mother's armpit by its sharp, recurved milk teeth. After a few days it is left at the roost while the mother forages. Often the young are left in a nursery cluster in the maternity colony, sometimes chaperoned by a small number of adults. Once the juveniles can fly they may accompany the mothers to forage for food, and learn to navigate and find their way back to the roost. In flying-foxes, the mother bat's investment in the young is considerable, with the young dependent on their mother for many months.

Juvenile females usually become sexually mature during their first year, and are ready to breed by the next breeding season. Males often take an extra year to reach sexual maturity.

# Echolocation

**F**ruit bats have large eyes and superb vision and find their way around at night entirely by eyesight. Microbats, although not blind, rely primarily on echolocation to navigate and hunt for food. They do this with startling efficiency: in controlled conditions a *Myotis* bat has been recorded capturing 1200 tiny fruit flies per hour, one every 3 seconds, while on the wing.

Echolocation calls are high frequency sound waves made by the bat forcing air through its vocal cords in the same way as we speak. Bat vocal cords vibrate very rapidly (thousands of times per second), creating sound impulses that are sent out either through the mouth or the nostrils. The calls bounce back from surrounding objects and the bat's sensitive ears detect the echoes of their calls. These faint echoes are converted by the bat's brain into information about the size, texture and distance of the surrounding objects. High frequency bat calls are described by the number of vibrations per second, more technically known as hertz (Hz).

There is a reason bats use high frequency sound. Think of an ordinary 30-cm ruler: it is calibrated in millimetres, centimetres and decimetres. The high frequency sounds correspond to the millimetre scale of the ruler because the markings are most frequent; low frequency calls would correspond to the decimetre scale. The most obvious thing about the millimetre scale is the smallness of the units, and how much more suitable they would be for measuring the length of a beetle than centimetres or decimetres. The number of vibrations per second of an average bat call is 50 000 Hz or 50 kilohertz (kHz) and corresponds to a wavelength of 6.8 mm, an ideal scale for measuring small insects. By contrast, a call of 5 kHz corresponds to a wavelength of 68 mm, an inconveniently large unit for measure. This is why bats don't use frequencies audible to humans (3–18 kHz) to find their food.

All echolocation calls provide the bat with information on the distance of objects, such as food or obstacles. When a bat sends out an echolocation call, the call strikes an insect, and some of it is bounced back as an echo. The time taken for the echo to return tells the bat how far away the insect is. Some bats use what is called constant frequency ultrasound. It has the advantage that the bat can determine not only the distance of its dinner, but also its speed, and direction of movement. This is achieved by means of the Doppler effect.

To make use of the Doppler effect the bat sends a constant frequency call. If the call strikes an insect that is moving towards the bat then the frequency of the call will be compressed by the speed of the insect. The returning echo will be of a higher frequency (due to compression) than the original call. The difference in frequency between the call and the echo tells the bat how fast and in what direction the insect is travelling. An insect moving away from the bat will cause the echo to have a lower frequency.

Constant frequency echolocation is amazingly efficient, even with small targets like mosquitoes. I have spent many nights camped by tropical waterholes, with hundreds of mosquitoes outside the mosquito net. Every so often there is a soft fluttering of wings as a dusky leaf-nosed bat, *Hipposideros ater*, a bat that uses constant frequency calls, circles the net. After only a couple of minutes every mosquito is gone.

There is a disadvantage to using a constant frequency sound. Each frequency is only useful for a specific distance and object size. To distinguish beetles from leaves or trees a bat needs to use a broad range of frequencies simultaneously. This is achieved by altering the tension on the vocal cords as the sound is being produced so that the frequency of the call decreases evenly, providing the high frequencies for detail and the low frequencies for larger objects. This is known as frequency modulation and is a characteristic of most bat calls.

High frequency sound doesn't travel as far as lower frequency sound. A bat such as the dusky leaf-nosed bat, *Hipposideros ater*, uses very high frequency sound (160 kHz) to catch its small prey. It flies very slowly, staying close to the ground or within the vegetation. This is because the range of its call is very short. When I have been sitting at cave entrances these bats have often come to 'investigate' me: circling and hovering, they stay within a distance of 30 cm because this is how far their echoes can travel. Contrast this with the white-striped freetail bat, *Austronomus australis*, whose call falls within the audible range of humans. These bats eat large beetles and moths and hunt for them at high speed above the tree canopy, and the low frequency echolocation calls are essential to give this species the distance information required to avoid collisions during fast flight. These bats can be heard during summer evenings cruising past with a loud ting.....ting.....ting.....ting.....ting.....

Frequency modulated calls do not provide the bat with details of an object's speed and direction of travel, but the bat compensates for this by making a large number of calls in a short time (up to 200 calls per second) and comparing the echoes of each call. As it gets closer to its target, the calls are made more frequently so that the bat has the most up-to-date information possible as it is about to grab its prey. These rapid calls are very distinctive when heard on a bat detector and are referred to as the terminal or feeding buzz. They indicate that a bat is hunting for food, not just flying past. The complexity of frequency modulated calls also provides bats with details on the texture and density of their targets.

Long-eared bats, *Nyctophilus*, have broadband frequency modulated echolocation calls. They forage using a variety of methods but often catch their food by a specialised technique called gleaning, where the complex textural picture built up by echolocation allows them to detect the presence of a moth camouflaged against a tree trunk. This would be almost impossible using vision alone. For more information see **Diet, flight and foraging**.

There is another way a bat call can use different frequencies simultaneously: the tissues around the vocal cords, the windpipe, the mouth and the nasal cavities are complex in shape and structure. As the vocal cords vibrate some of these tissues set up vibrations in sympathy, often at two, three or four times the frequency. These calls are called harmonics and they extend the number of frequencies used and improve the discriminating qualities of the call. Harmonics are used both by bats that rely on constant frequency calls and by those that use frequency modulation. The rostrum (muzzle) of the skull in horseshoe and leaf-nosed bats is considerably swollen beneath the nose-leaf and this may provide a resonating chamber for the calls, perhaps to produce the much-needed harmonics for these constant frequency bats.

It has been suggested that horseshoe bats may change the dominant harmonic, say from the second to the third, as part of the process of forming a new species, a process called harmonic hopping. It is interesting that all Australian horseshoe bats have dominant harmonics that are multiples of 13.5 kHz. By using the second (27 kHz), third (40.5 kHz) and fifth (67 kHz) harmonics they may prey on very different-sized insects.

Different species of bats have different echolocation calls, depending on their anatomy, habitat and hunting technique. The calls can be defined by their duration (sometimes as short as 1 millisecond), rate of repetition (up to 200 per second), whether they are constant frequency (CF), frequency modulating (FM) or a combination (e.g. FM/CF/FM), the number of harmonics, and the loudness (intensity, amplitude) at each stage of the call.

Although each species has a characteristic call, there is a lot of variation between individuals.

**ABOVE** The enormous ears and nose-leaf of the intermediate horseshoe bat, *Rhinolophus* species, are specialisations for echolocation. They emit the ultrasound through their nostrils.

BRUCE THOMSON

Every bat has a slightly different call, like each human voice, enabling it to recognise its own echoes when other bats are around. It has a repertoire of calls for orientation, foraging and communication with other bats.

It is interesting to imagine what it must be like to be a bat. I have stood at cave entrances and watched hundreds of thousands of bats leaving a cave in a few hours. At any time there are several thousand bats of the same species all flying out of the cave, all calling, all using the same frequencies and all listening to their own echoes returning from the cave walls and the other moving bats. Among the thousands of bats exiting at one time it is hard to imagine how a bat can recognise its own echoes from this incredible cacophony of sound let alone calculate the trajectories of all the other bats and avoid collision. However collisions are surprisingly rare, even in these circumstances.

Each call is modified by the bat in relation to the habitat it is using and what food it is hunting, which makes for considerable variation. Despite this, it is possible to identify many species by their echolocation call. Studying echolocation calls provides biologists with important insights into the ecology of bats, including information on habitat use, species competition for food resources, and the diversity of species using particular habitats. Details are given on bat detectors and their use in **How to catch and survey bats**.

The demands of echolocation are responsible for some of the strange and grotesque faces of bats. The large nose-leafs of the horseshoe, leaf-nosed and ghost bats are used to help focus or direct the echolocation call. In these species the call is emitted through the nostrils, which has the advantage that it is not restricted by eating and drinking as it is with simple-nosed bats that echolocate through the mouth.

Unlike vision, which is a passive sense relying on ambient light, echolocation requires a lot of energy. The bat must not only receive and interpret signals (as with vision) but must generate the sound to start with. Calls are synchronised to a large extent with the bat's wing beats; the bat's flight muscles are used for the inspiration and exhalation of air, which saves considerable energy with calling.

With all this sophisticated equipment for navigating you would think that bats would never collide with anything. In fact, they get so familiar with every twist and turn and stalactite of the home cave that they 'switch off' their echolocation and fly through on memory alone. Put an unfamiliar obstruction in the way, like a bat biologist doing an exodus count, and collisions do happen.

# Diet, flight and foraging

As a group, bats display as broad a range of food habits as almost all other mammals together. They eat fruit (frugivore), nectar and pollen (nectarivore), insects and other arthropods (insectivore), the flesh of vertebrates, frogs, reptiles, birds and mammals (carnivore), fish (piscivore) and blood (sanguivore).

Apart from blood, which is eaten by only three species of vampire bats in the tropical Americas, Australian bats use all of these foods.

Typical frugivorous bats are the flying-foxes and tube-nosed bats. They find ripe fruit primarily by smell, although some pale-coloured rainforest fruits are located by sight. They eat a large variety of native and cultivated fruits and will travel considerable distances at night in search of food. Flying-foxes need to eat a large amount of food each night while keeping their weight low enough to enable them to fly. To do this they take a bite of the fruit, chew it, squeeze out the juice by pressing it against the roof of the mouth with their tongue and spit out the almost dry wad of fibres. The energy-rich juice is rapidly digested. They supplement their diet with *Eucalyptus* and *Melaleuca* blossom, while some species, such as the little red flying-fox, *Pteropus scapulatus*, are almost entirely nectarivorous.

Blossom bats have elongated muzzles and a specialised long tongue with small mop-like projections at the tip, which enable them to probe deep into flowers to obtain nectar. They do eat some fruit but their teeth are very reduced, indicating that fruit eating is not greatly important to this species. Blossom bats usually have a well-used home range, with a group of favoured roost trees. They learn the flowering trees within their area and do the rounds of these trees each night. Because their energy needs are high they tend to forage throughout the night, becoming covered in pollen as they feed on flowers. Pollen, which they groom off their fur and eat, is an important source of protein for these bats.

By far the majority of Australian bats are insectivorous. The chief food items are moths and beetles but most bats are fairly opportunistic and will take whatever is going. At certain times of year flying termites become available in large numbers and all insectivorous bats, whatever their usual preference, become temporary specialists in eating these fat-rich insects. The bogong moths of New South Wales and Victoria are favoured prey for the same reason.

© JIRI LOCHMAN/LOCHMAN TRANSPARENCIES

**LEFT** Many bats, like this western falsistrelle, can eat up to half their own weight in insects in a night's foraging.

**RIGHT** Blossom bats have a long tongue specially adapted for collecting nectar.

Most insectivorous bats concentrate on aerial foraging, where the bat catches and consumes insects on the wing, allowing it to remain airborne for hours at a time. Many leaf-nosed bats, *Hipposideros*, use a flycatcher or perch-hunting technique where they hang from a suitable branch and sally forth to catch passing prey, returning to the perch to eat.

A surprisingly large number of food items are non-flying. For these, a specialised foraging technique called gleaning is used. The bats fly slowly and often hover, echolocating to identify insects against a background, such as leaves, branches or the ground, and pluck them from the surface. Tasmanian long-eared bats, *Nyctophilus sherrini*, eat mainly caterpillars, and there are many records of molossids foraging on the ground. One of the most interesting diets is that of the golden-tipped bat, *Phoniscus papuensis*, which specialises in eating orb-weaving spiders. Flying slowly through thick vegetation it uses echolocation to find spider webs then hovers to pluck the spider from its web.

Some long-eared bats, *Nyctophilus*, will also hunt from a perch by passively listening to the

sounds made by insects. They then catch them without echolocating and in this way are able to capture many of the moth species that can hear ultrasound and might otherwise take evasive action.

Piscivory, fish eating, has only been recorded in Australia in the large-footed myotis, *Myotis macropus*. This specialisation probably originated from the technique of catching insects on the water surface by raking its long sharp-clawed feet through the water, and subsequently using the same method to catch small fish and prawns.

Ghost bats, *Macroderma gigas*, are carnivorous, feeding on a variety of vertebrates, most commonly birds, small mammals and other bats, but also nocturnal reptiles, frogs and a variety of large insects. Their main foraging strategy includes active pursuit and capture on the wing; in the case of other bats, usually taking them from behind. This may be combined with the perch-hunting technique, or they may roost on a branch and listen passively to find small mammals, swooping down onto them without echolocating, enfolding

**LEFT** A ghost bat, *Macroderma gigas*, eating a rat that it has carried back to its cave.

them in their wings and then biting through their skulls. They return to the roost to devour their prey, dropping the less palatable items such as the legs, tail and muzzle. It is not known how they catch birds, but as they eat mainly diurnal species they are either captured on the wing as the bat is returning to its roost at dawn, or more likely, I suspect, they are taken from their perches during the night. The greater broad-nosed bat, *Scoteanax rueppellii*, is also carnivorous, eating bats at any opportunity. They are well known for eating bats in captivity but how common this behaviour is in the wild we have yet to find out.

Determining the diets of bats can be time-consuming and difficult. Insectivorous bats chew their food so finely that the insect remains in the stomach are almost unidentifiable. Details such as the feet and wing covers of beetles, the scales of moth wings, the venation patterns of insect wings, the eyes and mouthparts of bugs, and the hairs and eyes of flies are all the clues one gets to the identity of the prey. Interestingly, there is little difference in the results obtained from stomach content or scat analysis.

There are several advantages to examining scats. One is that much of the bulk has been digested leaving only the indigestible fragments, and it is these concentrated indigestible fragments that are used for identifying insect prey. An even bigger advantage is that scats are easily collected from every bat you ever catch. By placing the captive in a clean cloth bag for an hour you will usually obtain at least a few pellets. These can be dried and kept for an indefinite period before processing. Stomach content analysis can obviously only be done on dead bats.

The diet of frugivorous species is no easier to examine although direct observation can provide information on many food items. Scat analysis can be used to examine pollen grains, many of which have very distinctive shapes and can be identified to species level. Particles of fruit are usually not identifiable but ingested seeds may be; often, especially with rainforest fruit, the seeds need to be germinated and grown before they can be identified.

## Foraging guilds

The flight characteristics of different bats, their method of echolocation and the habitat they forage all influence foraging behaviour. Insectivorous bats can be separated into four major foraging groups, or guilds.

### OPEN SPACE AERIAL FORAGERS

These bats catch insects while flying in open spaces away from vegetation. Freetail and sheathtail bats typically use this foraging strategy.

They face the problem of having to search for insects over a wide area of empty space. They fly fast to cover large areas and have very loud low frequency calls that travel long distances. They typically have long gaps between their calls (often several wing beats) to allow time for the echoes to return.

Their wings are long and narrow, making them capable of fast flight, but are not very manoeuvrable. However, observations on flying molossids suggest that they can adjust their wing geometry and become capable of lower flying speeds with greater manoeuvrability.

Detecting prey at a distance gives them time to turn to intercept their prey rather than chase it. The greater the range at which prey is detected, the greater the opportunity for computing an intercept course. The range at which insects are first perceived is 4 to 15 m.

Their calls are usually narrow-band, shallow, frequency modulated (FM) calls of long duration, with long pulse intervals. In uncluttered air space, they hunt using narrow-band,

MICHAEL PENNAY AND TERRY REARDON

**ABOVE** The large-eared pied bat, *Chalinolobus dwyeri*, a typical edge space aerial forager.

short, constant frequency (CF) signals of 10 to 50 kHz. When they have detected and are pursuing prey, they introduce a frequency modulated component with a single harmonic. In the final closing with the prey, the frequency is lowered and the bandwidth widened. In more cluttered or confined situations, a multiple harmonic with several overlapping harmonics is used.

### EDGE SPACE AERIAL FORAGERS AND TRAWLERS

These bats catch insects while flying along the edges of vegetation or in gaps, or by trawling over smooth water. Most of the ordinary bats (vespertilionids) are in this category.

They typically use frequency modulated (FM) calls of moderate bandwidth. These calls enable bats to detect the relative position of their prey in three-dimensional space, and to describe its shape, size and possibly its texture, but provide very little information on the relative speed of the prey. They are not likely to locate or successfully pursue very fast prey. Their wings are moderately long and moderately broad. Flight varies from fast to moderately slow and they are typically very agile and manoeuvrable when chasing their prey.

The large-footed myotis, *Myotis macropus*, is also in this group although it catches its food (insects, shrimp and small fish) by raking its feet through the water surface over calm pools. Echolocation calls striking still water at an angle will be reflected not back but away, like light reflected from a mirror. Small ripples on the water surface made by fish below the surface would cause echoes to be returned in a very distinctive manner, enabling the bat to precisely pinpoint its prey. Similarly insects on the surface would produce echoes against a clear background free of echoes.

## GLEANING FORAGERS

These bats catch insects by gleaning from the ground or from vegetation, often within cluttered environments. Several vespertilionid bats (*Phoniscus, Murina* and *Nyctophilus*) exhibit these characteristics. Ghost bats also partially fit this category.

Echolocation calls are broadband frequency modulated (FM) calls of low intensity and short duration. They are distinctive in the use of very large bandwidths and extremely high frequencies and calls are produced at high pulse-repetition rates. The large bandwidth provides highly accurate target localisation, which is critical for bats hunting small prey within dense vegetation, while the high frequencies allow spectral discrimination of stationary prey, required for recognition of a moth against a tree trunk, for example.

The wing morphology of bats in this group, with its low aspect ratio and low wing loading, allows them to fly slowly within vegetation: the large tail membrane and broad wings enable them to make tight turns while flying and the rounded wing tips are associated with high manoeuvrability. They are also able to hover and to manoeuvre precisely in cluttered spaces.

## FLUTTER-DETECTING FORAGERS

This is the characteristic technique used by leaf-nosed and horseshoe bats. These bats forage in cluttered habitats and many species use perch-hunting. Their wings are usually rather short and broad allowing the bats to manoeuvre well in cluttered environments.

They use a very prolonged constant frequency (CF) call. The returning echoes from nearby structures overlap the emitted call and it would be hard to tell prey from clutter except that there is an increase in the strength of the returning echo each time an insect's wing is at right angles to the call. There is also a broadening of the sound spectrum as the insect wings move towards or away from the bat. These distinctive echoes are called 'glints' and they provide a very positive detection of flying insects.

The inner ear and auditory cortex of the brain is different from that of other bats. It is accurately tuned to the bat's calling frequency. These flutter-detecting bats may be able to identify the type of insect by analysis of the Doppler changes brought about by the amplitude and frequency of the insect's wing beat.

There is a potential disadvantage to this very accurate tuning to one frequency. There should be a Doppler-induced change in the returning echo when the bat is flying, and there would be except that the bat compensates by calling at a different frequency as soon as this starts to happen.

# Caves and conservation

oes it really matter if the odd bat cave or mine is destroyed? On the face of it you might think that bats would tolerate the loss of habitat better than other, less mobile mammals. After all, if their cave is destroyed they can simply fly off and find another cave, abandoned mine, road culvert or house. Unfortunately, it is not so simple.

Some years ago I studied cave bats in the Top End and looked at why they roost in different parts of caves. One thing I noticed was that some bats had very precise temperature and humidity requirements while others seemed to roost just about anywhere. Later I did a study with Russ Baudinette and others, looking at the metabolic reasons for these roost choices. We examined three species of cave bats, the orange leaf-nosed bat, *Rhinonicteris aurantia*, the large bentwing bat, *Miniopterus orianae*, and the ghost bat, *Macroderma gigas*.

From my previous work we knew that the orange leaf-nosed bat was known from only a few caves of the hundreds I searched in northern Australia and that even within those caves it was restricted to a very small zone. For example, they live in the 750-m long Cutta Cutta Cave near Katherine but roost only in the last 10 m, where the temperature is 32°C and humidity 98 per cent. We found that this bat is twice as sensitive to water loss as any other bat and seven times as sensitive as similar-sized rodents. For this bat the loss of a cave is no trivial matter. Its distribution is limited not by the number of possible caves but by the number of caves with a suitable microclimate. It is unable to maintain its body temperature in conditions below 30°C and in dry air can lose 20 per cent of its body weight from water loss in 12 hours. These stringent requirements have led to a situation where over 70 per cent of orange leaf-nosed bats live in a single small cave. This cave contains 25 000 of these bats and if it is destroyed we would probably lose a unique animal that has survived in Australia for over 25 million years.

Even the relatively unspecialised bats have their problems. The bentwing bat, *Miniopterus orianae*, is about the same size as the orange leaf-nosed bat, but has a great tolerance of water loss (with abilities comparable to desert-adapted rodents) and uses roosts with a broad range of temperatures. It is a widespread species that is found from the most northern to the most southern parts of the Australian mainland. In the tropics this bat has no difficulty finding roosts, but even this resilient animal can find a cave critically important in more temperate parts of its range. Recently a new subspecies of this bat was described (*M. o. bassanii*) from western Victoria and South Australia. It has been discovered that, although these bats use a great variety of caves for most of the year, they need very particular caves for giving birth. The caves must have a large chamber with a domed ceiling, which traps the rising warm air generated by large numbers of adult bats. These aggregations can raise the cave temperature by up to 15°C making a perfect humidicrib for the newborn babies. It appears that there are only two caves in their distribution that meet these criteria.

The third species, the ghost bat, was found to be moderately susceptible to water loss but surprisingly reliant on warm temperatures to maintain its body temperature. It preferred to roost in conditions of 28°C. In central Queensland (where the temperature is cooler) these bats also choose caves with domed ceilings, using their aggregate body heat to raise the cave's temperature by 3 to 4°C. So suitable thermal refugia are important for this bat, and this leads to another problem.

Genetic studies have shown that although there is gene flow between colonies of ghost

**ABOVE** Dusky leaf-nosed bats, *Hipposideros ater*, roost in hot humid caves.

bats in the northern part of their distribution, there is virtually none in the southern part. I surveyed many central Australian caves and found suitable caves were very uncommon and far apart. Because of this, the southern population of ghost bats is fragmented, living in isolated caves and having virtually no contact with other cave populations. The bats occupying a particular cave have no ability to recruit from other colonies in the event of disturbance or ecological change; each time a cave population is lost it is gone for good.

This makes them especially vulnerable and there has been a striking reduction in the distribution of ghost bats over the past century. In the Riversleigh fossil deposits of 25 million years ago ghost bats and orange leaf-nosed bats were the dominant bat fauna. Sub-fossil remains of ghost bats show that they were once widespread throughout the continent and in living memory were known over much of central Australia.

In 1983 I was doing survey work on the distribution of ghost bats with Peter Helman. One area we particularly wanted to study was the remote hill and range country on the border where the Northern Territory, South Australia and Western Australia meet. Ghost bats were known from the area, but there were few recent records, the latest being two isolated specimens from 1958 and 1961.

We approached the traditional Aboriginal custodians of this land to arrange a meeting, hoping to inform them of our objective, obtain their permission to be on their land, and find out if they knew of any caves or colonies.

As it happened, there was a meeting of traditional owners and tribal elders at Uluru. We were invited to discuss our study and received with courtesy. Knowing that many of the older people would not speak English, I had prepared a study skin of a ghost bat to pass around. I was sure that if it was in the area they would recognise such a distinctive animal. When the moment came and I held up the bat there was a collective gasp of shock. Women present at the meeting hurriedly covered their faces. The men looked stunned. It was a terrible moment. In my ignorance I had offended the very people whose help I needed. It turned out that this animal had great spiritual significance to their people and that it had to do with men's business. As a female I had committed a serious faux pas. Embarrassed, I hastily returned the bat to its box. Peter finished explaining what our project was about and we left the meeting.

Later the elders, forgiving my blunder, told us that they would like the project to go ahead. It was important to them to know where the bats were living. There was a problem, however, as the caves were sacred sites connected with men's business. I was extremely disappointed but suggested that Peter could continue this part of the study without me and we sat and arranged the details.

The following morning we were called back and told that the elders had discussed our problem during the night. They had talked carefully through the story of the ghost bat and found, away back in the legend, that there was one woman involved in the story. Therefore, they reasoned, it would be fine for one woman, me, to go to these areas. I was delighted and touched by all the trouble they had taken to make my participation possible.

We travelled with several old men from different communities in an old Landcruiser. There were no maps and most of the caves had not been visited for many years. One involved a 100-km drive cross-country through the sand dunes to a cave that couldn't be seen if you stood more than 3 m from its small vertical entrance. The old men who guided us were navigating by the shape of the sand dunes. They would stop every now and then and sing a long song to help them remember the landmarks of the journey. At each new locality the old men would try to tell us (there were some serious language barriers) the Dreamtime story of the ghost bat, or explain the ring of standing stones near a cave mouth, and sing the songs that they learned as young men. They even pointed out the woman in the story, a large rock on one of the ridges above a cave.

Each cave we visited was bare of ghost bats, although there was ample evidence of previous occupation. Even the caves of Uluru are a metre deep in mummified ghost bat droppings. But the ghost bats had left. With each disappointment our Aboriginal mentors became more distressed and more anxious to check the next site. As we ran out of caves a great sadness overtook the men, and some of these dignified old gentlemen were in tears. It was a humbling experience and we wished there was something we could do.

These men had grown up in the traditional life of the desert Aborigine. So much had changed, and we sensed that much of what they were showing us was part of a mourning and a final goodbye to parts of that earlier life.

The loss of the ghost bat is a severe blow to these people as it was central to the man-making ceremonies. The old men blamed themselves for the loss of the ghost bat, believing it was their fault for neglecting to perform the ceremonies.

Non-Aboriginal people might find other explanations: changing fire regimes, population

**ABOVE** An Arnhem Land cave painting of a flying-fox.

isolation, natural and induced climate change, and natural and feral animal mediated loss of small mammals, birds and reptiles.

Whatever the cause, it is our shared loss and the message is to not be complacent about the resilience of nature. It is not as simple as flying off and finding another cave.

# Bats and emerging viral diseases

The last decade and a half has seen the emergence of a number of previously unrecorded illnesses caused by viruses that have succeeded in jumping from their usual animal host to humans—such an illness is called a zoonosis. Bats have been implicated as the primary reservoir of these infections, although, apart from Australian Bat Lyssavirus, there has been no evidence of direct bat to human spread. Three of the viruses, Hendra and Nipah (sometimes referred to as Henipah), and Menangle are paramyxoviruses, a group that includes measles, dog and seal distemper, rinderpest and various forms of equine encephalitis.

The story starts in 1994 in the Brisbane suburb of Hendra. Twenty-one horses came down with a mystery respiratory infection. Fourteen horses and a trainer died. Possible human and animal sources of the outbreak were sought. All four Australian flying-fox species were found to have antibodies and seemed to be the natural hosts and reservoir of the virus. It was also prevalent in flying-foxes in New Guinea. The Hendra virus seems not to cause bats serious illness but if it jumps host to a horse the animal may die. In general, horse to horse transmission is not usual, and the first outbreak may have been made worse by human efforts to limit the spread. At the time of writing there have been seven outbreaks, but human cases have resulted from contact with horses rather than bats. There is no vaccine, but at this stage it seems not to be a problem for bat people. It may be that habitat destruction has led to formation of flying-fox camps near stables by smaller, more isolated, more susceptible groups of bats. Your own natural history observations could help to shed light on this.

The next virus was the Menangle virus which struck a large commercial pig farm in New South Wales in 1997 resulting in pregnancy problems in the pigs. Two people at the farm caught an influenza-like disease and had Menangle virus antibodies as they recovered. Grey-headed and little red flying-foxes shared a colony 200 m from the piggery and antibodies to this virus were later found in one-third of blood samples taken from flying-foxes in New South Wales and Queensland, including sera collected in 1996, before the outbreak.

Then, in 1998, Nipah, a new viral infection of pigs in Malaysia, spread to humans with a mortality of 105 people out of 265 infected. Over a million pigs were slaughtered to control the outbreak. Nipah virus antibodies were subsequently found in Malaysian flying-foxes. Since then there have been outbreaks of Nipah virus in Bangladesh in 2001, 2003, 2004 and 2005, spread from human to human, with high mortality. No intermediate animal vector has been identified there.

Flying-foxes seem to be the main hosts of all these viruses. This is not surprising as they are so numerous and gregarious, travel long distances, form dense mixed colonies, and spend periods of time in groups isolated from others of the same species, which allows for the development of new, susceptible populations. It is no surprise either that the viruses are present in New Guinea and East Timor flying-foxes. These are probably ancient viruses that co-evolved with flying-foxes so that they cause them relatively mild illness with lasting immunity. It would be interesting to know more about the behaviour of these viruses in the wild.

Flying-foxes are not the only source of zoonoses: SARS virus has been found in a horseshoe bat in China, and the yellow-bellied sheathtail bat, *Saccolaimus flaviventris*, is a significant carrier of Australian Bat Lyssavirus, a zoonosis spread directly from bat to human.

**ABOVE**  A rescued baby flying-fox enjoying a piece of fruit.

## Australian Bat Lyssavirus (ABLV)

In 1996 a new virus of the Lyssavirus group, which includes the rabies virus, was isolated from the brain of a black flying-fox. This was the first intimation of a rabies-like virus in Australian bats and tragically, a short time later, a bat carer from Rockhampton died, apparently from a second strain of Lyssavirus acquired from a yellow-bellied sheathtail bat, *S. flaviventris*. Then, in 1998, a woman from Mackay died 2 years after being bitten by a flying-fox.

This is a different situation. Here we have the emergence of a known disease from unrecognised viruses (which we could term Pteropus-ABLV and SF-ABLV), and the spread is directly from bat to human. The natural history of ABLV in bats is unknown, but the fact that there are healthy bats with antibodies suggests that some bats may either recover or have silent infections.

The human risk must be taken seriously: to say Australian Bat Lyssavirus infection is not rabies is splitting hairs. For practical purposes it is rabies and should be treated as such. However, the diagnosis of rabies is difficult. There are no tests to make the diagnosis before the onset of clinical disease. If the disease is diagnosable clinically it is too late to treat it. On the other hand, treatment can be effective before the onset of symptoms even if months have elapsed since the exposure.

So, what precautions need to be taken? The normal person who does not go out of their way to handle bats need take no precautions. Bats have no reason to bite humans. Living near a flying-fox colony or a bat cave or having bats in your roof is no danger. There would certainly be no justification for destroying bat colonies on the pretext of public health. But bat researchers and those that care for sick and injured bats do have a problem.

## Some thoughts for wildlife carers

Over the years many generous-hearted people have skilfully nursed thousands of sick, injured and orphaned bats. Australian flying-foxes in particular have proved intelligent and lovable creatures, winning the respect of their keepers.

The recognition that some bats carry a potentially fatal virus makes it necessary to think seriously about the implications of this work. Your risk of exposure to virus is much greater than that of other bat handlers precisely because you are selecting sick animals to handle.

A partly paralysed animal in the wild has no access to other bats. In your care, virus spread

### SOME GUIDELINES

1 **HAVE** the pre-exposure rabies vaccination and keep it up to date.
2 **TAKE** precautions against getting bitten or scratched—use gloves to handle bats. Wash with soap or iodine to help inactivate the virus.
3 **BE** willing to have suspiciously sick bats put down and tested. Be particularly suspicious of bats that cannot fly, that cannot take food or show an undue tendency to bite.
4 **REMEMBER** that a bat that has been free of symptoms in captivity for weeks is not necessarily safe.
5 **ALL** flying-foxes are potential carriers of this disease but microbats are also a risk. Be particularly careful with sick yellow-bellied sheathtail bats, *S. flaviventris*; one study has shown that 60 per cent of rescued *S. flaviventris* have the virus. It has also been isolated from long-eared bats, *Nyctophilus* species, and might affect others.

BAT RESCUE INC.

**ABOVE** An orphan flying-fox being fed at a bat rescue centre.

between captive bats may be unnaturally easy. A rare virus may become common. Wild bats do not approach humans but a rehabilitated orphan may consider itself to be human and contact humans for comfort if it becomes ill. If you choose to continue this work you owe it to yourself, and to the bats, to be meticulous about your precautions.

Remember that treatment after a bite from an infected animal is urgent and should never intentionally be deferred. On the other hand, if there has been an unavoidable delay it is still worth starting when circumstances permit.

It is hard to know what to make of these new zoonoses and their relationships to bats. I don't think it means bats are especially prone to carry disease, but believe it relates to bat lifestyle and changes caused by human activity. It is confusing for older bat biologists who look back on thousands of bat bites with no ill effect. It is particularly sad for those trying to educate a younger generation to respect and care about these animals. I think we will see more emerging viral diseases in the years to come.

I can only say that the situation will make the knowledge you gain as naturalists, carers or educators just that much more valuable.

# How to catch and survey bats

**N**ovice bat catchers may want to start out by contacting experienced bat researchers. The state museum, wildlife authority or university will be able to give you the names of people to contact. The Australasian Bat Society is also a good starting point to find people interested in bats (www.abs.ausbats.org.au). Most bat biologists are keen to share their knowledge about bats and would appreciate some help with their work.

## Permits

Australian bats are protected fauna and it is illegal to catch or keep them in captivity without a permit. Even flying-foxes considered pest species by commercial fruit growers require a permit for capture. Permits are issued by your state national parks or wildlife authority. You will also require valid reasons for catching, handling and keeping bats, which will be assessed when you apply for a permit.

## Equipment and techniques for catching bats

### HAND NETS

One of the most useful tools for catching bats is the simple hand net or butterfly net. This is usually attached to a 1-m telescopic pole (2 m when extended) and has a large 50-cm diameter hoop. The net is of simple mosquito mesh and long enough that a bat in the end of the net can be trapped with a twist while you catch a second animal. When using hand nets be careful not to strike too hard: if the bat's wing is hit by the hoop of the net it can easily be broken. I usually use a hand net to catch bats inside caves, mines and in buildings, but I have also had some success in luring bats to within striking range by throwing small stones in the air where bats are foraging around a street light. The bat swoops low to chase the pebble and can be caught in the net.

**ABOVE** Using a hand net to capture bats in a cave.

### MIST NETS

Mist nets are a common, cheap and convenient way to catch bats. They are lightweight, fold into small bundles and are very transportable. Mist nets are made of nylon or terylene.

Terylene nets are stronger, softer and more durable than braided nylon and are highly effective. Monofilament terylene nets are hard to come by but are the best nets for catching microbats as the fine mesh is difficult for bats to detect by

**ABOVE** The parts of a mist net.

echolocation. Nylon nets are stiffer, but they are cheaper and useful for rough environments, such as caves and mines.

Mist nets for catching bats have a mesh size of 36 mm and are 50 or 70 denier/2 ply. For catching flying-foxes a larger and heavier net is needed as they quickly damage finer nets. These have a mesh size of up to 100 mm and are usually 2 m high with four pockets (or benches). They come in a variety of lengths, most commonly 5.5-, 9-, 13- and 18-m lengths. Mist nets can be purchased from several suppliers. Monofilament nets are available from Ecotone in Poland: www.ecotone.pl/index.php. Other nets are available from Avinet, PO Box 1103, Dryden, New York, 13053-1103, USA; The Australian Bird Study Association, PO Box A313, South Sydney, NSW 2000; British Trust for Ornithology, Beech Grove, Tring, Hertfordshire HPZ3 5NR, UK.

## MIST NET POLES

Mist net poles can be made of rough bush poles, lengths of bamboo or anything handy that is strong enough. I have always used poles made of aluminium tubing. The most convenient are 1-m lengths with two joined together for each pole. I also make a few 50-cm and 25-cm lengths to add to the poles when on uneven ground. Tubing 2 cm in diameter is strong enough and light. At the top of each pole insert 10 cm of a 25-cm length of the next size smaller telescopic tubing. This is glued in place with epoxy resin. Fifteen centimetres of the insert that protrudes from the top of the pole will neatly fit into the base of another identical pole. I have successfully stacked up to six together for a pole 6 m high.

To avoid damaging the base of the poles I use pole holders. These are 40-cm lengths of 25-mm diameter galvanised water pipe with one end flattened to a spade point. The pole holders are hammered directly into the ground with a small sledgehammer. They support the pole while the nets are set and often nothing else is required, making the erection of several nets and complex patterns of multiple nets from a single pole quite easy. Once the nets are set it is then a simple matter to attach guy ropes where they are needed to keep the nets at the right tension.

## HOW AND WHEN TO SET UP MIST NETS

Nets should be set with a slight sag and with the pockets loose and baggy. This causes the bat to become well tangled. If they are too tight the bats may hit the net and just bounce off.

Most bats are caught in the 2 hours immediately following dusk when there are plenty of insects out in the warmth of the early evening. At this stage the bats have just emerged and are not as agile in their flight. They are hungry and thirsty and not as alert as later in the evening. After the first 2 hours, capture rates usually decline although there may still be plenty of bats flying around; by this time they usually know where the nets are and avoid them.

To reduce the chance of accidentally catching birds, I usually set out the nets about half an hour before sunset and plan to have them ready by dusk. It is also possible to set the nets earlier and furl them—just be sure to tie the nets in the furled position otherwise the wind will open them. High nets on long poles take much longer to set up and require longer poles, considerable lengths of string, pulleys and guy ropes.

Nets must be monitored continuously for the first 2 to 3 hours and then, once most of the bat activity has ceased, checked at least every 15 minutes. Otherwise you will find your nets either full of holes or full of extremely tangled and stressed bats. I usually find that sitting quietly in the dark next to one of the poles allows me to see the bats entering the net, and puts me in a good position to shine a light along the nets every few minutes.

## MACRO MIST NETS

Several nets can also be joined together at the top and bottom to make macro-nets. These large nets are raised on long poles up to 10 m high and cover a large vertical catching area. The nets are raised and lowered on pulleys or metal loops to remove captured bats. Small yacht masts have been used as poles for macro-nets with the bench strings attached to sail slides in the mast. These can be raised and lowered with ease.

## REMOVING BATS FROM NETS

First, grab the bat in the net to stop it from struggling or fluttering its way back out again. Next, determine what side the bat entered the net. This is not always easy. It is important that you remove the bat the way it came in. I find that a leather glove on my left hand is useful for holding the bat and giving it something to chew on. My right hand is then free to untangle the net. It is often easiest to remove the bat tail first, untangling the feet, then one wing, then the head and body, and finally the other wing. Disentangling one wing first, then feet and tail also works well. It helps to start with the least tangled parts; often if the tail and feet are carefully untangled then the whole bat will lift free of the net. The wings can be quite difficult at times and the strands of net have to be carefully lifted over the wrists and thumbs without putting too much strain on the finger bones.

Getting to the bat as quickly as possible after capture makes removal much easier as the bat has had less time to struggle and chew the net. It is a good idea when you are first using nets to carry a pair of fine scissors with you. That way when things appear impossible a few strands can be cut away. This reduces the stress on both bat and handler. It just takes practice and a little patience.

Each bat should be placed in its own clean cloth bag. If there is a shortage of bags then two or three individuals of the same species can be put in together. Only do this with the small vespertilionids. Most other bats should be kept separately, particularly rhinolophids and hipposiderids as they become stressed easily. Most of the emballonurids, molossids and pteropodids can inflict quite nasty bites on each other and carnivorous species such as the greater broad-nosed bat, *Scoteanax rueppellii*, will make a meal of their companions.

I usually mount a couple of bent wire hooks at the top of the net poles and hang the bags of bats on these. This keeps the bats off the ground (and away from feet in the dark) and has the added advantage of attracting other bats to the nets to investigate the calls coming from the bags.

## WHERE TO SET NETS

At night, bats leave their daytime roost and head for their preferred foraging area. They often use a regular pathway, called a flyway. These are an easy route through the vegetation, such as a road through a forest, along a cliff line or over a stream. Flyways are some of the best places to catch bats as they are less alert while commuting and will often blunder into the net or trap before they realise it is there.

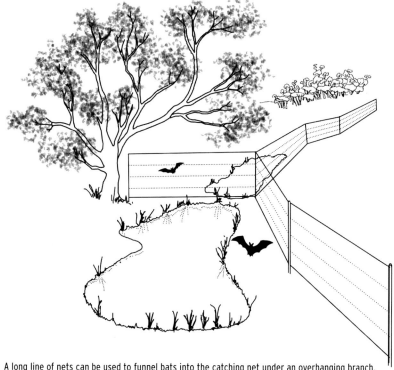

**ABOVE** A long line of nets can be used to funnel bats into the catching net under an overhanging branch.

A mist net in the open is very obvious to most bats so it pays to be sneaky, using vegetation and geography to your advantage. For example, place a net over a creek under a large overhanging tree or branch. When the bat ducks under the branch, as it does every night, it will fly into the net. Alternatively the net can be set just after a sharp bend in the creek. Bats learn fast and after an initial period of capture, success will decline even though there may still be many bats flying around. Once they have worked out where the net is they are very good at avoiding it; for this reason a second night trapping at the same locality is rarely very successful. If you do work the site again, you can try a different net configuration, but it is likely that the bats will be more wary for the next few nights. There are different ways to discover flyways: you can sit and watch for bats at dusk to see where they go, or you can monitor their activity using a bat detector. Over time you will get a feeling for the routes bats use.

It is worth setting nets over water, particularly in northern and inland Australia. Insect numbers are usually higher around water than away from it, particularly in more arid areas, and bats come to water both to drink and to catch insects.

When set over water, the nets should be low enough to stop bats from flying underneath, but not so low that the netted bat will be hanging in the water. Also keep in mind that nets tend to sag as the evening progresses and you may need to adjust the bottom bench string from time to time.

Nets should be placed to maximise the screening effect of background or overhead features such as vegetation. Bats tend to fly along walls of vegetation, roads, cliff lines and creeks, so placing the net diagonally across a roadway or out from a creek bank is usually effective. Placing nets at right angles across the flight path of a bat is usually too obvious: the bat will detect the net and avoid it. I have found that diagonal nets, for example in a Z pattern, guide the bats into the net's corner and before they have a chance to really work out what is happening, they are caught.

In open areas I have found that a long line of nets can be used to funnel the bats into a catching net or trap. This is particularly effective along mostly dry river beds, where the catching net is over water.

In water that is too deep to wade in, I use a pivot net that is set on two pole holders along one bank. The net is swung across the water using the pole to keep the net taut to a third pole holder. As each bat is captured the net is swung away from the water to remove the bat and then back again to catch the next one.

Take some trouble before putting your nets away to remove any twigs, leaves, beetles and so on that have become entangled. This will save considerable frustration at your next trapping site.

## BAT TRAPS (HARP TRAPS)

These wonderful devices can be used in a wide variety of localities and situations. They consist of a rigid square aluminium tube frame that supports two banks of vertical strands of fine fishing line. The fishing line is hard for bats to detect and when they hit it, they usually become caught between the two banks. The bat then struggles and slides down the lines into a large cloth holding bag at the base. The whole contraption is set up on legs that are adjustable for uneven terrain. Traps can be set during the day and left unattended at night. They work for the whole night and many traps can be set over a wide area by one or two people. They are very useful in places such as cave entrances where large numbers of bats may

**LEFT** A dusky leaf-nosed bat has been caught in the strings of a bat trap. As it tries to fly it will slide down the strings into the catching bag.

be captured in a short time. Mist nets in these situations can be a nightmare as you cannot remove the bats from the net fast enough to take down the net.

An excellent range of bat traps is available commercially from Faunatech, PO Box 1655, Bairnsdale, Victoria, www.faunatech.com. They have 2-, 3- and 4-bank models and two sizes available, one with a 4.2-m$^2$ catching area and a narrower, more portable trap with a 3.2-m$^2$ catching area. It is also possible to build your own: see Tidemann and Woodside (1978) for the design.

Bat traps need to be adjusted carefully; fishing lines should be firm when pressed with the open hand. It is worth spending some time sitting quietly by the trap to watch the bats being caught. If the lines have been set too tight most of the bats will bounce off; if too loose they will fly through without getting caught. If you are targeting a particular type of bat you can adjust the trap appropriately. Set the trap tighter than normal for fast flying bats or looser for slow flying bats.

Where possible it's good to check the bat traps several times during the night and remove the captured bats. These bats can then be measured and released during the night. This avoids bats dying from dehydration and cold (particularly horseshoe and leaf-nosed bats), or predation. It also enables lactating females to be released to return to their young as soon as possible.

## SETTING BAT TRAPS
Although bat traps have a much smaller catching area than mist nets, they can be amazingly successful when set in the right places. They are most suited to restricted flyways in forest, such as along tracks and waterways, but can

**RIGHT** A bat trap set up along a flyway over water.

also be used in open areas when placed next to large or unusually shaped trees. They can be used near water and are excellent when used in conjunction with mist nets. The rigid frame of a bat trap makes it easy to hoist into the canopy with ropes, and in one case bicycle wheels were attached to the four corners of the trap and used to lower it down a cliff to a cave entrance.

Bat traps and mist nets will often catch different species of bats in the same locality, so a combination of both methods is the most productive. In most surveys bat traps are moved to a new place each day, but for some bat species, such as flute-nosed bats, *Murina florium*, capture rates are much higher when the traps are left in the same place for at least 5 days.

## FLYING-FOX TRAPS

A giant bat trap has been invented by Tidemann and Loughland (1993) that is designed to capture flying-foxes. It uses the same principles as a bat trap, but on a much larger scale with a catching area of 220 m².

**ABOVE** A bat trap.

It is erected on cables strung between two yacht masts and the whole setup can be dismantled and carried on the roof of a car. It takes three people to set it up and must be monitored continuously. There is no catching bag and bats are grabbed as they slide to the bottom of the trap. When handling large numbers of flying-foxes the handlers use stainless steel mesh butchers' gloves under long leather gloves.

## TRIP LINES

Trip lines provide a convenient method of catching bats where water is too deep to allow access to mist nets. Trip lines are made using fine fishing line (about 3-kg breaking strain is ideal) that are criss-crossed across the water body several times at 5 to 10 cm above the surface. The taut line catches the bat as it comes down to drink and flips it into the water.

Most bats cannot fly off from the water surface (although eastern horseshoe bats, *Rhinolophus megaphyllus*, and some long-eared bats, *Nyctophilus*, can) and will swim rapidly to shore. The bat can be grabbed as it scrambles onto the bank but you will need to be quick. Be careful to keep your light off the bat as it will turn around and swim away from the light. Alternatively, this can be used to your advantage by employing two people, one on each side of the pool.

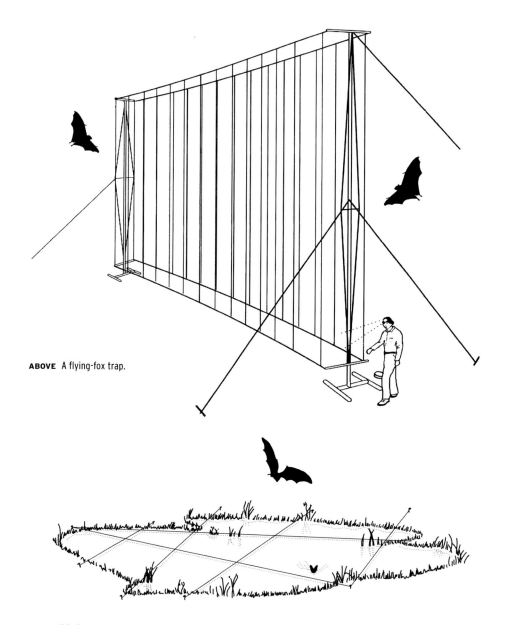

**ABOVE** A flying-fox trap.

**ABOVE** Trip lines set over a pool of water.

## BAT DETECTORS

Ultrasound detectors, or bat detectors as they are more commonly called, are used to listen to bat echolocation calls. The simplest bat detectors reduce the frequency of a bat call by 10 times, bringing it to within the range of human hearing. These detectors are very useful for obtaining information on the presence or absence of bats, locating the best flight paths, finding bats in crevices and tree roosts, etc. Some types are tuneable, providing information on the dominant frequency of the call. They are not usually very useful for identifying frequency modulated (FM) calls, but they can identify some constant frequency (CF) bats in flight.

There are many bat detectors on the market with a wide variety of price tags. It depends on your interests as to what type of detector you should use. A widely used bat detector in Australia is the Anabat detector (Titley Electronics, PO Box 19, Ballina, NSW 2478; www.titley.com.au). This unit can be used alone to listen to calls or can be coupled to a device that analyses calls (called a ZCAIM) and then recorded onto digital storage or a small tape recorder for later, or viewed directly on a portable computer. This records a graphic signature of the bat's call (using zero-crossing analysis) that is displayed as frequency against time. The shape of the call, the upper and lower frequencies, as well as the duration of the call can all be used to help identify the species. These units have been used in Australia for many years, and there are many reference calls available, including several regional guides, that can help you with identification.

## SURVEYING WITH BAT DETECTORS

There are two main methods of surveying with bat detectors–passive recording and active monitoring.

Passive recording is useful when several sites are to be monitored on a single night or when a variety of survey methods are used concurrently. Passive recording is done using a detector and a digital storage card or portable computer. The unit is left to record the calls automatically. It is usually set on the ground with the microphone pointing up or along a flyway. This system enables high quality recordings of calls and complete nights of data to be collected. The detectors can be set late in the afternoon and collected soon after dawn.

Active monitoring is done by conducting walking transits or from the back of a car while it is driven slowly along roads and tracks. Use a spotlight and a hand-held bat detector connected to a recording device. When a bat is spotted it can be followed with the detector. This maximises the length of the call sequence recorded and gives a better chance for good quality calls. This also provides valuable information on the foraging behaviour and flight characteristics of each bat.

An innovative approach to increasing the success of bat traps and bat echolocation call surveys is to use ultraviolet lights to attract insects and concentrate bat activity where you are sampling (black light insect traps are available from Australian Entomological Supplies, Bangalow, NSW). It can also increase the number of quality bat calls recorded, as bats stay in range longer to forage, and can improve bat species inventories particularly in communities where overlap in call characteristics among species is common.

If you are recording near water and the bat activity levels are high, move 10 to 20 m away and record the bats approaching the area. Too many bats recorded simultaneously makes identification difficult.

**LEFT** A bat detector and ultrasonic microphone in a waterproof box will passively record the calls of bats flying past during the night.

Other bat detectors, such as a Pettersson D980 (Pettersson Elektronik, Tallbacksvagen 51, S-756 45 Uppsala, Sweden; www.batsound.com), have three independent systems: scanning heterodyne, retained amplitude frequency division, and time expansion systems. More appropriate for detailed research into echolocation, this detector, combined with a storage device or computer, will record the entire bat call. It allows the analysis of all aspects of the call including peak frequency (FPEAK) values, call harmonics, sonograms and details of signal amplitude. These details can assist with the identification of species such as long-eared bats, *Nyctophilus*. Bat detectors also differ in the quality of the microphones, which strongly influences the frequency range and distance at which the calls can be detected.

Bat detectors have become increasingly valuable in bat survey work. Major advances have been made with the use of small portable computers and easy-to-use bat detectors, but the technique is not as simple as it sounds. It requires patience, skill and a considerable knowledge of bat calls.

Currently it is not possible to identify all the Australian species by their calls and it is unlikely that we will ever be able to confidently identify every call. This is because bats don't have a single consistent call. Many species actually modify their calls in different habitats: the same bat will use a short linear downsweep call in cluttered habitats and a longer, flatter call in open spaces. Combine these features with the fact that many species have calls that are very similar to those of unrelated species, and some of the problems can be appreciated.

In spite of these limitations there has been a great deal of valuable information obtained from bat detectors. Surveys have shown that many species that are difficult to catch by more direct methods are easily recorded using bat detectors. They are passive and cause the bats no stress or injury, they can be used all night and in any habitat, and they are not restricted by the availability of suitable sites for nets or traps.

When surveying bats in a new area it is essential that you catch the bats, identify them and then record their calls when you release them. This will give you an echolocation reference call or signature for that species at that locality. The signature may be surprisingly different from that of the same species at another locality. By building up a library of bat call signatures we will be able to confidently identify more species of bats in flight.

A newly released bat will tend to use a short linear sweep initially, with the call becoming flatter and more diagnostic as it becomes more settled in open space, by which time it may be out of detector range. It is not easy to get good reference recordings, but the following tips may help.

Release the bat in the widest space possible (Chris Corben suggests the size of a football field). Choose an area with no other bats (making sure the ones you have already released have left). Don't use a really bright spotlight to follow the bats as they will fly directly away from it. Instead, keep them just in the edge of the light and they are more likely to circle around and provide good calls. Small pieces of adhesive reflective tape on the bat's belly make it easier to see. Light tags can also be used. Make sure the bats are warm and ready to fly before release, as chilled bats readily enter torpor. Don't throw the bat: let it launch itself. Keep captive bats of the same species nearby (no other species), as the released bat is more likely to return to them. And finally, keep other people away to reduce background noise. One good helper to handle the spotlight is probably all you need.

## CAPTURE AND SURVEY AT ROOST SITES

Bats can be captured at their daytime roosts in caves, mines, buildings, road culverts or trees. Searching for bats in these situations usually involves a good light source and looking for signs of bats as well as the bats themselves. Fresh bat droppings are often the best indication of a roost. When searching caves and mines I spend as much time searching the floor for droppings as I do looking at the ceiling for bats. This is also a useful technique in the roofs of buildings where bats often roost in small crevices.

Once found, the bats can usually be caught with a hand net or by hand. Flighty species can be captured by rigging a mist net inside the cave between the bat and the entrance. If the bats are roosting out of reach they can usually be captured using a bat trap or mist net at the entrance at dusk.

Bat colony sizes can be estimated in the cave by counting a group of, for example, 20 bats and estimating the area of cave wall occupied by those bats. Extrapolate the number of these areas that will fit into the total area occupied by bats and multiply the result by the number of bats originally counted, in this case 20. Estimations of colony sizes are not always possible as in many cases

**LEFT** The author using the first edition of this book to identify bats in the Great Victoria Desert.

BRUCE THOMSON

**LEFT** A cluster of eastern horseshoe bats roosting inside a hollow tree.

the bats may be in inaccessible areas of the cave.

Bat counts can be done at the cave entrance at dusk, using a low-powered light shone across, rather than into, the entrance, so the bats do not see the light until they are outside the cave. Most species of bats have different flight patterns and behaviour; with a bit of practice it is possible to count the bats of each species as they leave the cave (I use a couple of hand-held laboratory click counters). This can provide useful information in terms of numbers, time of exit, foraging times, flight behaviour and predator avoidance behaviour. Entrance watches can be very useful for caves that are large or difficult to explore and for dangerous old mine workings (particularly vertical shafts).

Finding tree roosts of microbats is a matter of being in the right place at dusk when the bats emerge or radio-tracking a bat to its roost tree. Colonies of flying-foxes can often be found by watching their flight patterns at dusk, asking local people, or by their distinctive odour and characteristic squabbling noise in the late afternoon.

Flying-fox counts can be conducted by watching the bats fly out from their camp at dusk. Flying-foxes usually circle the camp several times before peeling off towards a favoured feeding area. There are often several streams of bats heading in different directions. It requires several people (depending on the size of the colony), with each person counting a different stream. Try to count from a spot with a good clear section of sky. Counts need to be conducted over several nights as weather conditions (cloud, wind and light levels) can greatly influence the results.

## LIGHT TAGGING

A cheap and easy method of obtaining information on foraging and flight behaviour is to use light tags. These are chemical lights in small plastic vials (called fishing lights, from Glowstix Australia, www.glowstix.com.au) that come in a range of colours—the bright green ones usually give the greatest range. These are glued directly onto the belly fur using skinbond glue.

The lights remain bright for several hours and can be seen over a considerable distance in open country. The bats groom them off in a few hours. Trying to follow a bat through the forest in the middle of the night can be challenging, but usually quite rewarding. Don't forget to carry a compass or GPS; it can be embarrassing when you can't find your car afterwards.

### RADIO-TRACKING

Radio-tracking small microbats has only been feasible for the last few years with the increasing miniaturisation of components. Bats should not be burdened with more than 5 per cent of their body weight. This means that for a 10-g bat the transmitter must weigh less than 0.5 g. Titley Electronics (PO Box 19, Ballina, NSW 2478) produces a 0.3-g transmitter (suitable for bats as small as 6 g) with a battery life of 11 to 12 days. These transmitters are attached to the back of the bat with skinbond glue after the fur has been trimmed short. The bats usually seem to be able to groom them off after only a few days.

Radio-tracking is a valuable method for obtaining information on roost sites. Bats captured in nets or traps can be fitted with transmitters and followed back to their roost. Usually the roost can be searched for during the day, although it can be difficult to find the bat even when you have located its roost. Foraging behaviour can also be studied by radio-tracking the bat at night.

Flying-foxes can carry quite large transmitters, which have a greater range and a longer battery life. Some very valuable work has been done on the long-term movements of flying-foxes by monitoring radio-tagged animals from aircraft. More recently it has been possible to use satellite tracking transmitters fitted with small solar cells to recharge the battery. These have provided information on the long-distance movements of flying-foxes up to 2000 km per year—and have shown that black flying-foxes, *Pteropus alecto*, can fly from northern Australia to southern New Guinea and back.

## Voucher specimens and samples

Correct identification of the bats being studied is crucial to the outcome of any work, as incorrect or unresolved identifications can invalidate your conclusions. This is true regardless of the type of research being conducted (physiological, anatomical, biochemical, behavioural or some other aspect of the bat's biology) and whether the work is in the field or the laboratory. Conservation needs are impossible to assess without the ability to recognise and differentiate species. The taxonomy of Australian bats is still in such a state of flux that in order to do reliable survey work it may be necessary to collect voucher specimens and/or material for genetic studies.

Voucher specimens received by museums are of immeasurable value, quite apart from confirming your identification. They become the basis for all future research into taxonomy, phylogeny, conservation, distribution, diet, and reproductive biology of that and related bat species. All bats accidentally killed should also be collected. They can be preserved in 70 per cent alcohol or frozen. It is essential that you accurately record the location where the specimen was collected as well as the date on which it was collected.

Often there is a need for genetic material to study cryptic species. There are two main types of genetic samples used: DNA and allozymes.

DNA is the fundamental genetic material in cells and it can be obtained from most biological material, including skin, liver, muscle, and even hair follicles. It needs to be stored in 70 per cent alcohol, or if transport is difficult it can be stored in DMSO (dimethyl sulphoxide)

**ABOVE** Two bat traps set together over a pool near a cave entrance in the Kimberley.

6M NaCl solution. A small circle of skin 3 to 4 mm in diameter can be removed from the wing with a small leather punch. Alternatively, small samples of blood can be collected from a wing vein. It is especially important to preserve (either frozen or in alcohol) small samples of tissue from specimens that are to be preserved in formalin (as formalin chemically alters the structure of DNA).

Allozymes are alternative forms of enzyme proteins. They are obtained from very fresh tissue such as blood, liver, kidney or muscle (liver is the best source). It needs to be frozen immediately in liquid nitrogen.

# Handling, measuring and examining bats

**B**ats should be measured, examined and released as soon as possible after catching. The standard measurements of weight (measured with a spring balance) and forearm length, as well as any distinctive measurements (for example, ear length for long-eared bats, *Nyctophilus* species) useful for identification, should be measured with callipers. Other measurements are optional but can be taken to compare with the measurements recorded in the species account and help confirm identification. Although less accurate, plastic callipers are preferable because they are much less likely to damage a struggling bat. Field measurements do not require the level of accuracy obtained from expensive steel callipers.

Holding bats gently but firmly enough that they don't get away takes a bit of practice, especially when you are trying to measure them. Try to take the measurements in a car, tent or room; this gives you a second chance if the bat escapes.

To measure the bat, hold it in the palm of your left hand, with its face towards you and with your thumb on its belly. In this position most measurements can be done with a minimum of manipulation. It is also possible to examine the bat's sex and reproductive condition, and its teeth. To avoid being bitten it is recommended that a glove is worn on the left hand, although this makes the handling a bit more clumsy. When measuring wingspan be careful not to stretch the bat too much and try to hold the bat by the wrists and forearms rather than the wingtips as a struggling bat may break its delicate finger bones.

## Sex, age and reproductive condition

Each bat should be examined to determine sex, age and reproductive condition. Field observations of the reproductive condition of bats relative to time of year are of great value in helping to understand their life cycle. Sexing a bat is easy as the males have an obvious penis.

### AGE

There are generally three age classes of bats. **Adults:** bats that are in reproductive condition or have reproduced in previous years. Their wing bones are fully formed and the joints have no indication of cartilage between the bones. Adults also often have worn teeth and numerous small scars on their wings and ears. **Sub-adults:** bats that are adult size but have not yet reached sexual maturity. They generally have unworn teeth. In the females the nipples are minute; in males the testes have not descended into the scrotum and there is no sign of an

## MEASUREMENTS USED FOR BAT IDENTIFICATION

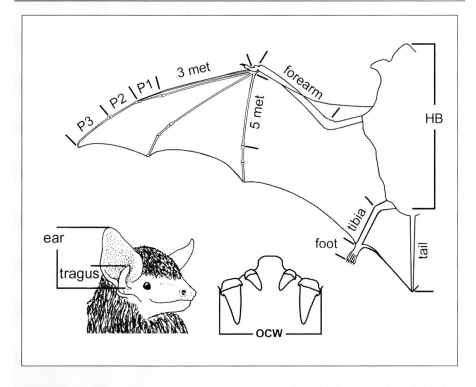

**Wt**—weight in grams (g)

All measurements below are in **millimetres**.

**Fa**—forearm length

**Ear**—length of ear from notch to tip

**Trag**—length of tragus in ear

**Foot**—hind foot length; from heel to toe tips, excluding claws

**Tibia**—tibia or lower leg length

**5 met**—length of metacarpal of fifth digit of wing

**3 met**—length of metacarpal in third digit of wing

**P1**—length of first phalanx of the third digit in the wing

**P2**—length of second phalanx of the third digit in the wing

**P3**—length of third phalanx of the third digit in the wing

**Tail**—tail length; from tail tip to anus

**HB**—head and body length; from nose tip to anus

**WS**—wingspan; from wingtip to wingtip

**Head**—head length; from junction with neck to nose tip

**Skull**—greatest length of the skull

**OCW**—outer canine width; the distance between the outer edge of the upper canines at the gum-line

**HS**—horseshoe width

**Sella**—sella width

epididymal sac. Their wing joints are smooth (not knobbly) and have one or two bands of cartilage and blood vessels clearly visible at the joint when held up to the light.
**Juveniles:** are smaller than sub-adults and adults and often have darker and greyer fur. They may be obviously juvenile and attached to the mother's teat, or flying but not yet fully grown. The wing joints are obviously knobbly.

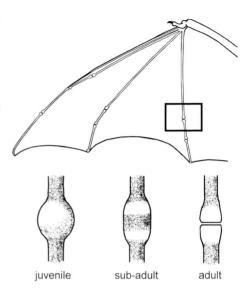

## REPRODUCTIVE CONDITION

The reproductive condition of bats can be assessed to a large extent by observation.

   **Female** bats should be examined for evidence of current, recent or previous pregnancy. The appearance of the teats in the never pregnant, previously pregnant, lactating and post-lactating bats is

| juvenile | sub-adult | adult |

characteristic. Bats have two teats, one near the armpit on each side of the body. Teats can be examined by gently blowing the chest hairs apart and working out towards the 'armpits'; the fur will often part around the teat. Sub-adult or nulliparous females (i.e. that have never given birth) have minute teats (usually just a small dot) which are often very hard to find. **Pregnant** bats in later stages of pregnancy are heavier than other bats and the foetus can often be

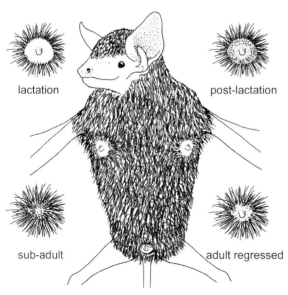

**ABOVE** Changes in teat appearance

detected by feeling the abdomen (but beware of well-fed bats with full stomachs). The foetus usually lies sideways across the belly. The teats become enlarged and at the birth of the young they are obviously swollen. During **lactation** the fur around the nipple becomes worn away and the nipple stretched and distorted. It is usually possible to see the white milk through the skin around the teats. When the young have recently been weaned the mother is said to be at the stage of post-lactation. There is no white patch beneath the skin, but still a circular bare area around the teat and large

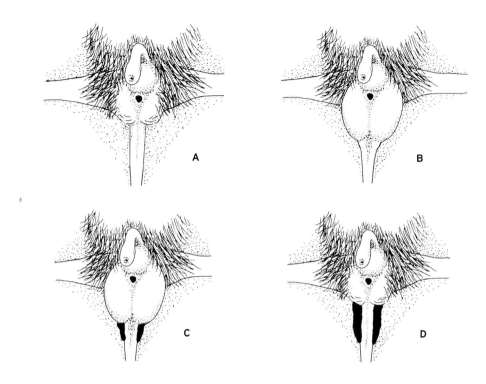

**ABOVE** Changes in testicular and epididymal appearance in vespertilionids. **A** Testes not enlarged: non-reproductive. **B** Testes enlarged: sperm production. **C** Testes enlarged and epididymis distended: sperm production and storage. **D** Testes regressed and epididymis distended: sperm storage.

nipples. In the **regressed** stage, the fur starts to grow back around the nipple and the teat slowly shrinks but remains three to four times the size of the teat before the first pregnancy. The skin around the teat usually becomes darkly pigmented.

Horseshoe bats, leaf-nosed bats and the ghost bat all have an additional pair of **false teats** (or pubic teats) in the pubic region. These do not produce milk but are used by the young to cling to the mother when in flight. Adults that have previously given birth will have large and obvious pubic teats. Sub-adult females have only minute pubic teats. Pubic teats are often easier to find than the true teats and may help to distinguish sub-adult from adult females.

**Male** bats are identified by an obvious external penis. Testes may or may not be obvious. Sperm production is not continuous and is associated with enlargement of the testes. As the testes enlarge they become apparent as swellings in the scrotum at either side of the base of the tail. Sperm is then stored in the epididymis for final maturation before mating. Field observations should record whether the testes are scrotal or not and whether the epididymal sacs are distended. The epididymides lie alongside the tail just behind the scrotum and their degree of enlargement is not necessarily synchronised with the testes. The sac is used for sperm storage in some species. Look also for secondary sexual characteristics such as a throat pouch, which may indicate a readiness to breed.

Testicular patterns vary considerably. Some bats such as leaf-nosed bats do not have a scrotum but retain the testes abdominally except during the mating period when they lie at either side of the penis. Testes in flying-foxes are known to descend to the scrotum or return to the abdomen with changes in temperature. This may even happen when a cloud obscures the sun!

For identification of some bats, such as *Vespadelus* and *Scotorepens*, it will be necessary to examine the **glans penis**. This is the tip of the penis beneath the foreskin. To examine the glans penis you must carefully draw back the foreskin. This can be difficult to do with such small bats but practice makes it easier. You will need a magnifying lens to see the details properly. Try to find a lens that can be held with your eye (such as jewellers use) as you will need both hands.

## Examining teeth

Teeth can usually be examined by placing your index finger on the top of the bat's head or muzzle and gently pulling the skin back away from the mouth. This usually causes the bat to open its mouth and pulls the lips away from the upper teeth. Again a magnifying lens is useful to see the details of the teeth. The upper incisors will be the main ones examined. Luckily these are at the front of the mouth and easy to see.

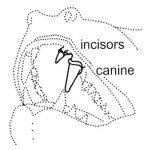

## Releasing bats

Release bats immediately after they have been examined, measured and identified. If it is a cool night many bats may enter torpor and they must be warmed up again before they can fly. You can put them in a cloth bag and place them inside your shirt. Your body temperature should warm them up within 5 minutes so they will be ready to fly. If they are still reluctant to fly then place them on a branch of a tree and they will fly away when they are ready. **Don't try to force them to fly by throwing them into the air.**

It is also important to try to release the bats at night, near to where they were captured, as bats flying during daylight hours quickly fall prey to birds such as falcons and butcherbirds. One difficulty with bat traps is that the bats are removed from the bag in the early morning when it is too late to release them. In this situation the bats can be kept during the day and released the following night. Be sure to keep them at a comfortable temperature, in the shade. When you have no choice but to release them during the day it is often possible to find an old tree with cracks and hollows. Place the bat on the tree and often they will find a crevice to rest for the day.

Blossom bats suffer rapidly from lack of food and water when held in a bag for more than an hour. Make up a concentrated sugar (or honey) and water syrup in a glass and then feed it to the bats with a teaspoon. They lick it up avidly once they get started and recover very quickly.

Part II

## The Species

# Key to bat families

**1a** Tail membrane absent or, if present, not joined between legs; claws on thumb and second finger of wing (except *Dobsonia* which has furless back); eyes large, head dog-like; no fleshy nose-leaf; navigates using eyesight.
→ ● **Family Pteropodidae** (page 62)

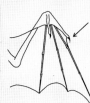

**1b** Tail membrane joined between legs; no claw on second finger of wing; eyes relatively small (except ghost bat); may have fleshy nose-leaf and/or complex folds; navigates using echolocation. → **2**

**2a** Tail fully enclosed within the tail membrane *or* tail is absent. → **3**

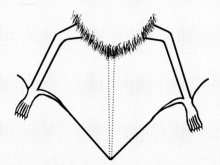

**2b** Tail not fully enclosed in tail membrane → **7**

**3a** Large elaborate nose-leaf covering large portion of face. → **4**

**3b** Nose-leaf absent or small simple ridge on muzzle. → **6**

**4a** No tail but full tail membrane; large bat; prominent eyes; large ears joined above head; forked tragus of ear.
→ ● **Family Megadermatidae** (page 82)

**4b** Tail present; eyes small; tragus absent. → **5**

**5a** Nose-leaf covers most of face; lower leaf a distinct horseshoe shape; large projection (sella) protrudes from the centre of the nose-leaf and the upper leaf is pointed; toes with three joints each.
→ ● **Family Rhinolophidae** (page 84)

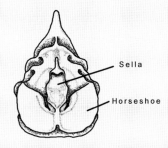

Sella

Horseshoe

**5b** Nose-leaf less extensive; a flattened square or oval disk; no sella protruding from the centre, but small club-shaped structures may be present; the upper  leaf is square or rounded; toes with two joints each.

→ ● **Family Hipposideridae** (page 90)

**6a** Terminal phalanx of the third digit of wing is a similar length to the second phalanx.

→ ● **Family Vespertilionidae** (page 104)

**6b** Terminal phalanx of the third digit of wing is at least three times the length of the second phalanx.

→ ● **Family Miniopteridae** (page 179)

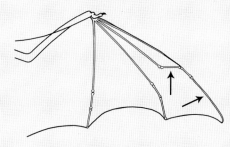

**7a** Substantial portion of tail extends beyond the tail membrane.

→ ● **Family Molossidae** (page 188)

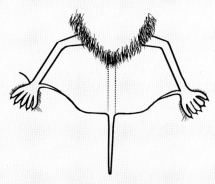

**7b** End of tail projects through the upper surface of tail membrane into a sheath of skin.

→ ● **Family Emballonuridae** (page 205)

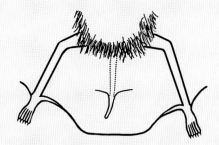

# Fruit Bats
## Family **PTEROPODIDAE**: Key to Species

**B**ats of the family Pteropodidae have no nose-leaf. The ear is simple, with no tragus, with the edge forming an unbroken ring. These bats do not echolocate. They use their large, well-developed eyes and sense of smell to navigate and find food. The thumb is long with a well-developed claw. The second finger is relatively independent of the third finger, and usually bears a small claw (*Dobsonia* is an exception). The tail membrane, if present, is a narrow band of skin inside the legs. The tail is either short or absent and not attached to the tail membrane.

**1a** Large size; forearm length greater than 100 mm. → **2**

**1b** Small to medium size; forearm length less than 75 mm. → **7**

**2a** Wing membranes joined along the midline of the back, forming pockets between the wing and back giving the impression of a naked back; no claw on second digit of wing; short tail; forearm length 138–155 mm.
→ *Dobsonia magna* (page 64)

**2b** Wing membranes attached along sides of body; no tail. → **3**

**3a** Only on Christmas Island, Indian Ocean; forearm length 110–140 mm.
→ *Pteropus natalis* (page 74)

**3b** Not on Christmas Island. → **4**

**4a** Wings red-brown and translucent in flight; usually roost in dense clusters often low to the ground; fur reddish to pale brown, sometimes with a pale yellow-brown mantle on back of neck; forearm length 116–140 mm.
→ *P. scapulatus* (page 78)

**4b** Wings dark and opaque in flight; usually roost with space between individuals and higher in trees; fur mainly black or grey.
→ **5**

**5a** Head and body fur grey; rusty brown mantle completely encircling neck; legs hairy to toes; forearm length 151–177 mm.
→ *P. poliocephalus* (page 76)

**5b** Head and body fur mainly black; mantle on shoulders when present does not fully encircle neck; lower legs not furred. → **6**

**6a** Prominent pale yellow eye rings and yellow mantle; forearm length 150–183 mm.
→ *P. conspicillatus* (page 72)

**6b** Eye rings absent or inconspicuous; mantle brown or absent; forearm length 153–191 mm. → *P. alecto* (page 70)

**7a** Medium size, forearm length greater than 60 mm; long tubular nostrils; obvious tail; wing  membranes spotted with yellow; upper incisors present, lower incisors absent.
→ *Nyctimene robinsoni* (page 68)

**7b** Small size, forearm length less than 50 mm; nostrils not tubular; no tail or tail minute; wings uniform brown. → **8**

**8a** Minute tail; interfemoral flaps of skin about 5 mm wide along the inside of the legs; four small lower incisors of equal size with a gap between inner pair; mature males have a naked V-shaped gland on chest.
→ *Macroglossus minimus* (page 66)

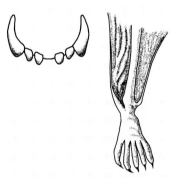

**8b** No tail; no interfemoral flaps of skin along inside of legs but fringe of long hairs instead; outer lower incisors much larger than inner pair without gap; no chest gland in males.
→ *Syconycteris australis* (page 80)

# Bare-backed fruit bat

## *Dobsonia magna* Thomas, 1905

● **DISTRIBUTION** N. Qld from Cooktown to Cape York; and Torres Strait. A single individual recorded from Chillagoe. Extralimital distribution in New Guinea and islands adjacent to n. and w. coasts of New Guinea.

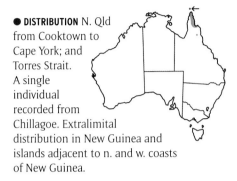

● **DESCRIPTION** This large and distinctive fruit bat differs from flying-foxes in its unusual wings that join along the mid-line of the back rather than along the sides of the body. The furless wings give the impression of a hairless back. The back is fully furred under the wings where deep pockets have been formed on either side of the body. The fur on the shoulders and head is black-brown. The belly is a lighter grey-brown and sparsely furred. There is a short tail. Claws on the thumbs and feet are white and there is no claw on the second digit of the wing. The unusual wing shape causes this bat to have a characteristic sound in flight, a hollow 'pock-pock-pock'.

● **ROOST HABITS** Bare-backed fruit bats live in small colonies of less than 100 in Australia, although they are found in colonies of many thousands in New Guinea. They usually roost in twilight conditions in caves, under boulder piles, and in disused mines and concrete bunkers, as well as in dark rainforest thickets and large tree hollows. A colony of 13 that I came across near Iron Range was roosting in a pile of large granite boulders 2–3 m above the ground. Initially the bats were hanging from the walls alone or in pairs, but when disturbed they flew off and on return roosted together clumped into a single tight mass with their feet intertwined and their bodies pressed against each other. Every so often one bat would leave the group and fly over to where we sat, hovering only a metre above our heads for up to 30 seconds, before returning to the roost. Inside the cave they flew slowly, in a very upright position.

● **HABITAT** Rainforest, gallery forest and tropical woodlands.

● **DIET AND FORAGING** They feed on a variety of native fruits (particularly *Ficus*, *Terminalia* and *Callophylum*), and eucalypt blossom, such as bloodwood. They also eat cultivated fruits including bananas and pawpaw. Like flying-foxes they tend to follow water courses when commuting between roost and feeding areas but unlike them they forage alone and are silent at night. Their flight is more controlled and manoeuvrable than that of flying-foxes, enabling them to fly slowly within the forest canopy. This gives them

| MEASUREMENTS | New Guinea | | | | | | | | |
|---|---|---|---|---|---|---|---|---|---|
| | | Wt | Fa | Ear | Foot | Tibia | Tail | HB | WS |
| | MEAN | 425 | 148.8 | 32.1 | 39.7 | 68.8 | 33.7 | 212 | 1010 |
| | MIN | 325 | 138 | 28.8 | 37.0 | 63.6 | 26.8 | 192 | - |
| | MAX | 525 | 155 | 37.4 | 43.0 | 74.4 | 39.0 | 230 | - |
| | NO | 54 | 54 | 9 | 6 | 4 | 9 | 9 | 1 |

Dwyer 1975; Flannery 1995a.

BRUCE THOMSON

access to food not easily available to flying-foxes such as cauliflorous fruits and flowers.

● **REPRODUCTION** Females develop folds of flesh around the vagina and both sexes develop glands on the cheek and at the shoulder from April to June. These glands probably produce the bat's characteristic musty odour and are thought to have a role in courtship. Copulation occurs in May and June. A single young is born between September and November after a 5-month gestation. The newborn weighs about 55 g and has a forearm length of 63 mm. The mother carries the young bat for about 1 month and nurses it for a further 3–4 months. It is weaned at the height of the wet season, in January to February. Males become sexually mature at 2 years of age. In New Guinea the timing of reproduction is variable.

● **NOTES** The strange structure of the wings pushes air into the pockets between the wings and the back, making the wings clap together at the top of the up-stroke, producing the characteristic flight noise. The additional surface area of the wing is thought to create extra lift, contributing to their ability to hover and manoeuvre in flight. They can also fly fast and in New Guinea have been seen to fold their wings and drop 300 m, almost vertically, into the entrance of a cave.

**REFERENCES** Bonaccorso 1998; Dwyer 1975; Flannery 1995a, b; Hall, in Strahan 1995; Robson 1986; Wilson 1985.

# Northern blossom bat

## *Macroglossus minimus* (Geoffroy, 1810)

● **DISTRIBUTION**
Kimberley, WA;
across Top End
to Cape York
Peninsula;
along Qld coast
s. to Tully.
Extralimital
range: s.e. Asia to Solomon Is.

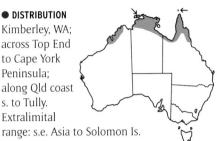

● **DESCRIPTION** A miniature flying-fox with **long pointed muzzle** and **very long tongue**. The fur is a uniform **light reddish brown**, slightly paler on the belly. **Very similar to the eastern blossom bat,** *Syconycteris australis*, but **differs** in having a very **small stub of a tail**, a narrow (5–10 mm) **flap of skin extending along the inside of the legs** from the base of the tail to the calcar on the ankles and **lower incisors of uniform size** but with **an obvious gap between the inner pair**. In the **adult male** there is a **V-shaped sternal gland**, like a thick pink welt across the chest.

● **ROOST HABITS** They roost alone or in small groups of two or three, among thick foliage, in bamboo thickets or in palm fronds. They have also been reported to roost in the rolled-up leaves of bananas and under the eaves of huts.

● **HABITAT** Rainforest, monsoon forest, mangroves, paperbark swamps, bamboo thickets and riverine vegetation. They can also be found in eucalypt woodlands adjacent to these habitats.

● **DIET AND FORAGING** Northern blossom bats rely mainly on nectar and pollen, although they do eat some fruit, such as *Ficus* (figs) and *Timonius*. Their long tongues collect nectar with rows of modified lingual papillae that form a nectar-absorbing mop. They feed on heavily flowering *Melaleuca* and *Syzygium* trees, mangrove (particularly *Sonneratia*), and banana flowers. These bats are capable of hovering in front of a flower but more often they land, usually quite awkwardly, and hang sprawled across the flower. Their fur becomes covered in pollen in the process. The hairs are modified with rough scales to catch the pollen which is later groomed off and eaten. Pollen is their major source of protein. In New Guinea adults hold an exclusive home range of about 6 ha with core areas around food plants of 1.5 ha whereas sub-adults usually have overlapping ranges. Adults appear to defend their food resources from other bats by chasing the intruder, vocalising and wing clapping.

One hot humid night near Darwin, a northern blossom bat hovered repeatedly around my head. It then landed and licked the salty sweat from my forehead and face, returning for more several times over the next 10 minutes.

| MEASUREMENTS | | Wt | Fa | Ear | Tibia | 3 met | HB | WS |
|---|---|---|---|---|---|---|---|---|
| | MEAN | 12.8 | 40.0 | 14.1 | 17.5 | 30.1 | 58.5 | 288 |
| | MIN | 10.5 | 38.1 | 12.4 | 14.7 | 27.4 | 49.0 | 268 |
| | MAX | 19.5 | 43.0 | 16.0 | 19.2 | 33.4 | 67.0 | 314 |
| | NO | 46 | 39 | 31 | 23 | 8 | 33 | 8 |

S. Churchill; Kitchener et al. 1981.

● **REPRODUCTION** Young males become sexually mature at 7 months and develop the large V-shaped sternal gland. At this time the testes descend into the scrotum and males develop a strong, pungent odour. An adult male approaches a roosting female, mounts her, copulates for 10–15 seconds, and flies off. Captive animals in the Top End have at least two litters per year, with young born from February to March and from August to October. One female produced three successive litters in April, December and March. The single young is born with a fine covering of fur and a short muzzle. It clings to the female constantly for 6–10 days after which it remains at the roost while the female forages. The young can fly well by 40 days but hang onto the female at the roost (in captivity) until they are 6 months old. I once caught a lactating female (13 g) carrying a very large young (9 g) in early October at the McIlwraith Range.

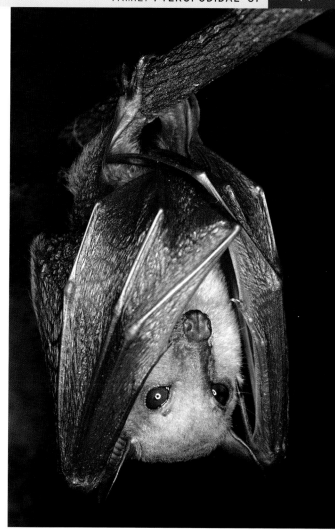

● **NOTES** These bats burn up energy very fast. When foraging their metabolic rate is twice the resting rate and although they live in the tropics they enter torpor for several hours every day. This drops their energy expenditure to 60–80% of a normal resting bat. Captured bats should be released promptly as they rapidly become low on energy and may die. I have found that feeding them a concentrated sugar and water syrup from a teaspoon gives them enough energy to get going again. It also creates an opportunity to watch their long tongues in action. Damian Milne tells me that they make a distinctive metallic call that can be heard at night in backyard gardens of Darwin.

**REFERENCES** Bartels et al. 1998; Birt et al. 1997; Bonaccorso 1998; Bonaccorso & McNab 1997; Flannery 1995a, b; Geiser et al. 1996; Hood & Smith 1989; Kitchener et al. 1981; McKean et al., in Strahan 1995; D. Milne (pers. com.); Webber 1992.

# Eastern tube-nosed bat

## *Nyctimene robinsoni* Thomas, 1904

● **TAXONOMY** This species has always been considered to be restricted to Australia but recent genetic work indicates it is also common in New Guinea, under several species names. Species identification and taxonomy in this genus is confusing. Although there are several records of *Nyctimene cephalotes* occurring on Cape York and Torres Strait Islands these are considered dubious. Examination of the literature gives no indication on how to separate *N. cephalotes* from *N. robinsoni*. Indeed they are the same size and have the same distinguishing features.

● **DISTRIBUTION** E. coast from n. NSW to Cape York Peninsula and Torres Strait and into New Guinea.

● **DESCRIPTION** A beautifully marked fruit bat distinguished by its **long, protruding, tube-like nostrils** and **bright yellow spots splashed across its wings and ears.** The **fur is grey to reddish brown** all over with a distinct **narrow black stripe along the spine.** The upper incisor teeth are present but it **does not have lower incisors** and the modified lower canines are almost touching. The tail is quite long. The bat makes a **distinctive whistling call** while in flight. In north Qld they can be heard in the forest most nights, often several bats calling at once. In NSW they call only in the warmer months from October to April and are usually solitary.

● **ROOST HABITS** Eastern tube-nosed bats roost during the day in foliage with their wings wrapped around them. They are very inconspicuous, even on quite exposed foliage. One evening after measuring two individuals I had netted, I placed them side by side on a low nearby branch, about 2 m above the ground. Expecting them to fly away during the night I gave them no further thought. The following afternoon when packing up camp I noticed they were still there although I must have walked within half a metre of them repeatedly for most of the previous night and all that day. Both animals watched me through slitted eyes whenever I approached, but made no other movement.

Some individuals roost at the same place each day for years, others roost in the last tree they were feeding in before dawn. They usually roost alone but groups of up to five animals have been found roosting together.

● **HABITAT** Tropical and subtropical rainforest, gallery forests and wet sclerophyll forests. In subtropical areas they favour streamside habitats within coastal rainforest and moist eucalypt forests with a well-developed rainforest understorey.

| | | Wt | Fa | Ear | Foot | 3 met | Tail | HB | WS |
|---|---|---|---|---|---|---|---|---|---|
| MEASUREMENTS | MEAN | 50.9 | 67.4 | 17.5 | 12.6 | 47.3 | 22.7 | 87.5 | 475 |
| | MIN | 42.3 | 65.0 | 15.8 | 11.0 | 46.4 | 21.0 | 82.0 | 455 |
| | MAX | 59 | 68.9 | 19.6 | 15.2 | 49.3 | 24.0 | 93.0 | 495 |
| | NO | 49 | 20 | 6 | 6 | 6 | 6 | 6 | 6 |

S. Churchill; J. Maclean; Spencer & Fleming 1989.

● **DIET AND FORAGING** They eat a variety of fleshy fruit from both understorey rainforest trees and canopy trees, favouring figs (*Ficus* spp.), *Eugenia*, *Syzigium* and *Randia sessilis*. They eat a lot of cauliflorous fruit which they consume either on the spot or carry away. In NSW they tend to forage in the canopy over 20 m above the ground on rainforest tree fruits, bangalow palm, mistletoe, and *Eucalyptus* blossom. They eat mainly firm fruit that they hold against their chest with their thumb claws and take large neat bites with their modified lower canines. They have large, broad wings for their size, enabling them to carry heavy loads of fruit (up to 30 g) and to hover, turn around in mid-air, and manoeuvre in dense vegetation. In NSW they forage at night usually within 200 m of their day roost. In Qld they forage further afield, usually 500 m, and up to 1 km from their day roosts.

● **REPRODUCTION** They give birth to a single young between October and December. Lactating females have been caught in November and December. The young is carried by the mother until quite large.

● **NOTES** They are capable of entering torpor and can drop their body temperature by as much as 8°C thereby reducing metabolic rates to only one-quarter of normal at temperatures of 25°C. They can rewarm very rapidly and are able to fly after only 20 seconds. These bats seem to be particularly vulnerable to being caught on barbed wire fences. Jenny Maclean at Tolga Bat Hospital had 14 tube-nosed bats suffering barbed wire injuries brought in during the month following Cyclone Larry in 2006.

**REFERENCES** Donnellan et al. 1995; Duncan et al. 1999; Hall & Pettigrew 1995; Hall et al., in Strahan 1995; J. Maclean (pers. com.); Milledge 1987; Richards 1986; Schulz 1995a; Spencer & Fleming 1989.

# Black flying-fox

## *Pteropus alecto* Temminck, 1837

● **DISTRIBUTION**
Widespread in n.
Australia from
Shark Bay,
WA, to n. NSW.
Since the 1930s,
s. limit of
distribution on e. coast has
moved s. from Rockhampton to
Sydney (over 1200 km).
Extralimitally in Indonesia and s. New
Guinea.

● **DESCRIPTION** A widespread and common bat
of northern Australia, it is a **large species**
with a **forearm length of 153–191 mm**. The
**fur is black**, often with a **reddish brown
mantle** on the **back of the neck**. The **black
belly fur is sometimes sprinkled with white
tipped hairs** giving a frosted appearance.
The **head is black** and some individuals have
faint red-brown eye rings. The **leg is furred
to the knee.**

● **ROOST HABITS** Black flying-foxes camp in
mangroves, rainforest, bamboo, *Melaleuca*
and monsoon forests. Camps comprise
500–30 000 individuals and may be
considerably larger. The same camp may be
used for many years. In southern Qld large,
reproductively important camps are formed
throughout summer (September to April),
after which the juveniles form winter camps
locally and adults disperse to distant smaller
camps. In the Top End the wet season
(summer) camps are in rainforest; in the dry
season (winter) the bats move only a short
distance, say 100 km, to camp in bamboo
thickets and mangroves, relying on blossom
rather than the fruit they lived on during the
wet. I have seen camps in the better lit
portions of large open caves at Chillagoe,
Qld, and Tunnel Creek, in WA, with some
individuals hanging from the cave roof over
40 m from the entrance.

● **HABITAT** A wide range of habitats in tropical
and subtropical woodlands. Monsoon
rainforest and *Melaleuca* open forests
provide a rich source of food when females
bear and raise young. The tall open eucalypt
forests provide widespread, rich and
abundant blossom. Mangroves and
floodplains are important for maternity
roosts, providing young with protection from
predators.

● **DIET AND FORAGING** Groups of bats will travel
up to 50 km from their camp to foraging
areas but usually remain within a 20-km
radius. Their preferred food is fleshy fruits
and the blossoms of eucalypts, *Melaleuca* and
turpentines as well as a variety of other
native and introduced blossoms. They have
been seen to eat the leaves of trees (*Albizia*)
by chewing the leaves into a bolus,
swallowing the liquid and then spitting out
the fibre. This provides the bat with most of

| | | Wt | Fa | Ear | Tibia | HB | Skull |
|---|---|---|---|---|---|---|---|
| **MEASUREMENTS** | MEAN | 674 | 171 | 34.4 | 86 | 250 | 68.8 |
| | MIN | 590 | 153 | 29.0 | 81 | 186 | 67.2 |
| | MAX | 880 | 191 | 37.0 | 90 | 280 | 70.2 |
| | NO | 53 | 70 | 9 | 4 | 19 | 9 |

Johnson 1964; Kitchener et al. 1981; M. Vardon.

the protein and nutrients from the leaves without the bulk. They often use the same technique for eating fruit, notably mangoes, spitting out the fibres after extracting the juice. I have watched them licking sap from incisions in eucalypt trees made by yellow-bellied gliders in north Qld.

● **REPRODUCTION** In southern Qld these bats congregate in large camps from early spring to late autumn. This is where the young are born, raised and weaned, and the next mating and conception occur. The adults mate in March and April, the females becoming pregnant before dispersing for the winter months. Pregnancy lasts for 27 weeks, with most births occurring from September to November. In the Top End births occur 3 months later, in January and February. It appears that the timing of reproduction varies according to the seasonal abundance of regional food resources. In the wet season the flying-foxes move to camps in rainforest where fruit is available. They remain here during pregnancy and birth and until the young are old enough to fly. The bats move in May to the dry season camps in mangroves and bamboo, when eucalypt and *Melaleuca* blossom are abundant. The young are weaned and the adults mate while in the dry season camps.

● **NOTES** Black flying-foxes have a sustained flight speed of 25 km/h. With wind assistance, speeds of 60 km/h have been recorded. Bats fitted with satellite tracking

BRUCE THOMSON

radio-collars have flown across Torres Strait between New Guinea and Australia, a distance of 150 km.

**REFERENCES** Breed 2006; Hall, in Strahan 1995; Johnson 1964; Kitchener et al. 1981; Lowry 1989; Markus 2002; Markus & Hall 2004; Martin et al. 1987; Nelson 1965a, b; Palmer et al. 2000; Palmer & Woinarski 1999; Pinson 2007; Ratcliffe 1931; Stager & Hall 1983; Tidemann et al. 1999; Vardon & Tidemann 1998, 2000; Vardon et al. 2001.

# Spectacled flying-fox

## *Pteropus conspicillatus* Gould, 1850

● **DISTRIBUTION**
Discontinuous distribution in n. Qld from Hinchinbrook Island, n. to Cooktown, including Atherton and Windsor Tablelands, several inland records near Charters Towers. Cape York Peninsula around Iron Range and McIlwraith Range and including Torres Strait Is. Extralimital distribution: Indonesia and New Guinea.

● **DESCRIPTION** A beautiful, **large black flying-fox** with **rings of pale yellow fur around the eyes**. There is a mantle of **pale yellow fur across the back of the neck and shoulders**. Occasionally pale yellow fur is found on the face and the top of the head. Their legs are furred to the knee.

● **ROOST HABITS** Spectacled flying-foxes roost in camps of many hundreds or thousands of individuals. This species does not often roost with other species of flying-foxes. Favoured camp sites are in tall rainforest and gallery forest trees, but they will also camp in mangroves, paperbark, eucalypt forest and tall *Acacia* trees.

● **HABITAT** In the wet season this species is capable of finding food in both coastal and upland rainforest but in the cooler months the tablelands are deserted in favour of the coast or the drier western fringe. They also make extensive use of woodland species, particularly flowering *Melaleuca*, so that woodland near rainforest may be as important as rainforest itself.

● **DIET AND FORAGING** Spectacled flying-foxes eat at least 35 species of rainforest fruits (primarily *Ficus, Terminalia, Syzygium* and *Eugenia*) and eucalypt blossom to a lesser extent. Plant foliage (*Albizia*) is occasionally eaten by chewing and spitting out the fibre. Preferred rainforest fruits are commonly light coloured, perhaps because they are easier to find visually from above the canopy. While feeding in a tree, these flying-foxes defend a feeding territory of several cubic metres, fighting and squabbling with other individuals that enter this space. Evicted individuals usually carry a piece of fruit a considerable distance before roosting to eat it. This behaviour helps in the dispersal of rainforest seeds. After a severe cyclone they have been observed to land on the ground in search of fallen fruit. They have recently been observed eating large numbers of scarab beetles that had infested a *Glochidion* tree. They chewed the beetles thoroughly and spat out the exoskeleton. They will also drink sea water.

| MEASUREMENTS | | Males | | | Females | | | Both | | |
|---|---|---|---|---|---|---|---|---|---|---|
| | | Wt | Fa | Head | Wt | Fa | Head | Ear | Tibia | HB |
| | MEAN | 626 | 168 | 79.0 | 570 | 166 | 76.5 | 31.3 | 82.8 | 233.5 |
| | MIN | 380 | 150 | 64 | 420 | 150 | 64 | 25.0 | 76.0 | 225 |
| | MAX | 950 | 183 | 92 | 806 | 182 | 84 | 36.0 | 87.5 | 247 |
| | NO | 232 | 236 | 232 | 237 | 240 | 237 | 14 | 14 | 7 |

S. Fox; J. Maclean.

BRUCE THOMSON

many months, the peak mating season is in March and April when most females become pregnant. Scapular glands regress in May and sperm production declines rapidly to its lowest level in June. Females ovulate from late February through to May, with peak conception occurring around early April. Pregnancy lasts for 27 weeks and the single (though occasionally twins) young is born between October and December. For the first 4 weeks the young cling tightly to the mother's belly fur with their oversized feet and thumb claws, their mouth firmly clamped to a nipple, while they are carried on nightly foraging trips. After 4 weeks of age the young are too heavy to be carried, and are left at camp each night while the females feed. The juveniles fly out increasing distances each night with the adults and are then left together in nursery trees often many kilometres from the camp. They are brought back to the main camp again each

● **REPRODUCTION** The reproductive patterns of the larger flying-foxes are similar and are summarised briefly here. Spermatogenesis starts in September with testicular size increasing and the testes descending into the scrotum in December. The testes are scrotal from December until April with maximum sperm production in February and March and epididymal storage peaking in April. At this time the males establish small, clearly defined territories that they defend from other males. They mark their territory with secretions from their scapular glands. Although occasional mating occurs over

morning. After 5 months of lactation the young are weaned from March to May at which time they congregate in nursery trees within the camp. Females are capable of breeding at 1 year of age but, in captivity, few of these young survive. Males probably do not breed for 3 or 4 years. Their natural lifespan is unknown but captive individuals have lived for 17 years.

**REFERENCES** Andersen 1912; Flannery 1995a, b; S. Fox (pers. com.); Garnett et al. 1999; Hall 1987; Pinson 2006; Richards 1987, 1990a, b; Richards & Spencer, in Strahan 1995; Spencer 2005; Tidemann 1993b.

# Christmas Island flying-fox

## *Pteropus natalis* Thomas, 1887

● **DISTRIBUTION**
Endemic to
Christmas Island,
Indian Ocean, an Australian
territory.

● **DESCRIPTION** A small
flying-fox; males and
females are the same size. The
fur is a **uniform blackish or dark brown**,
occasionally with a **slightly paler wash on
the back of the neck**. The **fur is peppered
with greyish white hairs**, particularly on the
belly. This is the only species of fruit bat on
Christmas Island.

● **ROOST HABITS** They roost in camps of up to
several hundred, but also roost alone or in
groups of two or three throughout the
island. All camp sites are located in semi-
deciduous rainforest on the coastal terrace or
around the first inland cliff. The population
has declined significantly in recent years.
Andrews in 1897 describes them as being so
common as to be a nuisance. In September
1984 there were five well-used camps
containing 3700 individuals; three of these
were used as maternity camps and occupied
year round, while the other two camps were
used seasonally by juveniles. The total
population was estimated to be about 6000.
In September 2006 a population count of
1400 was made. These bats are not easy to
locate and earlier in 2006 it had appeared

that there were no more than 500
individuals, with three of the five known
camps occupied. The reasons for the
population decline are not known.

From the time of their discovery these
bats have been largely diurnal, with the peak
activity period several hours before sunset
and briefly again at dawn. This provides
access to diurnal flowers and allows use of
the daily wind patterns to commute from
foraging to roosting areas. With declining
population they have become less diurnal
and are now rarely seen prior to 2 hours
before sunset.

● **HABITAT** Being highly mobile, the flying-
foxes use most of the vegetated habitats
present on Christmas Island. They forage and
roost in semi-deciduous rainforest on lower
terraces, semi-deciduous rainforest on
shallow soils of higher terraces, evergreen
rainforest on deeper plateau and terrace
soils, mangrove forest, and perennially wet
areas. They also feed in the urban regions
and mining areas. In the large areas of
regenerating forest (where the rainforest was
cleared for phosphate mining) a small South
American tree (*Muntingia calabura*) was
planted widely. It has become a favoured
food plant of the flying-foxes and the seeds
of this plant have been spread to many areas
of disturbed forest. As *Muntingia* bears fruit
while still quite a small shrub, the flying-
foxes often feed in these low bushes very

| MEASUREMENTS | | Wt | Fa | Ear | Foot | 3 met | Skull |
|---|---|---|---|---|---|---|---|
| | MEAN | 350 | 128 | 26 | 40 | 87.7 | 55.2 |
| | MIN | 220 | 110 | 25 | 37.5 | 83.0 | 54.5 |
| | MAX | 500 | 140 | 27 | 42.5 | 92.5 | 56.0 |
| | NO | 110 | 110 | 12 | 12 | 12 | 12 |

Andersen 1912; Tidemann 1985.

close to the ground where they are caught and eaten by feral cats.

● **DIET AND FORAGING** They eat predominantly fruit but will also eat blossom and occasionally leaves. They are known to feed on over 35 species of plants. The most common native food items are the fruits or flowers of *Barringtonia*, *Celtis*, *Dysoxylum*, *Ficus*, *Inocarpus*, *Macaranga*, *Maclura*, *Planchonella*, *Syzigium*, *Terminallia* and *Tristiropsis*, as well as introduced species such as *Cocos*, *Eugenia*, *Muntingia* and *Mangifera*.

● **REPRODUCTION** They have a polygamous mating system with a small proportion of the males monopolising most of the adult females. They breed once a year and a single young is born after a 4–5-month gestation. There is a peak in births from December to February but the timing appears to vary slightly in different years. The females are sexually mature at 6 months and conceive in their first year, while the males do not mature until about 18 months of age. In adults, there is a strongly skewed sex ratio with three times as many females as males.

● **NOTES** They make an unforgettable sight as they ride the updrafts from the trade winds in the late afternoon, to swirl and glide to their foraging sites.

REFERENCES Andersen 1912; Andrews 1900; James et al. 2006; Nelson 1965a; Tidemann 1985, 1987; Tidemann et al. 1994.

GLENN HOYE

# Grey-headed flying-fox
## *Pteropus poliocephalus* Temminck, 1825

● **DISTRIBUTION** Coastal e. Australia from Maryborough, Qld, through NSW to s.w. Vic. In last 150 years, n. limit of range has contracted s. by 750 km from Cape Upstart to Maryborough. Presently dist. extends w. to about the 800-mm rainfall isohyet. Endemic to Australia.

● **DESCRIPTION** The only Australian flying-fox to have a **mantle of rusty brown fur fully encircling the neck.** The **fur on the back is dark grey** although some individuals have a pronounced silver frosting to the hairs. The **head is covered with light grey fur** and the **belly fur is grey, often with flecks of white and ginger.** The **fur extends down the legs to the toes.** Large males can attain a body weight of 1100 g and a wingspan of 1500 mm.

● **ROOST HABITS** Grey-headed flying-foxes will form camps in almost any dense vegetation greater than 3 m in height. Throughout summer these camps may comprise up to several thousand individuals depending on local blossom availability. In winter the young form winter camps while the adults disperse up to 750 km away. Some adults remain in the winter camps when food is plentiful. Camps may be shared with little red flying-foxes, *P. scapulatus*, throughout their range and with black flying-foxes, *P. alecto*, in the north. They do not move camp as a unit but as individuals or small groups. This causes intermixing of the populations over large areas.

● **HABITAT** They roost, usually near water, in stands of native vegetation such as mangrove, rainforest, *Melaleuca*, *Casuarina* or introduced trees. Grey-headed flying-foxes live much further south than any other megabat and can tolerate a few degrees of frost, though their recent 450-km extension of range to the city of Melbourne has depended on the fact that human activity has changed the local climate, making it warmer, with less frost and higher rainfall and humidity. The fact that there are 350 000 street trees providing abundant food does no harm either! The sight and sound of these huge bats brings a welcome touch of the exotic and tropical to this southern city. They have sophisticated vocal communication with over 20 situation-specific calls identified.

● **DIET AND FORAGING** Grey-headed flying-foxes forage at night up to 50 km from their camp. Their diet consists of the fruit, flowers, pollen, nectar, and in rare cases, leaves of 201 plant species from 50 families. Almost half of these are Myrtaceae, including their

| | | Wt | Fa | Ear | Foot | Tib | 3 Met | HB | WS |
|---|---|---|---|---|---|---|---|---|---|
| **MEASUREMENTS** | MEAN | 781.5 | 163.5 | 29.7 | 38.1 | 78.3 | 112.1 | 244.0 | 1131 |
| | MIN | 410 | 151.6 | 19.3 | 34.6 | 72.0 | 105.1 | 220.0 | 1050 |
| | MAX | 1270 | 177.0 | 39.2 | 43.6 | 86.0 | 120.5 | 280.0 | 1180 |
| | NO | 226 | 225 | 49 | 38 | 47 | 38 | 10 | 10 |

A. Divljan; C. Kuiper.

BRUCE THOMSON

foraging resources, particularly eucalypt blossom, is related to rainfall in a highly complex way which is still poorly understood. Spring and summer rainfall is regular in most years, enabling seasonal breeding, but extreme droughts, commonly followed by periods of well above average rainfall, make food supplies unpredictable.

● **REPRODUCTION** Male fertility, responding to photoperiod, peaks in March and mating is followed by a 6-month gestation. Pregnant females congregate into maternity camps of at least 1500 females a couple of weeks before giving birth to a single young in September to October. Initially the female carries the young when foraging, but from late October to December they are left at camp and suckled on her return. In January and February the young are seen flying out to forage with the females. They are weaned in late February or March and segregate into separate roosting trees at the outer edge of the camp to avoid

major food source, *Eucalyptus* blossom. They also eat fruits from a variety of tree species, particularly native figs (*Ficus*), and have been found to chew leaves; they appear to eat the salt glands from mangroves. They are known to raid orchards of cultivated fruit and have been responsible for considerable crop losses, particularly in years with poor blossom abundance. The availability of the adult males now joining the camp to establish territory, mate and restart the cycle.

**REFERENCES** A. Divljan (pers. com.); Eby 1991; Eby & Lunney 2002; Hall 1987; Nelson 1965a, b; Parris & Hazell 2005; Parry-Jones & Augee 1991, 2001; Spencer et al. 1991; Tidemann 1999, 2002; Tidemann & Nelson 2004; van der Ree et al. 2006; Williams et al. 2006.

# Little red flying-fox

**Pteropus scapulatus** Peters, 1862

● **DISTRIBUTION** From Shark Bay, WA, through Top End to Qld and s. through NSW into n. Vic. More nomadic than other flying-foxes; they range far inland depending on availability of flowering trees. Occasional records from SA. Extralimitally, s. coast of New Guinea; one windblown waif recorded in New Zealand in 1927.

● **DESCRIPTION** A smaller flying-fox with **rich reddish brown to light brown fur** all over its body, often with **grey fur on the head**. Some individuals have a yellow patch on the back of the neck and shoulders. The **legs are sparsely furred or naked**. Wings are red-brown and **translucent in flight**. There are distinct patches of light creamy brown where the wing membrane and the shoulder meet.

● **ROOST HABITS** Little red flying-foxes are nomads, whose movements depend on the availability of blossom, a sporadic food resource. They congregate in large camps of up to one million individuals in early summer and frequently camp beside water. Typically they hang close together and their combined weight when in large numbers often causes severe damage to their roost trees. They commonly share the camps of other flying-foxes, although their camps are more temporary than those of other species, usually lasting only 4–6 weeks. A colony of 200 000 little red flying-foxes was observed displacing resident grey-headed and black flying-foxes from a permanent camp. They moved into the centre of the camp and pushed the other species to the edges. They also tended to displace the resident species from local feeding areas.

● **HABITAT** A broad range of habitats, from semi-arid areas to tropical and temperate eucalypt forests, paperbark swamps and monsoon forests.

● **DIET AND FORAGING** They feed predominantly on blossom. All dominant tree and shrub species within their range are included in the diet. The flowering time of many Australian plants is very variable and largely dependent on climatic conditions: eucalypt trees, for example, produce large amounts of blossom one year and little the next. A nomadic lifestyle enables this bat to utilise this unpredictable food supply. Fruit, sap and insects are also eaten, and cultivated fruit is eaten when other food resources are not available. The bats sometimes leave their camp before dark and in northern Australia can be seen foraging during the day on

BRUCE THOMSON

| | | Wt | Fa | Ear | Foot | 3 met | HB | WS |
|---|---|---|---|---|---|---|---|---|
| **MEASUREMENTS** | MEAN | 384 | 123.6 | 31.9 | 34.4 | 82.3 | 163 | 867 |
| | MIN | 258 | 116.3 | 28.3 | 30.0 | 77.8 | 122 | 815 |
| | MAX | 500 | 140.0 | 39.6 | 43.5 | 91.6 | 200 | 1005 |
| | NO | 13 | 16 | 12 | 12 | 10 | 11 | 11 |

S. Churchill.

overcast days during the wet season. The flight of this species is direct and of moderate speed. They are not very manoeuvrable as evidenced by their crashlandings in trees. They are pretty helpless on the ground, and need to climb a tree to become airborne again. In dry years individuals are commonly found entangled in barbed wire fences or drowned in water tanks in the western areas of the species' range. Loss of habitat from land clearing and drought conditions drives them to coastal areas but during wet years they are able to exploit extensive areas of inland Australia.

● **REPRODUCTION** The pattern of reproduction is similar to other *Pteropus* but is out of phase by 6 months and is not dependent on photoperiod. Mating occurs from November to January when the adults congregate in large camps. Males obtain harems of two to five females in small territories that they actively defend from other males. After a gestation of about 5 months the young are born in March or April in predominantly female camps from which the males have dispersed. The young are carried by the mothers for the first month and then left at the roost while she forages at night, returning at intervals to feed them. By 2 months the young are flying and move around between the trees within the camp. The female suckles and cares for the young for several months of semi-independence, while they develop basic food-finding skills, following her from the camp at night. Both males and females become sexually mature at 18 months of age.

**REFERENCES** Birt & Markus 1999; Daniel 1975; Dwyer 1965; Hall 1987; McCoy, in Strahan 1995; Nelson 1965a, b; O'Brien et al. 1993; Prociv 1983.

# Eastern blossom bat

## *Syconycteris australis* (Peters, 1867)

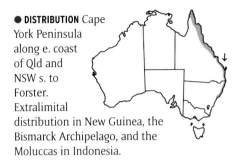

● **DISTRIBUTION** Cape York Peninsula along e. coast of Qld and NSW s. to Forster. Extralimital distribution in New Guinea, the Bismarck Archipelago, and the Moluccas in Indonesia.

● **DESCRIPTION** A miniature flying-fox, its **fur is fawn to reddish brown**, slightly lighter on the belly. It has **large eyes** and a **long thin muzzle** with raised nostrils, and a **very long tongue**. It is **similar to the northern blossom bat**, *Macroglossus minimus*, but **differs** in having the **outer pair of lower incisor teeth larger than the inner pair with no gap** between them and **lacking the skin flaps along the inside of the legs**. There is a strip of long fur in this area instead. **Males lack the large scent gland** found on the chest of northern blossom bats. Individuals in NSW are considerably heavier than those in north Qld.

● **ROOST HABITS** They roost only in rainforest, most commonly in the sub-canopy but occasionally in the canopy. Roosts are among large leaves (sometimes dead), often on the growing tips of saplings or among dense vines. They usually select a different roost every night but stay in the same vicinity (within 50 m) for the season. During the winter they roost near the forest edge, but in summer they select roosts deep within the forest where it is cooler. They leave the roost at sunset and commute to foraging areas in heathlands up to 4 km away, taking 2–3 hours for the trip as they sample food resources along the way. They remain actively foraging for nearly half the night before returning to their day roost shortly before dawn. They are influenced by the brightness of the moon and bats will delay departure by up to 4 hours on strongly moonlit nights.

● **HABITAT** The combination of heathland and coastal rainforest is essential for this species in northern NSW. They have a foraging area of about 13 ha of heathland and use the same area each night. Further north they live in rainforest, wet sclerophyll, monsoon and *Melaleuca* forests.

● **DIET AND FORAGING** They are specialist nectar and pollen feeders. Their tongues are long and covered in rows of papillae forming a nectar-absorbing mop. Pollen is a valuable food resource but is only eaten when they groom it from their fur and wings after nectar feeding. Microscopic examination of their fur reveals pollen-trapping scales on their hairs. In NSW they feed predominantly on *Banksia* and *Callistemon* nectar and

| | NSW | North Qld | | | | | | |
|---|---|---|---|---|---|---|---|---|
| | Wt | Wt | Fa | Ear | Foot | 3 met | HB | WS |
| MEAN | 19.2 | 15.4 | 40.9 | 14.7 | 8.9 | 31.7 | 62.5 | 304.1 |
| MIN | 17.5 | 13.7 | 38.6 | 13.0 | 7.9 | 28.0 | 57.0 | 290 |
| MAX | 23 | 17.1 | 42.8 | 16.6 | 10.2 | 35.5 | 71.0 | 314 |
| NO | 20 | 9 | 11 | 8 | 8 | 8 | 8 | 8 |

MEASUREMENTS

S. Churchill; Law 1993.

BRUCE THOMSON

chasing the intruder, vocalising and clapping their wings. They are capable of hovering but usually land on a flower to feed, getting their chests covered with pollen that they groom off and eat later. They actively forage for most of the night and continue to forage in rain. In the adult population, density is related to the availability of nectar rather than pollen, and population densities vary from one to 18 bats per ha.

● **REPRODUCTION** In NSW one young is usually born in October or November and another between February and April. Pregnancy lasts about 4 months and lactation a further 3 months. Eastern blossom bats are able to enter short periods of torpor when pregnant, which enables them to reduce their metabolic rates to less than half of normal.

● **NOTES** Eastern blossom bats differ from northern blossom bats, *M. minimus*, in their behaviour when captured. While being removed from mist nets they bite and squirm constantly, usually emitting a loud, high-pitched screech and plaintive cries (often attracting other blossom bats into the net). The northern blossom bats tend to be quiet and much less prone to biting.

pollen, no fruits or insects being eaten. In northern Qld they eat *Melaleuca, Banksia, Grevillea* and *Eucalyptus* blossom as well as the nectar of many rainforest plants, particularly the cauliflorous *Syzigium*. They tend to eat more fruit, particularly figs, in northern areas. Individuals appear to defend their food resources from other bats by

**REFERENCES** Bartels et al. 1998; Birt et al. 1997; Bonaccorso & McNab 1997; Coburn & Geiser 1998; Flannery 1995a, b; Geiser et al. 1996, 2001, 2005; Geiser & Coburn 1999; Law 1992, 1993, 1994, 1995, 1997, 2001; Law & Lean 1999; Law & Spencer, in Strahan 1995; Nelson 1964.

# Ghost bat
## *Macroderma gigas* (Dobson, 1880)

● **DISTRIBUTION** Once dist. across most of inland and northern Australia as far south as Flinders Ranges, SA. Recorded until 1970 in central Australia but now restricted to tropical n. Australia. Endemic to Australia.

Pre 1970

● **DESCRIPTION** A spectacular bat, this is the **largest echolocating bat in Australia** and one of the largest in the world. It has **pale grey or light brown fur with a lighter belly**. Individuals tend to be paler, almost white, in more inland populations. The wing membranes are pale cream to brown. It has **no tail** but retains a full tail membrane. The **very large ears** are **joined above the head** and there is a **large forked tragus**. It has **large eyes** and a **long simple-shaped nose-leaf** extends along the top of the muzzle.

● **ROOST HABITS** Ghost bats roost in shallow sandstone caves along cliff lines, under boulder piles, in deep limestone caves and in abandoned mines. They have a preference in the Top End for caves with roost microclimates of 27–29°C and 80% relative humidity. They roost either individually or in colonies of 30 to 200, with one colony of over 1500. The females congregate in maternity roosts, these are usually in larger caves but I have also found females with young roosting in boulder piles and shallow escarpment overhangs. At this time the males disperse. These bats commonly roost hanging from the ceiling about 25 cm apart but they roost more closely when they have young. Ghost bats make a distinctive twitter and a cricket-like chirp when disturbed at the roost and before they leave the cave at dusk. These calls can also be heard in the forest at night.

● **HABITAT** A broad range of habitats including arid spinifex hillsides, black soil grasslands, monsoon forest, open savannah woodland, tall open forest, deciduous vine forest and tropical rainforest. Their distribution is influenced by the availability of suitable caves and mines for roost sites.

● **DIET AND FORAGING** They eat birds, bats, small mammals, frogs and geckos. More than 50 bird species have been recorded as prey; these are almost all small diurnal species that either aggregate to roost or are ground-dwelling. I have watched ghost bats repeatedly catch cave bats on the wing as they leave the roost at dusk, swooping on them from behind. They commonly eat large invertebrates, particularly locusts and beetles, but also centipedes, millipedes, spiders, cockroaches, moths, caterpillars and cicadas. They often return to their cave roost

| | | Wt | Fa | Ear | Trag | Foot | 3 met | 5 met | HB | WS |
|---|---|---|---|---|---|---|---|---|---|---|
| MEASUREMENTS | MEAN | 104.6 | 102.8 | 52.0 | 25.4 | 23.9 | 73.2 | 85.3 | 107.4 | 686 |
| | MIN | 74 | 96.3 | 43.8 | 20.6 | 20.5 | 67.1 | 77.5 | 98 | 640 |
| | MAX | 144 | 113 | 56.3 | 29.1 | 26.8 | 78.4 | 89.6 | 118 | 720 |
| | NO | 64 | 65 | 16 | 16 | 15 | 16 | 16 | 16 | 12 |

S. Churchill.

LINDY LUMSDEN

20 g with a forearm length of 45 mm. The young remain with the mother for several months. They are initially carried by the foraging mother, but are later left in a nursery. Once the young can fly, at 7 weeks, it is common to see bats leave the roost to forage in pairs. They are fully weaned by March.

● **NOTES** Although common in the Top End, elsewhere they occur only in small or widely scattered colonies. They have undergone a dramatic reduction in range over the last 100 years. This is thought to be due to population isolation and long-term climate change coupled with recent changes in land management. They no longer occur in central Australia although they were there in Aboriginal living memory (See **Caves and conservation**). In open areas of grassland they often become entangled in barbed wire fences. Their flight is usually just above the vegetation and they often fly without echolocating. They are particularly vulnerable to new fences.

to eat, dropping the less palatable portions. Ghost bats use several techniques for catching prey: active hunting with echolocation, perch-hunting using eyesight, and passive listening for noises made by prey. Radio-tracking studies have shown they forage about 2 km from the roost cave, and use the same foraging areas (about 60 ha) each night. Within this area the bats hunted from tree perches, moving to a new vantage point every 15 minutes. Foraging areas were not exclusive and up to 20 bats had overlapping ranges.

● **REPRODUCTION** They mate in April to May when males have enlarged testes and are aggressive towards each other. The females give birth to a single young in July and August after 11–12 weeks' gestation. In the Pilbara the young are born in late October or early November. The newborn young weigh

**REFERENCES** Armstrong & Anstee 2000; Baudinette et al. 2000; Boles 1999; Churchill 1991a; Churchill & Helman 1990; Douglas 1967; Milne & Burwell (unpubl.); Nelson 1989; Pettigrew et al. 1986; Tidemann et al. 1985; Schulz 1986; Toop 1985; Worthington-Wilmer et al. 1994, 1999.

# Horseshoe Bats

## Family RHINOLOPHIDAE: Key to Species

The tail membrane of Rhinolophidae totally encloses the tail. On the muzzle there is a complex nose-leaf, consisting of a horseshoe-shaped structure at the front, a triangularly pointed, pocketed lancet at the rear, and a conspicuous mid-line sella, projecting forwards from the nostrils. The ears are large to extremely large and have no tragus.

**1a** Ears large; length less than 22 mm; forearm less than 50 mm in northern Qld; range elsewhere 44.5–52.2 mm; sella of nose-leaf is less than one-third the width of the horseshoe.
→ ***Rhinolophus megaphyllus*** (page 85)

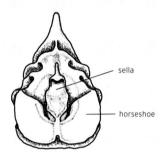

sella

horseshoe

**1b** Ear length greater than 25 mm; forearm greater than 50 mm; nose-leaf and ears disproportionately large. → **2**

**2a** Ears very large; ear length less than 28 mm; forearm length averages 51.4 mm (50.0–53.5 mm); sella of nose-leaf is less than two-thirds the width of the horseshoe.
→ ***Rhinolophus* species** (page 88)

**2b** Ears enormous; ear length greater than 29 mm; forearm length averages 55.8 mm (52.3–59.0 mm) (where distribution overlaps with *Rhinolophus* species the forearm length is larger: 56.0–59.0 mm); sella of nose-leaf is greater than two-thirds the width of the horseshoe.
→ ***Rhinolophus robertsi*** (page 87)

**LEFT** Three species of horseshoe bats caught together in the same mist net at Iron Range: the eastern horseshoe bat (left), the intermediate horseshoe bat and the large-eared horseshoe bat.

# Eastern horseshoe bat
## *Rhinolophus megaphyllus* Gray, 1834

● **DISTRIBUTION** E. coast Australia from Cape York Peninsula to central Vic. Most colonies are in coastal plains or e. slopes of the Great Dividing Range. Two subspecies are known, *Rhinolophus megaphyllus ignifer* in Qld and *R. m. megaphyllus* from s. Qld to Vic. Extralimital distribution in New Guinea.

● **DESCRIPTION** The only Australian horseshoe bat to extend its range to outside the tropics. This bat has **greyish brown fur**, which is slightly lighter on the belly. The fur has white tips and a grey base and is long and fine. In Qld there is a bright rufous form that may be found roosting among grey individuals. The **nose-leafs, wings and ears are pinkish grey**. It can be distinguished from other *Rhinolophus* by its **smaller ears and smaller size**. The **sella** of the nose-leaf is **less than one-third the width of the horseshoe**.

● **ROOST HABITS** Eastern horseshoe bats are cave dwellers, inhabiting a wide variety of caves and abandoned mines, but are also found in rock piles, buildings, tree hollows, old railway tunnels, tree roots in undercut creek banks, stormwater drains and culverts.

Many roosts have a restricted entrance with a narrow vertical drop. They roost mostly in complete darkness but may be found within the twilight zone near the cave mouth. Colonies are typically small, less than 20 bats, but females congregate in maternity colonies of 15–2000 bats in spring and summer. A maternity colony of over 10 000 was recently found in a sandstone cave near Sydney. To rear their young they select warm and humid caves (85–95% relative humidity) with little air circulation. In temperate latitudes these bats disperse in winter and are found roosting singly in the cooler parts of caves in a torpid state. In the tropics they are active and forage nightly throughout the year. On Cape York Peninsula, I have found colonies of several hundred to 2000 during the winter dry season. These are not maternity sites, but large aggregations of both sexes in non-breeding condition.

● **HABITAT** Tropical and temperate rainforest, deciduous vine forest, dry and wet sclerophyll forest, open woodland, coastal scrub and grassland areas. They are much more active in mature forests than in regrowth and they commonly forage along tracks and waterways and avoid large cleared areas such as paddocks.

● **DIET AND FORAGING** They are well adapted to foraging in cluttered habitats, having short

| MEASUREMENTS | | Vic | | Northern Qld | | | | | | |
|---|---|---|---|---|---|---|---|---|---|---|
| | | Wt | Fa | Wt | Fa | Ear | 3 met | Tail | HB | WS |
| | MEAN | 11.5 | 49.2 | 8.4 | 46.6 | 19.1 | 35.2 | 24.6 | 47.7 | 293.0 |
| | MIN | 10.0 | 45.7 | 6.9 | 44.5 | 17 | 33.6 | 22 | 44 | 280 |
| | MAX | 13.0 | 52.2 | 10.2 | 48.6 | 21.1 | 36.5 | 28 | 53 | 305 |
| | NO | 129 | 130 | 90 | 98 | 24 | 24 | 22 | 24 | 22 |

S. Churchill; L. Lumsden.

BRUCE THOMSON

fertilisation do not occur until late June. At this time spermatogenesis is waning, but males continue to store sperm for at least another 4 months. There is no evidence of female sperm storage prior to ovulation and they do not produce a vaginal plug. The single young is born in November after a gestation of between 4 and 4.5 months. The young are nursed for about 8 weeks and reach adult size after 5–6 weeks. During this time they congregate at the roost. Pregnant females fly up to 20 km to maternity roosts in September or October each year and return to their caves in March or April the following year. The onset of sexual maturity is late in this species. Males are not sexually mature until 18 months and females may not mature until 36 months. The maximum longevity recorded is 7 years which implies they may have a very restricted breeding potential.

● **NOTES** When roosting, they cling to the ceiling by their toes, hanging free with their wings wrapped around their body. When approached they swivel, often hanging by one leg and flicking their ears alternately while echolocating to examine what caused the disturbance.

broad wings and low wing loading, which gives them a slow but highly manoeuvrable flight. They often hover and are able to manoeuvre successfully among the branches and foliage of dense shrubs. Both continuous flight and perch-hunting are used, prey being captured by aerial pursuit and gleaning. Moths (mainly non-eared species) are the dominant food. They also eat beetles, flies, crickets, bugs, cockroaches and wasps. Prey is often taken to a temporary roost to be eaten, the floor below the roost becoming littered with discarded wings and legs.

● **REPRODUCTION** Spermatogenesis is initiated in February and mature sperm is available in March, although copulation, ovulation and

**REFERENCES** Calaby 1966; de Oliveira et al. 1999; Dwyer 1965, 1966a; Hall 1989; Hall et al. 1975; Krutzch et al. 1992; Law & Chidel 2002; Law et al. 2002, 2004; Pavey 1998b; Pavey & Burwell 1998, 2000, 2004, 2005; Pavey & Young, in Strahan 1995; Schulz 2000a; Schulz & Wainer 1997; Vestjens & Hall 1977; Whybird 1998; Young 1975, 2001.

# Large-eared horseshoe bat
## *Rhinolophus robertsi* Tate, 1952

● **TAXONOMY** This bat was originally described as *Rhinolophus maros robertsi*. The name *maros* was later synonymised with *philippinensis*. A genetic study by Cooper et al. (1998) has found that this bat is not related to *R. philippinensis* so I have upgraded the subspecific name to species *R. robertsi*.

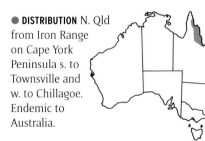

This species occurs sympatrically with the eastern horseshoe bat, *R. megaphyllus*, and another morphologically distinct undescribed species. Although the genetic study failed to resolve the relationships between the three Australian species they differ significantly in body size, nose-leaf shape, ear length and echolocation calls.

● **DISTRIBUTION** N. Qld from Iron Range on Cape York Peninsula s. to Townsville and w. to Chillagoe. Endemic to Australia.

● **DESCRIPTION** A bizarre-looking bat with **enormous ears and nose-leaf**. It has **long, fine, grey-brown fur** peppered with white hairs, and a lighter belly. The nose-leaf has a **large sella more than two-thirds the width of the horseshoe**. The nose-leaf, anus and penis or pubic teats may be either grey or bright yellow. The **size of this species varies with latitude** (forearm length averages 55.8 mm; 52.3–59.0 mm) becoming smaller in the south. In the northern part of its range (north of Coen) where the three species overlap in distribution it is considerably larger and heavier (with a forearm length of 56–59 mm and ear length of 32.1–33.3 mm, weight 11.5–16.2 g) than the intermediate horseshoe bat, *R. species*, which has a forearm length of 50.0–53.5 mm and ear length 25.2–27.3 mm, weight of 8.9–9.9 g and a sella less than two-thirds the width of the horseshoe. The eastern horseshoe bat, *R. megaphyllus*, is much smaller (forearm length of 44.5–48.6 mm and ear length of 17–21.1 mm) with a sella one-third the width of the horseshoe.

● **ROOST HABITS** One individual was captured in a disused mine at Iron Range where it was roosting alone, hanging free from the end of a small ledge in the wall. The roost conditions were 26°C and 78% relative humidity. It was sharing a roost with several hundred eastern

| | | Wt | Fa | Ear | Tibia | 3 met | Tail | HB | HS | Sella | WS |
|---|---|---|---|---|---|---|---|---|---|---|---|
| **MEASUREMENTS** | MEAN | 13.1 | 55.8 | 31.2 | 22.9 | 41.7 | 30.0 | 55.1 | 11.3 | 7.9 | 350 |
| | MIN | 10.1 | 52.3 | 29.3 | 21.4 | 38.7 | 25.0 | 48.0 | 10.0 | 6.7 | 334 |
| | MAX | 16.2 | 59.0 | 33.3 | 24.3 | 44.0 | 34.4 | 62.0 | 12.8 | 9.0 | 365 |
| | NO | 18 | 34 | 18 | 18 | 27 | 27 | 27 | 15 | 13 | 15 |

S. Churchill; Pavey 1999.

horseshoe bats, *R. megaphyllus*. It could be distinguished among this large colony by its large ears and larger size. A further six were seen in a mine at Mt Amos. They were roosting alone, hanging from the ceiling, scattered through the mine. The roost conditions were 26.5°C with 98% humidity. The mine was flooded waist-deep in water at the time and contained several thousand eastern bentwing bats, *M. o. oceanensis*, and several hundred eastern horseshoe bats, *R. megaphyllus*. Eighteen individuals were collected from this mine (the type locality) in 1950.

● **HABITAT** Lowland rainforest, along gallery forest-lined creeks within open eucalypt forest, *Melaleuca* forest with rainforest understorey, open savannah woodland, tall riparian woodland of *Melaleuca*, *E. tereticornis* and *E. tesselaris* and at the edge of a grassy clearing in the rainforest.

● **DIET AND FORAGING** Faecal pellets collected from pregnant females in late November contained predominantly moths and beetles with some grasshoppers or crickets. These bats foraged using continual flight, not perch-hunting. Their flight was slow and fluttery with sudden changes of direction and height. They flew below canopy height between 1 m and 8 m above the ground

within rainforest that grew both above and along the edge of a road. I have watched this bat catch a large moth near a light in an open house. It roosted in the dark corner of the room to eat its meal, discarding the wings before flying out again.

● **REPRODUCTION** A maternity colony of six heavily pregnant females was found roosting in a small abandoned mine at Mt Molloy in late October. No males were present and the roost conditions were very humid (25°C and 96% humidity) although the surrounding country was hot and dry. These bats were sharing a roost with 50 eastern horseshoe bats, *R. megaphyllus*. A female caught at McIlwraith Range in October and three females caught at Iron Range in late November were pregnant. A single young is born in October or November.

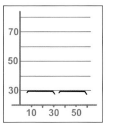

● **NOTES** Their echolocation calls are 28 kHz, one of the lowest frequency calls of any rhinolophid bat.

**REFERENCES** Churchill (unpubl.); Coles 2002; Cooper et al. 1998; Flannery 1995a, b; Kutt 2004; Pavey, in Strahan 1995; Pavey 1999.

# Intermediate horseshoe bat

## *Rhinolophus* **species** (undescribed)

● **TAXONOMY** This species occurs sympatrically with the eastern horseshoe bat, *R. megaphyllus*, and the large-eared horseshoe bat, *R. robertsi*. Although the genetic study (Cooper et al. 1998) failed to resolve the relationships between the three Australian species, they differ significantly in body size, nose-leaf shape, ear length and echolocation calls.

● **DISTRIBUTION** Known only from Iron Range and McIlwraith Range, n. of Coen on Cape York Peninsula, Qld.

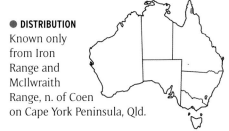

● **DESCRIPTION** Intermediate in size, this bat has long, **fine, grey-brown fur** peppered with white hairs and a lighter belly. The nose-leaf, anus and penis or pubic teats are usually grey. The **sella is** 5.3–5.8 mm wide, **less than two-thirds of the horseshoe width**. It is of intermediate size with a forearm length of 50.0–53.5 mm, ear length 25.2–27.3 mm, and weight of 8.3–9.9 g. The large-eared horseshoe bat, *R. robertsi*, is **considerably larger and heavier** where it overlaps in distribution (forearm length 56–59 mm, ear length 32.1–33.3 mm and weight 11.5–16.2 g) with a **sella width** of 6.7–9.0 mm, which is **greater than two-thirds of the horseshoe width**. The eastern horseshoe bat, *R. megaphyllus*, **is much smaller** (forearm length 44.5–48.6 mm and ear length 17–21.1 mm), with a sella less than one-third the width of the horseshoe.

● **ROOST HABITS** Intermediate horseshoe bats have not been captured at the roost and although they have been caught close to mines it is not known if they roost in them. Confusion with the large-eared horseshoe bat, *R. robertsi*, which has often been caught in caves and mines, has muddied the picture. Of the eight individuals on which I have information, all were caught in forest. They may roost in dense vegetation and tree hollows in more humid locations.

● **HABITAT** Rainforest and gallery forest.

● **DIET AND FORAGING** A light tag attached to a male bat in July showed it foraging within rainforest and around lights at a building in a small clearing. The bat used only continuous flight foraging to capture prey. When it roosted in a tree between foraging bouts it was either to rest or to consume prey. There was no evidence of perch-hunting. It flew at a height of 0.5–2 m above the ground; the flight was slow and fluttery with occasional sudden changes in direction to capture insects such as moths on the wing. It was also seen to catch an insect by gleaning from the ground. To reach the building the bat crossed more than 200 m of cleared area. Its flight across the grassland was fast and direct and it did not forage.

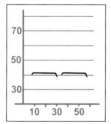

● **REPRODUCTION** Nothing known.

REFERENCES Churchill (unpubl.); Coles 2002; Cooper et al. 1998; Flannery 1995a, b; Pavey, in Strahan 1995; Pavey 1999.

| | Wt | Fa | Ear | Tibia | 3 met | Tail | HB | HS | Sella | WS |
|---|---|---|---|---|---|---|---|---|---|---|
| MEAN | 8.9 | 51.4 | 26.3 | 21.2 | 38.6 | 29.9 | 48.7 | 9.8 | 5.5 | 325 |
| MIN | 8.3 | 50.0 | 25.2 | 20.4 | 37.1 | 27 | 45 | 9.3 | 5.3 | 317 |
| MAX | 9.9 | 53.5 | 27.3 | 21.8 | 40 | 31.2 | 53 | 10.1 | 5.8 | 337 |
| NO | 6 | 8 | 6 | 3 | 6 | 6 | 6 | 3 | 3 | 3 |

MEASUREMENTS

S. Churchill.

# Leaf-nosed Bats
## Family HIPPOSIDERIDAE: Key to Species

In the Hipposideridae the tail is completely enclosed by the tail membrane. The second, third and fourth toes have only two phalanges each, unlike the Rhinolophidae and most other bats, which have three. The muzzle has a complex nose-leaf consisting of a rounded, flattened structure at the front (analogous to the horseshoe of the Rhinolophidae) and an irregular rear portion with folds, pockets and sometimes wart-like projections. There is no sella.

**1a** Nose-leaf flat and round with upper portion scalloped.
→ *Rhinonicteris aurantia* (page 102)

**1b** Nose-leaf squarish with raised upper portion. → **2**

**2a** Forearm length less than 55 mm. → **3**

**2b** Forearm length more than 65 mm. → **6**

**3a** Ears narrow and sharply pointed at tip; two club-shaped wart-like projections on central and upper nose-leaf. → **4**

**3b** Ears broad and rounded with slightly pointed tip; no club-shaped projections on nose-leaf. → **5**

**4a** Forearm length averages 47.1 mm (44.6–50.4 mm); distribution eastern Qld; wart-like projections on nose-leaf larger.

→ *Hipposideros semoni* (page 98)

**4b** Forearm length averages 44.1 mm (41.9–45.6 mm); distribution far western Qld, Top End and Kimberley;

wart-like projections on nose-leaf smaller.
→ *H. stenotis* (page 100)

**5a** Forearm length less than 41 mm (averages 38.5 mm; 34.4–41.0 mm); no secondary leaflet at the sides of nose-leaf.
→ *H. ater* (page 91)

**5b** Forearm length greater than 45 mm (averages 46.8 mm; 45.0–47.8 mm); two or three secondary leaflets at the sides of nose-leaf.
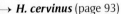
→ *H. cervinus* (page 93)

**6a** Forearm length greater than 77 mm (averages 81.8 mm; 77.5–85.1 mm); northern Qld.

→ *H. diadema* (page 94)

**6b** Forearm length less than 74 mm (averages 71.1 mm; 68.1–73.4 mm); NT, Top End. → *H. inornatus* (page 96)

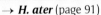

# Dusky leaf-nosed bat

## *Hipposideros ater* Templeton, 1848

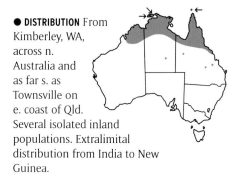

● **DISTRIBUTION** From Kimberley, WA, across n. Australia and as far s. as Townsville on e. coast of Qld. Several isolated inland populations. Extralimital distribution from India to New Guinea.

● **DESCRIPTION** Australia's cutest bat, the dusky leaf-nosed bat is a **small and delicate species**. It differs from the fawn leaf-nosed bat, *H. cervinus*, in its **small nose-leaf that lacks secondary leaflets. The ears are large, rounded and extend well beyond the top of the head. Fur long and very fluffy** making the bat appear much larger than its 4-g mass. Fur **colour is variable, usually pale grey-brown** but interestingly in caves where it coexists with the orange leaf-nosed bat, *Rhinonicteris aurantia*, it often takes on the same fur colour as that species, varying from orange to white.

● **ROOST HABITS** Dusky leaf-nosed bats roost in warm humid areas of caves or disused mines. The preferred roost microclimate is 29°C and 92% relative humidity. Colony sizes vary from solitary bats to groups of 300 but are commonly ten to 30. A colony of 11 has been recorded roosting in a large tree hollow in rainforest at McIlwraith Range on Cape York Peninsula.

● **HABITAT** A wide variety of tropical habitats are used including monsoon forest, scrubby open forest, mixed open forest, open woodland, vine thickets, savannah woodland and spinifex grasslands.

● **DIET AND FORAGING** They are primarily continuous flight foragers, capturing all of their prey while in flight. They do not use perch-hunting. They fly below the canopy, frequently in dense vegetation, in tall grass or close to the ground. Their flight is very slow and fluttery and they can hover. Their slow flight means that they do not travel far from their roost sites to forage. Studies in Qld have shown them to consume almost exclusively moths, and 90% of these were eared moths. The high frequency echolocation calls are beyond the moths' hearing range enabling the bats to hunt eared moths without their taking evasive action. In the Top End their diet is less specialised and as well as moths they eat beetles, termites, grasshoppers, ants, leaf-hoppers, mantis flies, lacewings and mosquitoes. They are a delightful companion in areas with high numbers of mosquitoes as they will circle you repeatedly, eating numerous mosquitoes on each pass until all are gone.

| MEASUREMENTS | | Wt | Fa | Ear | 3 met | Tail | HB | WS |
|---|---|---|---|---|---|---|---|---|
| | MEAN | 4.2 | 38.5 | 18.0 | 29.0 | 24.3 | 41.3 | 247 |
| | MIN | 3.4 | 34.4 | 16.0 | 26.6 | 22.0 | 33.0 | 230 |
| | MAX | 5.6 | 41.0 | 20.6 | 30.9 | 27.8 | 46.0 | 268 |
| | NO | 37 | 52 | 14 | 15 | 14 | 15 | 13 |

S. Churchill.

● **REPRODUCTION** In the Kimberley, females are pregnant by June and a single young is born between October and December. The young remain clinging to the mother's teat for the first 2 weeks. When the mother is going to fly the young invert their position and cling to the false pubic teats allowing the mother to better balance the load. After 2 weeks of age they often hang from the mother's shoulders as she hangs head down at the roost. From this position they practise flapping their wings (I told you they were cute). On several occasions, at night, I have encountered groups of up to 15 half-grown young at the roost with a single adult, indicating the young are left at the roost while the mother forages. Between 6 weeks and 2 months the young attain adult size and are capable of independent flight. For several weeks it is common to see these bats leave the roost to forage in pairs, one in front of the other (probably mother and young).

BRUCE THOMSON

● **NOTES** This is a delicate species that dies readily in captivity and in traps from dehydration and hypothermia. They have a constant frequency echolocation call that varies from 175 kHz in the Kimberley to 152 kHz in Qld. Such a high frequency can only travel a short distance, approximately 30 cm, and this is the distance they maintain while investigating unfamiliar objects, such as bat biologists at cave entrances. They can

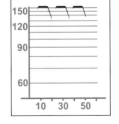

easily detect monofilament mist nets even in very cluttered habitats and will often flutter along the net until they find a hole large enough to fly through. They don't always manage to avoid nets; I once found a dead one caught in the web of a golden orb-weaving spider.

**REFERENCES** Bullen & McKenzie 2002b; Churchill 1991a; R. Coles (pers. com.); Flannery 1995b; Kitchener et al. 1981; McKenzie et al. 1975; Milne 2002; Milne & Burwell (unpubl.); Pavey 1995; Pavey & Burwell 1998, 2000, 2005; Shaw 1996.

# Fawn leaf-nosed bat

## *Hipposideros cervinus* (Gould, 1854)

● **DISTRIBUTION** Cape York Peninsula n. from Coen, and Torres Strait Is in n. Qld. Extralimital distribution includes Malaysia, Indonesia, Philippines, New Guinea, Solomon Is and Vanuatu.

● **DESCRIPTION** Widespread and common elsewhere, this bat only just reaches the northern tip of Australia. The **ears are broad and triangular**. The **nose-leaf is small and comparatively simple**, with **two well-developed supplementary leaflets** that project beyond the margin of the anterior leaf. The **fur colour varies from grey to greyish brown to orange**. In **males there is a small gland (the frontal sac) behind the rear leaf** of the nose-leaf. This can exude a clear and odourless fluid but its function is not known. It is represented in females by a depression containing a tuft of hairs.

● **ROOST HABITS** Fawn leaf-nosed bats roost in caves and mines in colonies of up to 900 individuals, more commonly 20–100. Occasionally individuals are found roosting in old sheds and buildings. They like warm and humid roost conditions. One colony of 180 bats roosted in 26°C and 94% humidity. Like dusky leaf-nosed bats, *H. ater*, they hang free from the ceiling by their toes, often from only one foot, and space themselves 10–15 cm apart. They roost in small passages or avons rather than in large chambers. They are always alert and fly readily when approached. When disturbed they hang from the ceiling and pivot their body in an arc from side to side, echolocating while their ears twitch rapidly. Fawn leaf-nosed bats do not enter torpor. They are thermoneutral in air temperatures of 31–35°C.

● **HABITAT** Rainforest, gallery forests along water courses, and open savannah woodland. They also forage around buildings and open parkland.

● **DIET AND FORAGING** Fawn leaf-nosed bats have a low metabolic rate, 58% of that

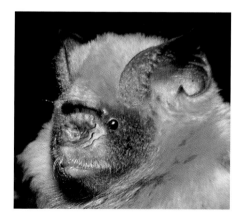

| MEASUREMENTS | | Wt | Fa | Ear | Foot | 3 met | Tail | HB | WS |
|---|---|---|---|---|---|---|---|---|---|
| | MEAN | 7.0 | 46.8 | 14.2 | 6.9 | 36.1 | 27.0 | 46.0 | 290 |
| | MIN | 5.6 | 45.0 | 12.7 | 6.3 | 31.9 | 24.0 | 41.0 | 283 |
| | MAX | 8.4 | 47.8 | 15.3 | 7.8 | 38.0 | 31.4 | 51.0 | 295 |
| | NO | 18 | 38 | 10 | 10 | 10 | 10 | 10 | 9 |

S. Churchill; Pavey 2000.

expected for a mammal of their weight. Perch-hunting is metabolically efficient compared with aerial foraging and is the main technique used by these bats in New Guinea. They select perches near an open space and 1–6 m above the ground. Many different perches are used during the night and they return to the perch to eat captured prey, discarding wings and unpalatable parts. In Qld they perch-hunt only 15% of the time, prey usually being captured by aerial pursuit and by surface gleaning. When foraging the flight is slow and fluttery, close to vegetation, from 1 m above the ground to just below the canopy. By contrast the flight when commuting is fast and direct, with slight changes of direction to avoid vegetation. They commute from roosting to foraging areas along established pathways, often creeks or gullies. Individuals or groups split off from the main group and fly into the forest to commence hunting; the return to the roost is a reverse pattern of the exit. They eat mainly moths and beetles with occasional bugs, cockroaches, flies and parasitic wasps.

● **REPRODUCTION** The single young is born in November to December, at the start of the wet season. They form maternity colonies in the same caves that they use as a roost all year.

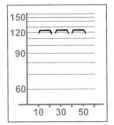

**REFERENCES** Bonaccorso & McNab 2003; Flannery 1995b; Jenkins & Hill 1981; Pavey & Burwell, in Strahan 1995; Pavey & Burwell 2000, 2005.

# Diadem leaf-nosed bat

## *Hipposideros diadema* (Geoffroy, 1813)

● **DISTRIBUTION**
N. Qld: Cape York Peninsula s. to Townsville and inland to Chillagoe. The Qld subspecies *H. d. reginae* Troughton, 1937 is endemic to Australia. Extralimital distribution of 15 other subspecies ranges from Burma to Nicobar Is, Thailand, Cambodia, Vietnam, Malaysia, Philippines, Indonesia, New Guinea and Solomon Is.

● **DESCRIPTION** A formidable bat, this is the largest *Hipposideros* in Australia. The fur on the back is a **pale grey to light brown** (there is also a deep burgundy red form) with a **distinct white patch on each shoulder**. The **ears are of moderate size**, broad at the base

and **acutely pointed**. The **nose-leaf is well developed**, with **three or four lateral supplementary leaflets**; the fourth is small and sometimes rudimentary. There is **no frontal sac**. The diadem leaf-nosed bat is distinguished from the Arnhem leaf-nosed bat, *H. inornatus*, by its larger size and white shoulder patches.

● **ROOST HABITS** Diadem leaf-nosed bats are most commonly found in caves and disused mines, but also in buildings and road culverts. They show a preference for large caves with large chambers and multiple entrances. I have recorded roost micro-climates of 25–26.5°C and 65–80% humidity. They usually hang from the ceiling by their toes, keeping separated from each other by 20–25 cm. A study at Chillagoe caves showed they used nine of the 18

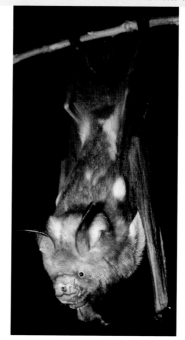

suitable caves. Colony sizes ranged from one to 65, usually less than ten with many solitary males. In 1981 about 2000 of these bats lived in a mine at Iron Range. The bats roosted close together, across the ceiling and down the wall. More recently the colony has ranged from 70 to 250 with 100 being typical.

● **HABITAT** Lowland rainforest, *Melaleuca* forests, eucalypt woodland, deciduous vine thicket and open woodland.

● **DIET AND FORAGING** These large bats are occasional carnivores. Recent work has found the remains of birds in their scats. Their more usual diet is hard-bodied insects such as beetles and grasshoppers, as well as large moths, bugs and wasps. A light-tagging study of these bats at Chillagoe showed that they exit from their cave soon after dusk and fly directly to regularly used individual foraging areas usually within 2–5 km of the cave. At the foraging area they hunted from perches that were 5–15 m above the ground. Foraging flights were observed at the edge of vegetation, in small clearings, and in open woodland. They spend between 2 and 7 hours foraging each night, usually in two activity peaks, and spend the remainder of the time roosting in caves. They often continue foraging for up to an hour after dawn. They have large cheek pouches for temporarily holding food while they are in flight. They have long broad wings and a high wing loading like the carnivorous ghost bat, *Macroderma gigas*.

● **REPRODUCTION** In a large mixed-sex colony at Iron Range, males had scrotal testes (indicating mating) at the end of September to early October. Pregnant females were caught in early October and late November. Births probably occur in early December. Lactating and post-lactating females have been caught in January.

● **NOTES** They have a formidable set of teeth, strong jaws for crunching beetles and an unpleasant and tenacious disposition. Heavy gloves are strongly recommended.

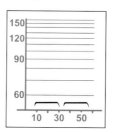

**REFERENCES** Bonaccorso & McNab 2003; Brown & Berry 1983; Hall & Richards 1979; Hall & Richards, in Strahan 1995; Hill 1963; Kitchener et al. 1992; Pavey 1994, 1998, 2000; Pavey & Burwell 1997; Troughton 1937.

| MEASUREMENTS | | Wt | Fa | Ear | Foot | 3 met | Tail | HB | WS |
|---|---|---|---|---|---|---|---|---|---|
| | MEAN | 43.9 | 81.8 | 26.3 | 13.3 | 62.8 | 42.4 | 83.8 | 492 |
| | MIN | 32.0 | 77.5 | 24.4 | 10.2 | 59.0 | 37.0 | 74.0 | 475 |
| | MAX | 57.0 | 85.1 | 30.2 | 15.2 | 65.8 | 47.0 | 96.0 | 515 |
| | NO | 53 | 53 | 21 | 21 | 21 | 21 | 21 | 20 |

S. Churchill; Pavey 2000.

# Arnhem leaf-nosed bat

## *Hipposideros inornatus* McKean, 1970

● **TAXONOMY** In a partial revision of *H. diadema* Kitchener et al. (1992) noted that the subspecies *inornatus* and *demissus* (from the Solomon Islands) were not closely enough related to other *H. diadema* to warrant inclusion in the revision. Flannery (1995b) accepted this finding to elevate both *H. demissus* and *H. inornatus* to full species status. Having examined large numbers of both *inornatus* and *diadema reginae* I agree with this assessment.

● **DISTRIBUTION**
Top End of NT. Known only from Arnhemland escarpment and previously Litchfield National Park. Endemic to Australia.

● **DESCRIPTION** A secretive bat that is better natured than its Qld cousin, the diadem leaf-nosed bat, *H. diadema*. The Arnhem leaf-nosed bat is **distinctly smaller with a forearm length of 68.1–73.4 mm, and lacks the white fur patches at the shoulders. The fur on the back is pale brown with slightly darker tips and is only slightly paler on the belly.** Bright orange individuals have also been recorded. The nose-leaf is similar to *H. diadema* but the **skull has smaller cranial crests** and there is a less developed frontal depression.

● **ROOST HABITS** They are known from only a few large sandstone caves with multiple entrances. These are characteristically draughty, cool (23–25°C and 75–85% humidity), and close to water. They have recently been recorded from a large abandoned mine in Kakadu National Park. In 1989 I located two cave colonies. One of these was at Mt Calanan, in Kakadu National Park, where a colony of 14 adults and eight young were roosting about 25 cm apart in a cool area of the cave, under large boulders, 1 m above the floor and only a few metres from a small stream running through the cave. In the other colony, at Dinner Creek near Oenpelli, up to 15 of these bats roosted in similar conditions in a large sandstone cave. Over a number of years I have revisited a colony in a sandstone cave with a collapsed roof at Tolmer Falls, in Litchfield National Park. The cave is cool and draughty and has a small spring running through it. This colony roosted 3 m above the ground. It had contained 15 individuals in 1978, eight in 1984 and none from 1987 to 1995.

● **HABITAT** Monsoon forest, tall open forest, sandstone monsoon forest and open woodland. Found only in sandstone escarpment areas close to water.

● **DIET AND FORAGING** At Deaf Adder Gorge in Kakadu National Park, a large number of these bats (92) flew through my camp site

| | | Wt | Fa | Ear | Tibia | Tail | HB | WS | Skull |
|---|---|---|---|---|---|---|---|---|---|
| **MEASUREMENTS** | MEAN | 26.5 | 71.1 | 25.1 | 29.6 | 39.0 | 77.0 | 415 | 27.6 |
| | MIN | 22.0 | 68.1 | 23.2 | 28.5 | 32.0 | 75.0 | 387 | 26.9 |
| | MAX | 35.0 | 73.4 | 26.6 | 30.9 | 45.6 | 78.0 | 441 | 28.2 |
| | NO | 30 | 30 | 12 | 13 | 13 | 13 | 12 | 11 |

S. Churchill; McKean 1970.

● **REPRODUCTION** Births probably occur in early November. A colony of 14 adults and eight young was observed in mid December. The young were three-quarters adult size and were a much darker colour (a uniform charcoal grey). Most were hanging against a female, with their feet clinging to the same part of the ceiling, but one was hanging alone. When disturbed a female with an attached young flew off, carrying her sizeable bundle with apparent ease. The young grasp the false pubic teat with their teeth and so face backwards when the female is flying.

● **ECHOLOCATION** The largest hipposiderid in the Top End, it has a much lower characteristic frequency than the other leaf-nosed bats (67.1–71.2 kHz). The distance over which calls of this species can be detected is estimated at around 10 m so it is easily recorded with ultrasound detectors.

one evening at dusk. The bats were flying along the edge of the creek through thick riverine monsoon forest, and many could be heard chewing and crunching as they flew past. While eating they flew straight with a gliding flight; when not eating had a fast and zigzagged flight. They flew well below the canopy at between 1 and 3 m above the ground. They were flying fast and moving quickly downstream, presumably so they could spread out to forage once outside the confines of the gorge. Stomach contents have been found to consist almost entirely of beetles, with some moths and traces of ants, bugs and cockroaches.

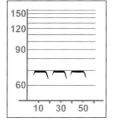

**REFERENCES** Churchill (unpubl.); Flannery 1995a, b; Kitchener et al. 1992; McKean 1970; McKean & Hertog 1979; Milne 2002; Milne & Burwell (unpubl.); Woinarski & Milne 2002b.

# Semon's leaf-nosed bat

## *Hipposideros semoni* Matschie, 1903

● **DISTRIBUTION** N. Qld, Cape York Peninsula to Townsville. Isolated population at Kroombit Tops, 70 km s. of Gladstone. Tentative records based on echolocation calls suggest it occurs in Mt Windsor Tableland area and as far s. as St Mary's State Forest near Maryborough. Extralimital distribution in New Guinea.

● **DESCRIPTION** A bat with exotic taste in accommodation, it is similar to the northern leaf-nosed bat, *H. stenotis*. The **ears are very long and narrow**, with an **acute narrow point**. The **fur is long, dark smoky grey** and has a ruffled appearance. It is **slightly lighter on the belly**. The nose-leaf is well developed, square shaped and covers most of the muzzle. There are **two wart-like protuberances**, one in the centre and one on the posterior edge of the nose-leaf. These are proportionally larger than those of the smaller northern leaf-nosed bat, *H. stenotis* (forearm length 44 mm; 41.9–45.6 mm).

● **ROOST HABITS** Semon's leaf-nosed bat has been found roosting in some strange places. These include an oven, a clothes closet, a picture rail in an unoccupied house and even hanging from the door handle of a car,

although they have more commonly been reported roosting in caves and in tree hollows. I have caught this bat in a small granite boulder cave with a roost microclimate no different to that of the surrounding rainforest. I suspect that this bat is primarily a forest roosting species but as it is difficult to see at its usual roost, it is more commonly observed in atypical places that are visited by humans. They have been caught in groups of up to eight individuals in mist nets in rainforest. Three were recorded near Cooktown, roosting alone in different rock fissures in limestone tower karst. Roosts were less than 7 m from the entrance in the twilight zone. The roost microclimates were very similar to outside conditions. Further south at Kroombit Tops two individuals were caught in a cave containing about 9000 other bats (*Miniopterus* and *Rhinolophus*). The warm and humid microclimate of this cave may have permitted these bats to be so far south of their known distribution.

● **HABITAT** Tropical rainforest, monsoon forest, wet sclerophyll forest and open savannah woodland.

● **DIET AND FORAGING** They are known to eat moths. The presence of huntsman spider and beetle remains under two cave roosts suggests that these may form part of their diet. To catch huntsman spiders the bats would need to be partial gleaners, taking

| | | Wt | Fa | Ear | Foot | 3 met | Tail | HB | WS |
|---|---|---|---|---|---|---|---|---|---|
| **MEASUREMENTS** | MEAN | 7.2 | 47.1 | 20.5 | 8.0 | 33.9 | 24.8 | 45.9 | 296 |
| | MIN | 5.7 | 44.6 | 17.3 | 7.2 | 31.2 | 22.0 | 39.0 | 273 |
| | MAX | 8.7 | 50.4 | 22.5 | 8.5 | 36.3 | 26.0 | 49.0 | 320 |
| | NO | 6 | 6 | 6 | 6 | 6 | 6 | 6 | 6 |

S. Churchill.

prey from surfaces such as rock faces, tree trunks or from the ground. Bats released in the rainforest flew low, within a metre of the ground. Like other species of *Hipposideros*, the flight was relatively slow and manoeuvrable as they carefully negotiated their way through the undergrowth. Bats observed exiting a cave roost after sunset, when it was dark but moonlit, flew without echolocating, relying on vision and memory to negotiate obstacles.

● **REPRODUCTION** A group of four of these bats caught in late October was made up of three heavily pregnant females and a single adult male with scrotal testes, a condition uncommon for hipposiderids unless they are sexually active. The females probably give birth in early November to a single young.

● **ECHOLOCATION** The echolocation calls of this species are unusual in that they show a sexual difference with males and females producing calls of different frequencies. Males call at 94 kHz and females call at 74 kHz.

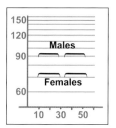

**REFERENCES** Bonaccorso 1998; de Oliveira & Pavey 1995; de Oliveira & Schulz 1997; Hall & Richards 1979; Hill 1963; Schulz & de Oliveira 1995; Thomson et al. 2001; Van Deusen 1973.

BRUCE THOMSON

# Northern leaf-nosed bat

## *Hipposideros stenotis* Thomas, 1913

● **DISTRIBUTION** From Kimberley, WA, through Top End of NT to Mt Isa in n.w. Qld. Endemic to Australia.

● **DESCRIPTION** This little bat formerly rejoiced in the wonderful name of 'lesser warty-nosed horseshoe bat'. It is a **medium-sized** *Hipposideros* with **long, sharply pointed ears** that extend well beyond the fur and which can be seen from a distance when the bat is roosting. The **fur on the back is grey-brown** and slightly lighter on the belly. Their **fur is very long and fine with a white base** to the hairs, giving a rather ruffled and untidy appearance. A distinctive feature is the large **wart-like projection in the centre of the nose-leaf** and the small secondary wart on the posterior nose-leaf. The function of these is unknown. It is similar to Semon's leaf-nosed bat, *H. semoni*, of eastern Qld which is larger (forearm length 44.5–50.5 mm) and has more prominent wart-like projections on the nose-leaf.

● **ROOST HABITS** Northern leaf-nosed bats have not been found in limestone caves despite extensive searches in the NT. It seems that they only use sandstone caves, boulder piles, road culverts and disused mines. They roost alone or in well-separated pairs in the less humid twilight zone (with a roost temperature of 27°C and 46% humidity). Most caves are small, shallow overhangs or splits in sandstone cliffs. These bats are easily overlooked. I have known one to wait quietly at its roost, 50 cm off the ground, in a boulder pile, as I crawled past it only centimetres away. I saw it for the first time as I turned around to leave the cave. In mines they appear to be more alert and slip away quickly and quietly when disturbed, usually flying outside rather than entering the deeper, more humid areas of the mine. They are seldom caught in mist nets or bat traps in the open. These bats could be confused with the dusky leaf-nosed bat, *H. ater*, but their long pointed ears are noticeable at the roost; while on the wing they are larger, with more direct flight.

● **HABITAT** Dense monsoon thickets, tall open forest, open eucalypt woodland, floodplains, open grassland and spinifex-covered hills usually in close proximity to rocky outcrops and escarpments. Their distribution is influenced by the availability of suitable roost sites. In the Kimberley, they have been captured along creeklines and pools.

● **DIET AND FORAGING** In the Kimberley, stomachs were found to contain mostly moths, beetles (chafers) and some ants. They have a slow fluttering butterfly-like flight

| | | Wt | Fa | Ear | Tibia | 3 met | Tail | HB | WS |
|---|---|---|---|---|---|---|---|---|---|
| **MEASUREMENTS** | MEAN | 5.5 | 44.1 | 18.8 | 21.2 | 31.4 | 24.9 | 42.3 | 262 |
| | MIN | 4.6 | 41.9 | 17.3 | 20.3 | 30.5 | 20.0 | 39.0 | 240 |
| | MAX | 6.7 | 45.6 | 20.9 | 22.7 | 32.1 | 28.0 | 45.7 | 275 |
| | NO | 8 | 11 | 9 | 7 | 4 | 9 | 9 | 4 |

S. Churchill; Kitchener et al. 1981; S. Murphy.

BRUCE THOMSON

and fly close to the ground, darting between grass tussocks and tree trunks in search of small insects. In the Top End, stomach contents included mainly beetles and moths with cockroaches and traces of crane flies, lacewings and ants. One individual released with a light tag had difficulty in controlling its height and direction while flying in windy conditions until it reached the cover of shrubs.

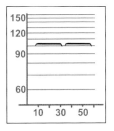

of about eight heavily pregnant females was found roosting together in a sandstone cave, further from the entrance than is usual for this species. Females with attached young have been reported in November and December.

● **REPRODUCTION** In the Kimberley some individuals are in the early stages of pregnancy in July and there is an extended birth season from October to at least the end of January. In the NT in November a colony

**REFERENCES** Hill 1963; Kitchener et al. 1981; McKenzie et al. 1978, 1995; Milne 2002; Milne & Burwell (unpubl.); Schulz & Menkhorst 1984, 1986; B. Thomson (pers. com.); Thomson 1991.

# Orange leaf-nosed bat
## *Rhinonicteris aurantia* (Gray, 1845)

● **DISTRIBUTION** N.w. Qld through Top End and into Kimberley, WA. Relict population in Pilbara region isolated by Great Sandy Desert. The Pilbara population is slightly smaller with a higher echolocation call. Genus is endemic to Australia.

● **DESCRIPTION** A beautiful bat, which, despite stringent roost requirements, has been around since before the Riversleigh deposits were laid down about 5 million years ago. It is a distinctive species, easily distinguished from other members of the family by its **elaborate rounded and scalloped nose-leaf**. Most commonly the **fur is bright orange** in contrast to the dark brown wings, but colonies of brown, yellow and white individuals occur. The colour of all the individuals within a colony can change over time.

● **ROOST HABITS** Orange leaf-nosed bats are dependent on caves and mines with very hot and humid roost sites (28–32°C and 96–100% relative humidity) during the tropical dry season. Caves and mines with these conditions are uncommon. These bats roost hanging freely from the ceiling or against the cave wall and separated from each other by 10–15 cm. Colony size varies from five to over 20 000. They abandon the dry season roost caves from November to February, during the wet season, when the outside climatic conditions are hot and humid and similar to the dry season roost microclimate. It is thought that these bats become forest dwellers at this time.

● **HABITAT** Monsoon rainforest, tall open forest, open savannah woodland, black soil grassland and spinifex-covered hills. They are more influenced by the availability of suitable roost caves than habitat type.

● **DIET AND FORAGING** They are opportunistic in their diet, eating primarily moths and beetles throughout the year. During the wet season, however, they prefer flying termites, which provide a fat-rich diet for the pregnant and lactating females. Over the year their diet is comprised of 70% moths, 17% beetles, 8% termites, with occasional ants, wasps, mantids, lacewings, bugs, flies and cockroaches. They fly rapidly (speeds of up to 26 km/h) with a fast wing beat and tend to forage with a zigzag flight pattern low to the ground. They are often seen flying along roads at night and their bright orange fur is very distinctive in car headlights.

● **REPRODUCTION** Males have enlarged testes and mate in July. Females give birth to a single young in late December or early

| | | Wt | Fa | Ear | Foot | 3 met | Tail | HB | WS |
|---|---|---|---|---|---|---|---|---|---|
| **MEASUREMENTS** | MEAN | 8.4 | 48.1 | 12.7 | 7.5 | 37.1 | 25.0 | 50.2 | 283.4 |
| | MIN | 6.5 | 45.2 | 12.1 | 6.6 | 33.4 | 23.0 | 44.8 | 245 |
| | MAX | 11.2 | 50.2 | 13.6 | 9.0 | 40.1 | 29.0 | 55.0 | 297 |
| | NO | 27 | 49 | 17 | 17 | 17 | 15 | 17 | 15 |

S. Churchill.

January after a 5-month gestation. They leave their dry season roost caves during late pregnancy and lactation, returning only after the young are weaned and independent. The young grow rapidly and are almost indistinguishable from the adults when they are weaned in late February. The females are reproductively mature at 7 months but males do not mature until their second year at 18 months.

● **NOTES** These bats are very susceptible to dehydration and hypothermia. Their rates of evaporative water loss have been found to be more than double that of other bats. Removed from the high temperature and humidity of their cave roosts they die within hours. For this reason they are difficult to hold in captivity and will die in bat traps if these are not checked frequently. They will abandon roost caves if disturbed unreasonably.

A large colony (over 20 000) of orange leaf-nosed bats is heavily preyed upon by ghost bats, *Macroderma gigas*, as they exit the cave at dusk. The ghost bats fly 15–20 m above the cave entrance, swooping down rapidly to gain speed and fly through the stream of outgoing bats to take them from behind. In June and July, when the ghost bats are in late pregnancy or nursing young, they eat far more orange leaf-nosed bats

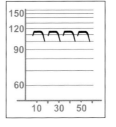

than at other times; the cave floor below the ghost bats' roost becomes littered with hundreds of discarded wings. Orange leaf-nosed bats exit the cave at high speed with an erratic zigzag flight pattern, and rapidly enter the thicker vegetation, presumably to avoid the ghost bats.

**REFERENCES** Armstrong 2002a, b, 2006a, b; Baudinette et al. 2000; Bullen & McKenzie 2002; Churchill 1991a, 1994, 1995; Churchill et al. 1988; Jolly 1988.

# Evening Bats
## Family VESPERTILIONIDAE: Key to Genera

**V**espertilionidae have an extensive tail membrane fully enclosing the tail. These bats have no nose-leaf or, at most, a low transverse muzzle ridge (*Nyctophilus*). Ears and tragus are variable. This is the largest family of Australian bats with many similar species that are difficult to identify.

**1a** Dark brown curly fur with bright golden-tipped hairs on body, forearms, legs and tail; muzzle pointed with overhanging top lip; ears funnel-shaped; tragus long, straight and narrow with a deep lateral notch at the base; upper canine long and grooved, and fits in pocket of lower lip when mouth closed.

→ ***Phoniscus papuensis*** (page 147)

**1b** Fur, muzzle, ears, tragus and canines not as in 1a. → **2**

**2a** Nostrils tubular and extend sideways from the end of the nose; long thick fur covers most of the tail membrane.

→ ***Murina florium*** (page 126)

**2b** Nostrils not tubular; tail membrane without long thick fur. → **3**

**3a** Ears long and joined above head by a ridge of skin; simple nose-leaf in the form of a ridge on muzzle and small flaps of skin around nostrils.

→ **Genus *Nyctophilus*** (page 107)

**3b** Ears not joined above the head; muzzle ridge absent. → **4**

**4a** Lobes (wattles) on the lower edge of the ear near the corner of the mouth and along the lower lip.

→ **Genus *Chalinolobus*** (page 106)

**4b** No lobes on the corner of mouth or on lower lip. → **5**

**5a** Forearm length greater than 45 mm. → **6**

**5b** Forearm length less than 45 mm. → **7**

**6a** Four upper incisors (two pairs); the outer pair being minute and easily overlooked; usually a gap between incisors and canines; ears meet easily when pressed together over the head, and overlap by about 5 mm; penis shorter and moderately hairy.

→ **Genus *Falsistrellus*** (page 107)

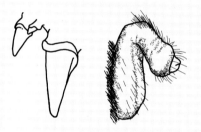

**6b** Two upper incisors (one pair); no gap between incisors and canines; ears barely touch above the head when pressed together; penis longer and relatively hairless.

→ ***Scoteanax rueppellii*** (page 153)

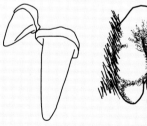

**7a** Foot disproportionately large, averages 10.1 mm (8.3–11.2 mm without claw); foot more than half the length of tibia; calcar long, extending three-quarters of the distance from ankle to tail tip; tragus very long, straight and slender.

→ ***Myotis macropus*** (page 128)

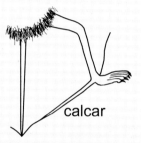

calcar

**7b** Foot not disproportionately large, less than 8.0 mm; foot less than half the length of tibia; calcar extends much less than three-quarters of the distance from ankle to tail tip; tragus not long, straight and slender. → **8**

**8a** Two upper incisors (one pair), simple, not forked; muzzle broad with naked, swollen, glandular pads.

→ **Genus *Scotorepens*** (page 110)

**8b** Four upper incisors (two pairs; outer pair may not be visible); inner pair of incisors forked (forked tips may be worn away in old individuals); muzzle not broad; glandular pads rarely swollen. → **9**

**9a** Inner upper incisors distinctly forked; the two lobes are side by side and easily seen from the front (forked tips may be worn away in old individuals); outer incisors are small to minute (they may be hidden beneath the gums, but it is possible to 'feel' them with the tip of a pencil); only a single pair of upper premolars are present.

→ **Genus *Vespadelus*** (page 111)

**9b** Inner upper incisors forked but difficult to see from the front as one lobe is behind the other; outer incisors obvious, only slightly smaller than inner pair; two pairs of upper premolars present, the forward premolar is only half the height of the rear premolar and lies slightly inside the tooth row.

→ **Genus *Pipistrellus*** (page 109)

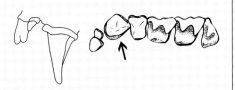

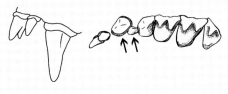

# Family VESPERTILIONIDAE: Key to Species

## GENUS *Chalinolobus*

These bats have a fleshy lobe at the lower margin of the ear and a second lobe either at the corner of the mouth or along the lip. The ears are short and broad and the curled tragus points inwards. The forehead is high and there may be glandular swellings on the muzzle.

**1a** Inner upper incisor forked; fur either uniform brown, or black with white stripes on the belly along the wings. → **2**

**1b** Inner upper incisors not forked; fur light to dark brown with darker head and shoulders or grizzled grey to black, without distinct white belly stripes. → **4**

**2a** Fur uniform brown all over, paler belly in some individuals; forearm length 33.0–42.4 mm; a small ridge of fur across the muzzle; lobe at corner of mouth small, lobe on lower lip easily seen.

→ ***C. morio*** (page 118)

**2b** Fur black except for a distinct white stripe along the junction of the belly fur and the wing membranes joining at the groin to form a white 'V'. → **3**

**3a** Forearm length usually greater than
37 mm (36.9–44.6 mm); ears large and
easily overlap by about 5 mm when
pressed together above the head.
→ *C. dwyeri* (page 114)

**3b** Forearm length usually less than 37 mm
(31.4–37.5 mm); ears small and barely
touch or do not touch when pressed
together above head.
→ *C. picatus* (page 121)

**4a** Fur brown, usually with a distinctly
darker, almost black, head and shoulders;
forearm length (35.5–47.2 mm) with
considerable regional variation, being
smaller in north and east; lobes around
mouth well developed.
→ *C. gouldii* (page 116)

**4b** Fur grey, dark at base with white tips
giving a frosted appearance, WA
specimens are much lighter than eastern
Australian (south-eastern Qld individuals
may be almost black); forearm length
averages 34.2 mm (31.6–37.1 mm); lobes
on lip thin.
→ *C. nigrogriseus* (page 120)

## GENUS *Falsistrellus*

The inner upper incisor is not forked, the
outer upper incisor is very small and
considerably outside the line of the tooth
row. There are two pairs of upper premolars.
The forward upper premolar is tiny, less than
half the size of the rear upper premolar. The
skull has a marked occipital crest.

**1a** South-west WA.
→ *F. mackenziei* (page 123)

**1b** South-eastern Australia and Tas.
→ *F. tasmaniensis* (page 124)

## GENUS *Nyctophilus*

The muzzle, which is only slightly hairy, has a
transverse muzzle ridge halfway along its
length. There are also foliations around the
nostrils that vary between species. These are
believed to act in conjunction with the
muzzle ridge to function as a nose-leaf. The
ears are joined over the head by a band of
skin and are ribbed along the rear edge
permitting them to be folded down when
the bat is at rest. The eyes are relatively large.

Within each species the size of
individuals varies considerably from north to
south, with smaller individuals in the north.
Within any one region forearm
measurements are a more useful guide to
identification than these keys indicate. **Ear
length is an important measurement for
identification and care must be taken not
to stretch the ear and distort the
measurement.** USE ONLY PLASTIC
CALIPERS.

**1a** Muzzle ridge well developed with distinct groove or split (Types 1 and 2). → **2**

 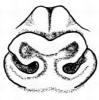

Type 1            Type 2

**1b** Muzzle ridge poorly developed without distinct groove (Types 3 and 4). → **5**

Type 3            Type 4

**2a** Muzzle ridge high and composed of two lobes joined at the top by a membrane of skin, forming a distinctive Y-shaped groove (Type 1); fur grey on the back with a white belly; forearm length 30–42 mm; ear length 17–26 mm.
→ ***N. geoffroyi*** (page 135)

**2b** Muzzle ridge moderate with two distinct lobes divided centrally by a vertical groove (Type 2). → **3**

**3a** Ears short, 10.7–14.1 mm; small size, forearm length 30.1–36.0 mm; weight 3.0–7.0 g; fur orange-brown on the back with a distinctly lighter belly.
→ ***N. walkeri*** (page 145)

**3b** Ears longer than 15 mm; size larger, forearm length usually greater than 36 mm. → **4**

**4a** Ears moderate length (16.3–21.5 mm); medium size, forearm length averages 37.4 mm (33.2–39.9 mm); fur colour light russet brown all over; occurs in northern WA, NT and western Qld; the glans penis is a square-ended cylinder with a flat circular urethral opening on the underside, near the tip.
→ ***N. arnhemensis*** (page 130)

**4b** Ears longer (24.3–30.1 mm); larger size, forearm length 36.3–47.7 mm; fur colour dark grey or greyish brown; south-western and south-eastern Australia extending north to Townsville; glans penis divided by a longitudinal groove into two cylinders, with the upper one projecting to give a distinctly beaked appearance, and a slit-like urethral opening; OCW less than 5.1 mm.
→ ***N. gouldi*** (page 137)

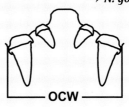

OCW

**5a** OCW is less than 5.5 mm; muzzle ridge low, rounded with slight depression in centre (Type 3); northern Australia and east coast to northern NSW. → **6**

**5b** OCW is greater than 5.6 mm; muzzle ridge low with no central depression (Type 4); southern Australia. → **7**

**6a** Occurs along the east coast of Qld from Cape York to northern NSW; forearm length 37.5–46.8 mm; ear length 19.2–27.1 mm; glans penis is not beaked (similar to 4a); baculum bifid.
→ *N. bifax* (page 132)

**6b** Occurs from western Qld to the Pilbara in WA; forearm length 38.3–45.8 mm; ear length 20.5–25.8 mm; glans penis distinctly beaked (similar to 4b); baculum not bifid. → *N. daedalus* (page 134)

**7a** Restricted to Tas; large size; weight averages 12.9 g (9.8–18.9 g); forearm averages 45.9 mm (43.9–48.0 mm).
→ *N. sherrini* (page 141)

**7b** Not in Tas. → **8**

**8a** South-eastern Australia; large size; weight averages 15.3 g (11.8–21.0 g); forearm averages 45.6 mm (41.3–49.4 mm); semi-arid habitats.
→ *Nyctophilus* species 2 (page 143)

**8b** Not in south-eastern Australia. → **9**

**9a** Inland SA and WA; weight averages 11.0 g (9.5–12.7 g); forearm averages 41.2 mm (37.6–45.3 mm); skull length less than 18.8 mm, skull width less than 11.2 mm.
→ *Nyctophilus* species 1 (page 142)

**9b** South-western and south coast of WA; weight averages 13.6 g (11.5–17.5 g); forearm averages 45.5 mm (43.2–48.4 mm); skull length greater than 18.8 mm, skull width greater than 11.6 mm.
→ *N. major* (page 139)

## GENUS *Pipistrellus*

These tiny bats are very similar in appearance to *Vespadelus*, but can be distinguished by their teeth. The inner upper incisors are forked, with the second lobe hidden behind the first when viewed from the front, and the outer upper incisors are almost as large as the inner ones. There are two pairs of upper premolars with the forward ones approximately half the size of the rear premolars. The muzzle is rather short and sparsely haired.

**1a** Larger size; forearm length averages 31.3 mm (29.6–32.7 mm); OCW is 3.9–4.3 mm; greatest skull length 12.0 mm (11.7–12.6 mm); ear more rounded at tip, tragus with a larger lobe at base and the rear edge more convex; glans penis with single fleshy tongue from lower lip; distribution in north Qld and the Top End, mainly associated with monsoon forests and rainforests but also near mangroves. → **P. adamsi** (page 149)

**1b** Smaller size; forearm length averages 29.1 mm (27.4–31.3 mm); OCW is 3.4–3.8 mm; greatest skull length 11.4 mm (11.1–11.9 mm); ear triangular, less rounded at tip, tragus with a smaller lobe at base and the rear edge less convex; tip of glans penis swollen, at the tip a circular depression full of small fleshy spines; distribution the Kimberley and Top End extending along the Gulf of Carpentaria into western Cape York Peninsula, virtually restricted to mangroves in WA.
→ **P. westralis** (page 152)

**1c** Christmas Island only.
→ **P. murrayi** (page 150)

## GENUS *Scotorepens*

The head appears almost square in outline when viewed from above. The muzzle is sparsely haired and has a swollen appearance due to the presence of glands on each side. They have only one pair of upper incisors. The forehead profile is flat, not elevated.

*Scotorepens* can be very difficult to identify. There are no reliable external characters that separate *S. sanborni* and *S. greyii.* **Distribution is useful in most areas.** Positive identification requires protein electrophoresis. In south-eastern Qld and northern NSW four species—

*S. orion, S. greyii, S. balstoni* and *S.* species—overlap in distribution. These four species also overlap in forearm measurements.

**1a** Forearm length more than or equal to 2.5 times tibia length; fur not markedly bicoloured; forearm length averages 35.1 mm (32.4–38.8 mm); moderate build, weight averages 9.3 g (7.0–14.0 g); coastal south-eastern Australia and Atherton Tablelands, Qld; glans penis with eight spines on head, in a nearly circular cluster; muzzle pug-like.
→ **S. orion** (page 158)

**1b** Forearm length less than 2.5 times tibia length; fur markedly bicoloured; glans penis with spines on head mainly in two long rows; muzzle not pug-like. → **2**

**2a** Forearm length longer, averages 35.6 mm (32.0–40.5 mm); robust build, weight averages 9.3 g (6.3–12.7 g); inland Australia; spines on glans penis smaller and more numerous, up to 22.
→ **S. balstoni** (page 155)

**2b** Forearm length intermediate, averaging 32.8 mm (31.0–34.6 mm); body less robust, average weight 7.4 g (6.1–9.0 g); distribution in northern NSW and south-eastern Qld only.
→ **Scotorepens species** (page 161)

**2c** Forearm length smaller, averaging less than 32 mm; small build, weight averages 6.5 g (4.0–9.1 g); spines on glans penis larger and less numerous, up to ten. → **3**

**3a** Widely distributed through northern and inland Australia, not on Cape York Peninsula; forearm length averages 31.3 mm (27.3–35.0 mm); pterygoid process of skull usually extends posterior to the forward edge of foramen rotundum. → ***S. greyii*** (page 156)

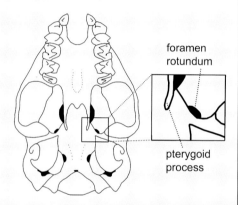

foramen rotundum

pterygoid process

**3b** Discontinuous distribution; on Cape York Peninsula forearm averages 33.3 mm (31.0–35.8 mm); in the Kimberley and coastal, western Top End forearm length averages 31.0 mm (27.9–34.0 mm); pterygoid process of skull does not extend posterior to the forward edge of foramen rotundum.
→ ***S. sanborni*** (page 160)

## GENUS *Vespadelus*

The small delicate skulls are without sagittal crests. The inner upper incisors are forked, the outer cusp being smaller than the inner cusp. The outer upper incisors are not forked and range in size from minute (from just above the inner incisor cingulum) to one-quarter the height of the inner incisor. There is only a single pair of upper premolars.

*Vespadelus* **species can be very difficult to identify.** Within the one species colour and size vary considerably from one region to another but within a given locality each species is usually consistent. Penis morphology is the most reliable identification method but wing bone ratios may help to identify females of some species. Comparison of size and colour with males from the same area that have been identified using penis characters will also help.

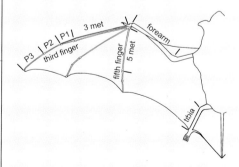

**1a** Forest bat; penis is either distinctly angular or pendulous and distinctly swollen; glans penis compressed dorsoventrally or not compressed; third finger: P3 divided by P2 is greater than 0.73. → **2**

**1b** Cave bat; penis pendulous but not distinctly swollen, penis short relative to body size; glans penis cylindrical and compressed laterally; third finger: P3 divided by P2 is less than 0.70. → **4**

**2a** Penis is distinctly angular without a swollen tip; glans penis is dorsoventrally compressed; third finger: P3 divided by P2 is generally greater than 0.84. → **3**

**2b** Penis clearly swollen, pendulous, never distinctly angular; glans penis not compressed; third finger: P3 divided by P2 is generally less than 0.84. → **6**

**3a** Smaller size; forearm length less than 33.0 mm; third finger: P3 divided by P2 averages 0.87; distribution Qld and northern half of coastal NSW.
→ ***V. pumilus*** (page 171)

**3b** Larger size; forearm length greater than 32.5 mm; third finger: P3 divided by P2 averages 0.92; distribution restricted to south-eastern coast and Tas (overlaps *V. pumilus* in northern coastal NSW).
→ ***V. darlingtoni*** (page 166)

**4a** Smaller size; forearm length less than 32 mm; forearm averages 29.5 mm (26.6–31.7 mm) (*V. finlaysoni* falls within this range only in the Pilbara region of WA); upper first molar ($M^1$) metacone-hypocone crista moderate; greatest skull length averages 11.2 mm (10.6–12.0 mm); distribution Top End and Kimberley.
→ ***V. caurinus*** (page 164)

**4b** Larger size; forearm length greater than 32 mm (except in the Pilbara region). → **5**

**5a** Fur colour grey with orange or yellow stain around mouth and nose; third finger: P1 divided by 3 met is less than 0.34 (average 0.32); distribution restricted to the Kimberley region of WA; forearm length averages 36.3 mm (34.3–37.8 mm); greatest skull length averages 12.8 mm (12.3–13.2 mm).
→ ***V. douglasorum*** (page 168)

**5b** Fur colour generally dark brown with light brown or rust tips; third finger: P1 divided by 3 met is greater than 0.34 (average 0.37); does not occur in the Kimberley region; distributed over most of inland Australia, generally not overlapping other cave-dwelling species; forearm length averages 32.8 mm

(29.8–37.6 mm); upper first molar ($M^1$) metacone-hypocone crista always absent; greatest skull length averages 12.4 mm (11.3–13.5 mm).

→ *V. finlaysoni* (page 169)

**6a** Glans penis bulbous with abruptly truncated tip, without furrow or lateral folds; third finger: P1 divided by 3 met is greater than 0.39 (average 0.42); forearm length averages 28.4 mm (23.5–32.8 mm); distribution Tas and south-eastern Australia extending inland; tragus often white; skull has a distinct rise on the bridge of the nose that can be felt with a finger; head is small and narrow with a smaller gap between the ears than *V. regulus*.

→ *V. vulturnus* (page 177)

**6b** Glans penis not bulbous; third finger: P1 divided by 3 met is less than 0.39. → **7**

**7a** Glans penis funnel-shaped and lacks a deep furrow on the underside; size smaller, forearm length averages 28.6 mm (26.5–31.4 mm), greatest skull length averages 12.1 mm (11.6–12.5 mm); distribution inland Australia generally not overlapping other forest species.

→ *V. baverstocki* (page 163)

**7b** Glans penis with deep furrow on underside; forearm length averages greater than 30.0 mm; greatest skull length averages 12.7 mm (11.9–13.4 mm). → **8**

**8a** Glans penis with distinct lateral urethral folds; head of penis relatively short and stocky; size smaller, forearm length averages 31.2 mm (28.0–34.4 mm); distribution across southern Australia and Tas, not extending far inland; tragus is usually dark; skull is flat; head is triangular when viewed from above, with a wider gap between the ears than *V. vulturnus*.

→ *V. regulus* (page 173)

**8b** Glans penis lacks lateral folds; head of penis laterally compressed and relatively elongate; size larger, forearm length averages 34.6 mm (32.3–36.4 mm); distribution eastern Qld and NSW.

→ *V. troughtoni* (page 175)

# Large-eared pied bat

## *Chalinolobus dwyeri* Ryan, 1966

● **DISTRIBUTION** Areas with extensive cliffs and caves from Blackdown Tableland in central-eastern Qld s. to Bungonia in Southern Highlands of NSW. Scattered records from New England Tablelands and n.w. slopes of NSW. Endemic to Australia.

● **DESCRIPTION** A caricature of a *Chalinolobus*, with its large ears and curly wattles, the large-eared pied bat has **uniform glossy black fur on the back**. The belly is washed with brown, usually with a **band of bright white fur along the sides of the body** where the wing membranes join. These **white lateral stripes converge in the pubic region to form a V-shape. Ears are very large** and easily touch when pressed together above the head. The **lobe** (wattle) at **the corner of the mouth is well developed**. A second lobe of skin along the side of the lower lip is also well developed.

● **ROOST HABITS** These bats roost in caves, crevices in cliffs and mines, in colonies of three to 40, clustered in indentations in the ceiling. They prefer the twilight areas of the caves not far from the entrance. Males have been found during the winter in deep torpor

roosting alone in abandoned mines and one juvenile male overwintered in an abandoned fairy martin nest. Colonies of up to four have been found in both intact and partially intact fairy martin nests in south-eastern Qld. In mid November a maternity colony of 40 females with their newborn twins was found in a sandstone cave near Coonabarabran. The bats were clustered into two separate cracks in the twilight area in the cave ceiling. The temperature ranged from 15.5–18.5°C and 51–76% humidity.

● **HABITAT** I have mist-netted these bats in a sandstone gorge in tall open eucalypt forest with an understorey of scattered small trees and palms. They are most commonly recorded from dry sclerophyll forests and woodlands, but they also occur in sub-alpine woodland, the edge of rainforest, wet sclerophyll forest, *Callitris*-dominated forest and sandstone outcrop country. In the Sydney basin they are common in areas of high fertility soils in wet sclerophyll forests along the edges of sandstone escarpments.

● **DIET AND FORAGING** These bats are insectivorous, but no details are known. They fly relatively slowly with rapid but shallow wing beats. Their flight is direct and moderately manoeuvrable. I have watched them fly low along a creek bed, but they also fly at mid-canopy level 6–10 m above the ground.

| | | Wt | Fa | Ear | Tibia | 3 met | Tail | HB | WS | Skull |
|---|---|---|---|---|---|---|---|---|---|---|
| **MEASUREMENTS** | MEAN | 7.7 | 40.1 | 16.0 | 18.5 | 38.5 | 41.4 | 46.2 | 277.5 | 13.7 |
| | MIN | 5.5 | 36.9 | 12.4 | 17.9 | 36.7 | 34.5 | 43.0 | 275 | 13.6 |
| | MAX | 12.2 | 44.6 | 17.5 | 19.2 | 40.3 | 48.3 | 50.1 | 280 | 13.8 |
| | NO | 77 | 112 | 9 | 5 | 7 | 9 | 9 | 2 | 5 |

S. Churchill; M. Pennay; Ryan 1966a.

● **REPRODUCTION** During the autumn and early winter the males have enlarged testes. At this time, the facial glands on either side of the muzzle become swollen and show a cream colour beneath the skin. They exude a milky secretion when compressed. It is possible that these glands have a secondary sexual function. It is not known whether mating occurs in the autumn or spring. Groups of 20–40 females have been recorded raising young in maternity roosts from November through to February in roof domes in sandstone caves. The females give birth, commonly to twins, in November, and the young are independent by late February. They leave the cave soon after and the females remain for another month before abandoning the roost in late March for the winter. They remain loyal to the same cave, returning each summer over many years.

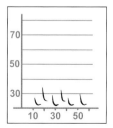

REFERENCES Duncan et al. 1999; Dwyer 1965, 1966b; Hoye & Dwyer, in Strahan 1995; Ryan 1966a; Schulz 1998.

# Gould's wattled bat

## *Chalinolobus gouldii* (Gray, 1841)

● **DISTRIBUTION** Tas and mainland Australia, except Cape York Peninsula and Nullarbor Plain. Formerly at Norfolk Is but now extinct there.

● **DESCRIPTION** An amazingly adaptable bat that is found in the full spectrum of Australian climatic zones. It has a delightful habit of murmuring to itself when held in the hand. The **fur is brown on the back and belly** with **contrasting blackish fur on the head and shoulders**. The **muzzle is short**, the **ears are short and broad**. There is **a large lobe of skin** (wattle) **at the corner of the mouth** and a secondary long narrow lobe along the lower lip. It shows variation in body size throughout its range. Individuals from northern Australia are smaller than those from the south and those from eastern Australia are smaller than western individuals. There is no significant difference in size between males and females.

● **ROOST HABITS** Gould's wattled bats roost most commonly in tree hollows and hollow limbs of mature living trees, particularly river red gums (*Eucalyptus camaldulensis*) and cypress pines (*Callitris*). Other recorded roosts include buildings, a tree stump, among leaves, in a roll of canvas, and even in the exhaust pipe of a tractor. Females form colonies of eight to 40 in tree hollows and up to 80 in buildings. Males are usually solitary but have been found sharing a tree hollow roost with feather-tail gliders (*Acrobates pygmaeus*) and several other bat species. They move daily between a number of roost sites within a small area, returning to the same roost every few days. One tree hollow, 5 m above the ground, was occupied throughout the year for at least 6 years. They hibernate in the cooler parts of their range and they are able to enter and spontaneously arouse from torpor at temperatures as low as 5°C or as high as 25°C. Evaporative water loss in these bats is usually high but by entering torpor they reduce the loss to less than 15%. This must be a significant advantage to a species that is so widespread in arid areas.

● **HABITAT** This ubiquitous bat is found in virtually all habitats throughout Australia from alpine regions to tropical rainforests, eucalypt forests and woodlands, deserts, grasslands, agricultural land and urban areas.

● **DIET AND FORAGING** Bugs and moths are the major food items, including bogong moths in the Southern Highlands of NSW. A wide variety of prey including winged and wingless ants, cockroaches, stoneflies,

| | Vic | | Northern Australia | | | | | | |
|---|---|---|---|---|---|---|---|---|---|
| | Wt | Fa | Wt | Fa | Ear | 3 met | Tail | HB | WS |
| MEAN | 13.8 | 43.7 | 9.8 | 41.2 | 10.5 | 38.1 | 40.1 | 52.4 | 295 |
| MIN | 10.0 | 35.5 | 6.8 | 36.6 | 7.2 | 31.8 | 31.0 | 46.0 | 273 |
| MAX | 20.0 | 47.2 | 15.8 | 45.9 | 13.3 | 44.5 | 46.0 | 60.4 | 330 |
| NO | 566 | 566 | 98 | 106 | 30 | 30 | 28 | 30 | 28 |

MEASUREMENTS

S. Churchill; L. Lumsden.

BRUCE THOMSON

winter. Ovulation and fertilisation occur at the end of winter. The pregnancy, usually twins, one in each uterine horn, lasts 3 months. The timing of births changes with latitude, becoming later further south. Births occur in late September in the north, in October in central areas and late November in the south. The young achieve adult size and independence in about 6 weeks. In the Mallee region of western Vic, females can breed in their first year but do not breed every year, with 20–30% of females non-breeding each year.

● **NOTES** They often emerge early after sunset when there is still a lot of ambient light. This makes them vulnerable

katydids, field crickets, cicadas, bugs, beetles, flies and caterpillars have been reported from scats and stomach remains. They regularly forage 5–10 km from their roost site and occasionally up to 15 km away. They fly just below or within the lower level of the tree canopy and along the forest edges, creeklines and around isolated paddock trees. Their agile flight is faster than most vespertilionids. They tend to fly on a fixed horizontal plane with abrupt zigzag changes of course, frequently rolling to near vertical banking angles during horizontal turns. They can fly at speeds of up to 36 km/h.

to predation, and they have been taken by owls, falcons, butcherbirds, currawongs and feral cats.

**REFERENCES** Calaby 1966; Dixon & Huxley 1989; Dixon, in Strahan 1995; Herr 1998; Hosken & Withers 1997; Hosken 1996; G. Hoye (pers. com.); Kitchener 1975; Lumsden & Bennett 1995; McKenzie et al. 2002; Menkhorst 1995; O'Neill & Taylor 1986; Rounsevell et al. 1991; Taylor & O'Neill 1986; Tidemann 1986; Vestjens & Hall 1977; Young 1980.

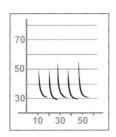

● **REPRODUCTION** In WA and Vic testicular enlargement peaks in February. Copulation takes place around May to June and sperm is stored in the female's uterine lining over

# Chocolate wattled bat

## *Chalinolobus morio* (Gray, 1841)

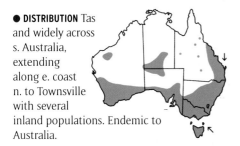

● **DISTRIBUTION** Tas and widely across s. Australia, extending along e. coast n. to Townsville with several inland populations. Endemic to Australia.

● **DESCRIPTION** A common species of southern Australia. The fur is a uniform **milk-chocolate brown on the back and the belly.** The **belly fur is sometimes slightly paler** in inland individuals. The **head is steeply domed with a short muzzle**, usually with a **distinct ridge of fur across the muzzle**. The **ears are short and broad** and will barely or not quite meet if pressed together across the top of the head. The tragus is short, broad and strongly curved forward with a pointed tip. There is a **moderate development of the wattle**; the lobe at the corner of the mouth is small, but the **secondary lobe along the lower lip is semicircular and easily seen**. These lobes and the shape of the tragus help to distinguish this species from the large forest bat, *Vespadelus darlingtoni*, which is a similar size and colour.

● **ROOST HABITS** These bats roost in tree hollows, houses, under the exfoliating bark of trees, in fairy martin nests, culverts and bridges as well as in caves (in the south-west and Nullarbor areas). Most roosts are in trees. Female colonies of six to 70 have been found. Males usually roost alone. Larger colonies of up to 400 have been recorded in buildings and caves. Colony sizes may be many times greater than the numbers observed at any one time as each bat has several roosts and they move almost daily to alternate roosts.

● **HABITAT** Rainforest, wet and dry sclerophyll forest, woodlands and mallee as well as shrublands and treeless regions such as the Nullarbor. In inland areas their distribution tends to follow water courses as these provide large trees for roosts. They prefer continuous forests to small forest patches.

● **DIET AND FORAGING** They are opportunistic foragers and choice of prey tends to reflect the availability of aerial insects. They feed predominantly on moths and beetles but also take termites and occasional flies, bugs, ants, lacewings and wasps. They forage up to 5 km from their roost site and use the same relatively small foraging area each night. They mostly forage in the open zone between the top of the understorey and the canopy, although they sometimes fly low along forest trails. Their flight is usually fast and direct, with rapid wing beats. Gliding attack-manoeuvres are carried out with considerable agility, usually with sudden vertical drops. They have been recorded at

| MEASUREMENTS | | Wt | Fa | Ear | Tibia | 3 met | Tail | HB | WS |
|---|---|---|---|---|---|---|---|---|---|
| | MEAN | 8.9 | 38.9 | 8.61 | 18.8 | 34.9 | 43.4 | 46.6 | 271.3 |
| | MIN | 5.5 | 33.0 | 7.7 | 18 | 33.6 | 39.3 | 40 | 266 |
| | MAX | 13.0 | 42.4 | 9.8 | 20.2 | 37.4 | 49.5 | 52.4 | 275 |
| | NO | 1110 | 1385 | 12 | 9 | 12 | 11 | 12 | 6 |

S. Churchill; M. Pennay.

BRUCE THOMSON

speeds of 28 km/h and are among the most agile bats.

● **REPRODUCTION** Spermatogenesis in males occurs in spring and summer. Sperm is stored in the epididymides as the testes regress. Mating occurs in autumn and winter. Females give birth to one, or two, young after a gestation of 4–5 months. The young are born in late spring and early summer, usually in October in Qld or November in the southern part of its range. Births are earlier at lower latitude and/or altitude. The young are 25% of the female's weight at birth and twins are 35% of her weight. They are born hairless, with a pink body and dark wings. Lactation is usually completed by early February. In Tas births are 1 month later than other bats but weaning occurs at about the same time indicating a shortened lactation period.

● **NOTES** In southern Australia they tend to be the last species to enter hibernation for the winter and the first to emerge in the spring. At these times there is a paucity of food available, but there is also less competition from other species. Males remain far more active in winter than females. They often mate with the hibernating females at this time.

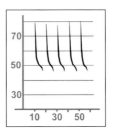

**REFERENCES** Bullen & McKenzie 2001; Hall 1970; Kincade et al. 2000; Kitchener & Coster 1981; Law 1994; Lumsden & Bennett 1995; Lumsden & Wainer (pers. com.); Lunney et al. 1985; Menkhorst 1995; O'Neill & Taylor 1986; Reardon & Flavel 1991; Schulz 2000a; Taylor & O'Neill 1986; Tidemann 1993a; Tidemann & Flavel 1987; B. Thomson (pers. com.); Young 1979.

# Hoary wattled bat

## *Chalinolobus nigrogriseus* (Gould, 1856)

● **DISTRIBUTION** From Kimberley, WA, across n. Australia to Cape York and down e. coast to Coffs Harbour, n. NSW; becoming less common s. of the tropics. Extralimitally in New Guinea.

BRUCE THOMSON

● **DESCRIPTION** A gentle animal, the hoary wattled bat has **dark grey to black fur on the back** and **greyish brown on the belly**, with a **frosting of white tips to the hairs**, giving a hoary appearance (some individuals have no white frosting). **The lobe** (wattle) at the corner of the mouth **is poorly developed** and the **secondary lobe is reduced to a thin ribbon of skin** along the lower lip. There is an east to west change in size and the amount of white frosting to the fur. WA individuals are smaller with considerably more frosting than Qld bats which may be almost black. The little pied bat, *C. picatus*, can be distinguished by the presence of a notch in the inner upper incisor.

● **ROOST HABITS** Hoary wattled bats are forest dwellers that roost in hollows in eucalypt trees. They have also occasionally been found to roost in rock crevices. In New Guinea a maternity colony of several hundred females and their young were found in the roof of a building in November. They can often be seen flying about at dusk, having left their roost site before other bat species have emerged.

● **HABITAT** Monsoon forest, tall open forest, open woodland, dry sclerophyll forest, river red gum riparian woodland, littoral rainforest, deciduous vine thickets, coastal scrub, sand dunes, spinifex-covered hills, grasslands and floodplains. They fly fast below the canopy level so forests with naturally sparse understorey layers may provide the best habitat.

| | | Wt | Fa | Ear | 3 met | Tail | HB | WS | Skull |
|---|---|---|---|---|---|---|---|---|---|
| **MEASUREMENTS** | MEAN | 6.0 | 34.2 | 9.3 | 33.0 | 33.6 | 43.6 | 253 | 12.3 |
| | MIN | 4.2 | 31.6 | 7.5 | 25.8 | 29.0 | 39.6 | 240 | 11.4 |
| | MAX | 10.0 | 37.1 | 11.3 | 37.0 | 39.0 | 48.0 | 276 | 13.4 |
| | NO | 119 | 119 | 33 | 33 | 28 | 33 | 29 | 40 |

S. Churchill.

● **DIET AND FORAGING** They show a preference for beetles, ants and moths but they also eat a wide variety of prey including spiders, mantids, earwigs, crickets, grasshoppers, cockroaches, cicadas, bugs, flies and lacewings. They commonly forage along water courses and in swampy areas in northern Australia, and are also found around isolated dams and waterholes in drier areas. They have been observed at twilight foraging along the edge of forest, along the tops of forest crowns and circling isolated trees about 5 m from the crown edge. Their foraging flight is moderately fast with speeds of up to 34 km/h recorded. They are agile and respond to prey at a range of 3–5 m, making frequent course changes in response to evasive manoeuvres by the prey.

● **REPRODUCTION** I have captured pregnant females in late July, August, October and late November. They usually give birth to twins during October and November. Most females are lactating in November and post-lactation in December.

● **NOTES** A commonly captured species in both mist nets and bat traps. They tend to emerge early in the evening, often in large numbers. They are gentle animals, easily handled, and rarely bite when being removed from the net. They often produce a low murmuring vibration while being held.

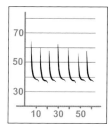

**REFERENCES** Law et al. 2000; McKenzie et al. 1995; Menzies 1971; Milledge et al. 1992; Milne & Burwell (unpubl.); Ryan 1966a; Van Deusen & Koopman 1971; Vestjens & Hall 1977.

# Little pied bat
## *Chalinolobus picatus* (Gould, 1852)

● **DISTRIBUTION** Qld and NSW just extending into SA and Vic. Generally semi-arid interior regions of e. Australia to w. of the Great Dividing Range; ventures to the coast in Qld. Endemic to Australia.

● **DESCRIPTION** This beautiful bat has **uniform glossy black fur on the back**, faintly **washed with grey on the belly**. There are **two white stripes running along the sides of the body that converge to form a 'V' in the pubic region**. The long black fur on the back extends well onto the tail membrane where it grades into a fringe of brownish black hairs. The **ears are small** and are too short to meet or only barely touch when pressed together across the top of the head. The **lobe at the corner of the mouth is poorly developed but the secondary lobe along the lower lip is easily seen**. It differs from the hoary wattled bat, *C. nigrogriseus*, in having a notch in the inner upper incisor.

● **ROOST HABITS** They roost in trees, caves, abandoned mines and buildings. One colony containing 38 bats (both sexes) was recorded in an abandoned house. Another large colony of about 50 (both sexes) has been roosting in a shed for over 20 years. Most colonies in caves and mines contain fewer than ten bats. Roost sites in caves are usually warm and dry but they can tolerate roost temperatures of over 40°C. Roosts have been found in *Casuarina pauper*, mulga, bloodwoods and other large eucalypts. Favoured hollows are in large mature trees with dead limbs, and dead trees that have fallen over leaving a hollowed stump. The hollow entrances vary in size but open into large cavities, midway up the trunk. Pied bats often roost alone and move roost location most days, although remaining in the same general area (all roosts within 200 m).

Michael Pennay made a remarkable observation of a colony that roosted in a clump of small dead mulga near Bourke in NSW. Each night they commuted 17 km to forage in a dry creek bed and in the morning returned to the same mulga clump, a 34-km round trip. It is not as though dead mulga were in short supply around Bourke! He also radio-tracked a male that roosted alone under a rock in a boulder pile.

● **HABITAT** Little pied bats appear to reach their greatest relative abundance in the mallee and mixed species woodlands of the Willandra Lakes area of NSW and the mulga and riverine open forest communities in central western Qld. They have also been caught in dry open forest, open woodland, chenopod shrublands, *Callitris* forest and *Casuarina pauper* woodlands.

● **DIET AND FORAGING** Their flight is fast and highly manoeuvrable, changing direction often. They fly close to the vegetation, and have been seen to glean from the canopy of *Casuarina* by flying among the foliage. They were observed to glean from the walls of a woolshed, with a distinct up and down sweeping action. The flight was composed of many darting actions and hunting involved rapid swoops and dives, flying at about 2–4 m above the ground. A single stomach content examination found only moths.

● **REPRODUCTION** I have caught a female in late October pregnant with two well-developed foetuses, indicating they give birth to twins in early November. Lactating females have been caught in late October, November and December.

**REFERENCES** Dominelli 2000; Lumsden & Bennett 1995; M. Pennay (pers. com.); Pennay 2002; Pennay & Freeman 2005; Richards 1979; Ryan 1966a; Schulz et al. 1994; Van Deusen & Koopman 1971; Young et al. 1996; Young & Ford 2000.

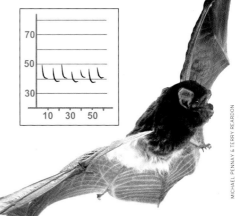

MICHAEL PENNAY & TERRY REARDON

| | | Wt | Fa | Ear | Tibia | 3 met | Tail | HB | WS | Skull |
|---|---|---|---|---|---|---|---|---|---|---|
| **MEASUREMENTS** | MEAN | 5.7 | 34.1 | 10.3 | 16.3 | 31.2 | 36.7 | 45.3 | 249 | 11.14 |
| | MIN | 4.3 | 31.4 | 8.6 | 16.0 | 30.3 | 29.3 | 40.6 | 239 | 10.7 |
| | MAX | 8.0 | 37.5 | 11.2 | 17.1 | 32.9 | 42.5 | 49.3 | 265 | 11.7 |
| | NO | 47 | 83 | 8 | 20 | 9 | 18 | 6 | 8 | 5 |

Dominelli 2000; G. Hoye; A. Young; Van Deusen & Koopman 1971.

# Western falsistrelle

## *Falsistrellus mackenziei* Kitchener, Caputi and Jones, 1986

● **DISTRIBUTION** S.w. Australia; range extends n. almost to Perth and e. to the w. margin of the wheatbelt. Endemic to Australia.

● **DESCRIPTION** The largest vespertilionid in WA, this is a **large and robust bat**. The fur **on the back is dark brown** with a **light cinnamon belly**. The snout is naked forward of the eyes; the slender **ears extend well above the head** and overlap when pressed together. The **ears are triangular** with a **rounded tip that curves backward** and there is a characteristic **notch on the outer margin** near the tips. The **tragus is more than half the length of the ear**, with a moderate-sized lobe at the rear base and narrowing to a slightly rounded tip. The penis is hairy. This bat has **two pairs of upper incisors**, but the outer pair are very small and hard to see. There is a gap between the upper canines and the incisor teeth. Differs from the eastern falsistrelle, *F. tasmaniensis*, by being slightly larger (greatest skull length is 19.2 mm compared to 18.3 mm).

● **ROOST HABITS** These gregarious bats roost in hollow trees, branches and stumps. They have been found in colonies of five to 30. A group of five bats released in the forest gathered around the canopy of one tree before settling together on a dead branch to roost. The sexes segregate for roosting, at least during much of the spring and summer.

© JIRI LOCHMAN/LOCHMAN TRANSPARENCIES

| MEASUREMENTS | | Wt | Fa | Ear | Trag | Tibia | Tail | HB | Skull |
|---|---|---|---|---|---|---|---|---|---|
| | MEAN | 21.0 | 50.7 | 16.7 | 9.2 | 22.1 | 46.2 | 61.7 | 19.2 |
| | MIN | 17.0 | 48.0 | 14.0 | 7.7 | 20.2 | 40.1 | 55.4 | 18.2 |
| | MAX | 26.0 | 53.7 | 18.3 | 10.6 | 23.6 | 53.2 | 66.6 | 20.1 |
| | NO | 32 | 41 | 48 | 48 | 48 | 45 | 48 | 50 |

Kitchener et al. 1986.

● **HABITAT** Western falsistrelles are restricted to areas in or adjacent to stands of old growth forest. It is estimated that 12–15% of the south-western forests remain as old growth. Typically these bats are found in wet sclerophyll forest dominated by karri (*Eucalyptus diversicolor*), and in the high rainfall zones of the jarrah (*E. marginata*) and tuart (*E. gomphocephala*) forests. They have also been recorded in mixed tuart-jarrah tall woodlands on the adjacent coastal plain. Marri (*E. calophylla*), sheoak (*Casuarina heugeliana*) and peppermint (*Agonis flexuosa*) trees are often co-dominant at their collection localities.

● **DIET AND FORAGING** Their flight is fast and direct as they forage for insects within the large spaces between the canopy and the understorey of these tall forest trees.

● **REPRODUCTION** The single young is born in spring or early summer.

● **NOTES** Their echolocation calls are of a relatively low frequency. They have been caught with mist nets on high poles between 4 and 8 m above the ground. I have caught them in bat traps set at normal height along forest tracks.

REFERENCES Duncan et al. 1999; Hosken & O'Shea 1994; Kitchener et al. 1986; Start & McKenzie, in Strahan 1995.

# Eastern falsistrelle
## *Falsistrellus tasmaniensis* (Gould, 1858)

● **DISTRIBUTION** S.e. Qld, NSW, Vic and Tas. Endemic to Australia.

● **DESCRIPTION** This is a **large and robust bat**. The **fur is dark brown to reddish brown on the back** with a slightly paler grey belly. The muzzle is sparsely haired. The **slender ears extend well above the head** and overlap when pressed together. There is a characteristic **notch on the outer margin of the ear** near the tip. The **tragus is more than half the length of the ear**; it has a moderate-sized lobe at the rear base and narrows to a slightly rounded tip. The **penis is hairy**. There are **two pairs of upper incisors**: the outer pair are very small and hard to see. There is a **gap between the upper incisors and the canines**. These features help to distinguish it from the greater broad-nosed bat, *Scoteanax rueppellii*. Differs from the western falsistrelle, *F. mackenziei*, by being slightly smaller (greatest skull length is 18.3 mm compared to 19.2 mm).

● **ROOST HABITS** Eastern falsistrelles generally roost in hollow trunks of eucalypt trees in colonies of three to 80. Colonies are usually almost entirely male or female groups although evenly mixed colonies sometimes occur. They have been recorded roosting in a cave at Jenolan, NSW, and they are occasionally found in old wooden buildings. In the Australian Alps roost trees are exclusively older smooth-barked eucalypts. These bats are often solitary but one roost

GLENN HOYE

contained a colony of 79 males, one female and three white-striped freetail bats, *Austronomus australis*. Radio-tracked individuals changed roosts almost every night, and returned to old roosts on different nights. Roosts on consecutive nights were usually less than 750 m apart, although one bat moved 3.5 km between roosts. They have a home range of up to 136 ha.

● **HABITAT** In Tas and on the mainland they are found in wet sclerophyll and coastal mallee. They prefer tall and wet forests where trees are more than 20 m high and the understorey is dense. They occur in open forests at lower altitudes. In Qld they have been captured within tall open forest, subtropical riparian rainforest, cool-temperate rainforest and open forest with *Eucalyptus acmenoides* and *E. tereticornis*.

● **DIET AND FORAGING** They tend to target the largest available prey items. On both the mainland and Tas they eat mainly beetles and moths with some bugs, ants and flies. Their flight is swift and direct, within or just below the tree canopy. They tend to fly fast in a fixed horizontal plane with sudden darting changes in course. One radio-tracked bat was found to move 12 km from where it foraged to where it roosted in a very large tree. They hunt in gaps and spaces within the forest and avoid thick rainforest understorey or dense regrowth. They are absent from small patches of remnant forest, preferring continuous forest where they forage along tracks, creeks and rivers. They are also capable of moving through cleared landscapes and have been recorded foraging in open areas.

● **REPRODUCTION** The males produce sperm in late summer and store sperm in the epididymides over the winter. Females produce a large 'hibernation follicle' in autumn. Ovulation, fertilisation and pregnancy occur in late spring and early summer. The single young is born in December. Lactation continues through January and February.

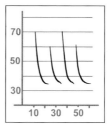

**REFERENCES** Hall & Richards 1979; Herr 1998; Kitchener et al. 1986; Law & Chidel 2002; Law et al. 1999; Menkhorst 1995; O'Neill & Taylor 1986, 1989; Parnaby 1976; Phillips et al. 1985; Phillips, in Strahan 1995; Taylor & O'Neill 1986, 1988; Taylor et al. 1987.

| MEASUREMENTS | | Wt | Fa | Ear | Trag | Tibia | Tail | HB | Skull |
|---|---|---|---|---|---|---|---|---|---|
| | MEAN | 20.5 | 50.7 | 17.0 | 9.4 | 21.9 | 47.0 | 62.3 | 18.3 |
| | MIN | 16.0 | 45.3 | 13.5 | 8.0 | 20.4 | 40.4 | 57.0 | 17.5 |
| | MAX | 28.5 | 56.3 | 19.0 | 10.5 | 23.5 | 51.2 | 66.3 | 19.0 |
| | NO | 307 | 420 | 43 | 44 | 42 | 39 | 43 | 56 |

Kitchener et al. 1986; L. Lumsden.

# Flute-nosed bat

## *Murina florium* Thomas, 1908

● **DISTRIBUTION** N. Qld
from Paluma n. to
Cedar Bay;
isolated
record at Iron
Range, Cape
York Peninsula.
Extralimitally in New Guinea
and e. Indonesia. Originally
collected by Alfred Russell Wallace
from Flores in Indonesia but not described
until over 50 years later. Found in Australia a
further 73 years later.

● **DESCRIPTION** This elusive and unusual bat
has **tubular nostrils** that diverge and **extend
sideways** from the **end of the nose**. The **fur
on the back is grey-brown to an orange
rufous brown** with the base of the fur dark
to light grey. The fur is long and woolly with
a grizzled appearance and is paler on the
belly. The **fur extends over most of the tail
membrane** and along the bones of the wings
and legs. The rear margins of the ears are
deeply notched and the wing membranes are
attached to the end of the outer toes. The
thumbs are unusually long. They **emit a loud
drawn-out, high-pitched whistle** while
foraging.

● **ROOST HABITS** These distinctive bats live in
the wet rainforests of north Qld. They roost
in the understorey 1–8 m from the ground
wherever they find suitable cover. They are

known to roost in suspended clusters of
fallen leaves, the curled dead base of
epiphytes, tree fern and palm fronds, disused
nests of fernwrens and yellow-throated
scrubwrens. The bird nests often have a hole
in the base that may have been made by the
bat. Over 80% of roosts are occupied by a
single bat but up to a dozen may share a
simple roost such as a curled dead tree fern
leaf. The same roost is used for up to 4 days,
before individuals move to another one from
a few metres to a kilometre away, often
reusing the original roost some days later.
One individual was found roosting in the
nest of a sacred kingfisher inside a termite
mound in a tree. Several bats released during
the day landed on broad leaves and wrapped
the leaves around them, holding the leaves
in this position with their feet and thumb
claws so that they could not be seen except
from directly below.

● **HABITAT** Captures have been in both upland
and lowland tropical rainforest (microphyll
fern-vine, notophyll vine and mesophyll
forest) often with emergent eucalypts. They
are also found in tall open forest of flooded
gums (*Eucalyptus grandis*) with or without
rainforest understorey and in gallery forests,
and there is one record from dry sclerophyll
forest.

● **DIET AND FORAGING** They forage in the sub-
canopy and canopy and avoid open areas.

| | | Wt | Fa | Ear | Trag | Tibia | 3 met | Tail | HB | WS |
|---|---|---|---|---|---|---|---|---|---|---|
| MEASUREMENTS | MEAN | 7.8 | 34.8 | 12.4 | 7.4 | 17.0 | 31.4 | 33.5 | 47 | 272 |
| | MIN | 5.0 | 32.2 | 10.5 | 5.6 | 15.2 | 29.2 | 30.6 | 39 | - |
| | MAX | 10.9 | 35.8 | 13.7 | 10.1 | 18.3 | 33.2 | 37 | 56.5 | - |
| | NO | 57 | 58 | 9 | 8 | 9 | 9 | 12 | 8 | 1 |

S. Churchill; Clague et al. 1999; M. Schulz 1999; M. Venz.

BRUCE THOMSON

They are very vocal while foraging. Their flight is slow and manoeuvrable and they are capable of hovering. Scat analysis has shown their diet to consist of two-thirds beetles and one-third spiders, with traces of moths and flies. Their echolocation calls are appropriate for active foraging in cluttered areas. Their wings have low wing loading and a low aspect ratio suggesting agile and manoeuvrable flight at low speed. Individuals emerging at dusk hover briefly under roosts and exit the roost area through vine tendrils, branches and other cluttered situations.

● **REPRODUCTION** Little is known. Births are probably around October or November as most females caught in December are lactating or post-lactation. Testicular and epididymal enlargement has been noted in males caught in December. Females caught in April and June were not pregnant.

● **NOTES** Flute-nosed bats emit low-intensity wide frequency range echolocation calls of short duration (1.5–2 milliseconds). The combination of manoeuvrable flight characteristics and broad frequency range echolocation calls indicates this bat is specialised for foraging within a cluttered environment. The high frequency calls are thought to allow sophisticated texture resolution enabling the spectral discrimination of stationary prey. Flute-nosed bats have extremely large olfactory areas in the brain and tube-like nostrils indicating that their sense of smell is very well developed, an unusual characteristic for echolocating bats.

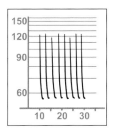

**REFERENCES** Clague 2000; Clague et al. 1999; R. Coles (pers. com.); Duncan et al. 1999; Flannery 1995a, b; Kingston et al. 1999; Kutt & Schulz 2000; Richards et al. 1982; Schulz & Hannah 1996, 1998; H. Spencer (pers. com.).

# Large-footed myotis

## *Myotis macropus* (Gould, 1855)

● **TAXONOMY** A recent clarification of the species boundaries of *Myotis* by Cooper et al. (2001) has shown that there is only one species, *Myotis macropus*, in Australia and that it is a different species to Indonesian *M. adversus*. *M. macropus* and an undescribed species occur in New Guinea.

● **DISTRIBUTION** Primarily coastal, from Kimberley, n. WA, to n. Qld and along e. coast of Qld and NSW to Vic and SA. Further inland along major rivers such as Murray River in s.e. Australia and Fitzroy River in Kimberley.

● **DESCRIPTION** This fascinating fishing bat can be distinguished from all other Australian vespertilionid bats by its **disproportionately large feet**: over 8 mm long, they are **greater than half the length of the tibia**. Its fur colour varies from dark grey to reddish brown. The ears are long and the tragus is long, straight and slender. The calcar is very long, extending three-quarters of the distance from the ankle to the tail tip.

● **ROOST HABITS** Large-footed myotis roost near water in caves, tree hollows, among vegetation, in clumps of *Pandanus*, under bridges, in mines, tunnels, road culverts and stormwater drains. They are commonly found roosting alone or in pairs in abandoned, intact fairy martin nests. They will select caves that overhang pools even when these are rather exposed. Colonies of several hundred are known but more commonly they roost in groups of less than 15. They have been found to form small harems with a single male and one to 12 females. Other males roost alone or in small all-male clusters.

● **HABITAT** They have a strong association with streams and permanent waterways, most frequently at low elevations and in flat or undulating country and usually in areas that are vegetated rather than cleared. They will live in most habitat types as long as it is near water.

● **DIET AND FORAGING** They commonly forage over water for small fish, prawns and aquatic insects such as water boatmen, water striders, backswimmers and whirligig beetles. These species mainly live on or just below the water surface and are caught by trawling. The bats fly 15–100 cm above the water, frequently dipping their big feet into the water and briefly raking them along the surface. Sometimes several bats follow each other while foraging along similar flight

| | Vic | | Northern Australia | | | | | | | | |
| MEASUREMENTS | Wt | Fa | Wt | Fa | Ear | Foot | Trag | 3 met | Tail | HB | WS |
|---|---|---|---|---|---|---|---|---|---|---|---|
| MEAN | 11.3 | 39.9 | 8.3 | 38.4 | 13.7 | 10.1 | 7.0 | 38.1 | 36.9 | 45.6 | 281 |
| MIN | 9.0 | 37.2 | 5.0 | 36.0 | 8.9 | 8.3 | 5.8 | 36.1 | 33 | 35 | 267 |
| MAX | 14.9 | 42.9 | 10.4 | 40.7 | 15.6 | 11.2 | 9.4 | 40 | 42.3 | 50 | 292 |
| NO | 114 | 115 | 103 | 96 | 27 | 26 | 26 | 26 | 26 | 26 | 25 |

S. Churchill; L. Lumsden.

BRUCE THOMSON

paths. They have a preference for large still pools rather than flowing streams, and it is thought that they use echolocation to detect the small ripples made by prey on the water surface. These bats are also aerial foragers, usually hunting insects that fly over water, but in the Top End their diet is more terrestrial with scats containing mostly termites, flies, ants, moths, beetles, spiders, cockroaches and bugs.

● **REPRODUCTION** The number of pregnancies per year varies with latitude. In Vic there is one pregnancy with the single young born in November or December. In northern NSW they produce two litters of single young in October and January. The first ovulation occurs in early August and the second occurs soon after the birth of the first litter. Both pregnancies last 12 weeks despite the first pregnancy occurring during cooler months. During the second pregnancy females are

still lactating with the first young. Lactation lasts about 8 weeks. Mother and young forage and roost together for a further 3–4 weeks after weaning. Males show two peaks of testicular development; in April to June and in September to November. Only a small proportion of the males mate with the majority of the females. The dominant males establish a territory, collect a harem of one to 12 females and defend them from other males. In northern Qld females may have three pregnancies per year.

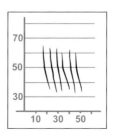

**REFERENCES** Anderson et al. 2006; Barclay et al. 2000; Caddle 1998; Cooper et al. 2001; Dwyer 1970a, b; Jansen 1987; Kitchener 1978; Kitchener et al. 1995; Law & Anderson 1999; Law & Urquhart 2000; Law et al. 2001; Lloyd et al. 1999; Mackey & Barclay 1989; Milne & Burwell (unpubl.); Robson 1984; Schulz 1998.

# Arnhem long-eared bat
### *Nyctophilus arnhemensis* Johnson, 1959

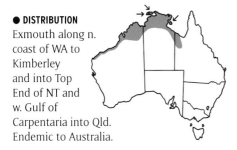

● **DISTRIBUTION**
Exmouth along n. coast of WA to Kimberley and into Top End of NT and w. Gulf of Carpentaria into Qld. Endemic to Australia.

● **DESCRIPTION** An attractive bat in appearance and disposition, the Arnhem long-eared bat is a **medium-sized species** (forearm length 33.2–40.0 mm) with **moderately long ears** (16–21.5 mm). The **fur is usually light russet brown**, with dark bases to the hairs. The fur shades to a **slightly lighter colour on the belly** but is not distinctly different. The **muzzle ridge is moderately developed and has a central depression** (Type 2). The **glans penis is a square-ended cylinder** with a flat circular urethral opening on the underside, near the tip. The northern long-eared bat, *N. daedalus*, has longer ears (20.5–25.8 mm), larger size (forearm 38.3–45.8 mm), less developed muzzle ridge (Type 3) and the glans penis has a distinct beaked appearance. The pygmy long-eared bat, *N. walkeri*, has much shorter ears (10.7–14.1 mm) and smaller forearms (30.1–36.0 mm) with the belly fur distinctly paler than back. The lesser long-eared bat, *N. geoffroyi*, has a well-developed muzzle ridge (Type 1).

● **ROOST HABITS** These bats have been found roosting 2–3 m above the ground under hanging flaps of the soft, flexible bark of large paperbark trees (*Melaleuca leucodendron*). They will also shelter in houses, within rainforest foliage and among *Pandanus* leaves.

● **HABITAT** In and around mangroves as well as monsoon forest, open savannah woodland, tall open forest, and *Melaleuca*- and *Pandanus*-lined waterways and over waterholes in sandstone country. In the Kimberley they were observed foraging in rainforest patches, in groves of cajuput and *Melaleuca argentia* forest that fringe water courses, in woodlands of *Tristania grandiflora* and *Melaleuca acacioides* around freshwater swamps. They are common in mangrove forests along WA's northern and western coast. Their distribution tends to correspond to the areas that receive an annual rainfall of over 500 mm.

● **DIET AND FORAGING** They hunt among the foliage of dense vegetation. Prey is gleaned from surfaces or caught in flight at relatively slow speeds of 5 km/h, although they can fly at up to 16 km/h when commuting. The slow fluttering flight of their short, wide wings is well adapted to confined spaces where manoeuvrability is preferable to speed. They are often seen flying through the vegetation or quite low along tracks and

| | | Wt | Fa | Ear | Tibia | 3 met | Tail | HB | WS |
|---|---|---|---|---|---|---|---|---|---|
| MEASUREMENTS | MEAN | 6.8 | 37.4 | 18.4 | 17.9 | 35.7 | 37.8 | 44.4 | 269 |
| | MIN | 5.2 | 33.2 | 16.0 | 17.2 | 33.2 | 35.6 | 40 | 255 |
| | MAX | 9.6 | 39.9 | 21.5 | 18.2 | 38.6 | 41 | 50 | 288 |
| | NO | 36 | 48 | 31 | 8 | 13 | 13 | 13 | 13 |

S. Churchill; D. Milne.

BRUCE THOMSON

waterways. They forage in mangroves in the Kimberley, and within dense thickets in monsoon forest and along *Pandanus*-lined waterways in the Top End, where their diet is predominantly termites, water-beetles, cockroaches, field crickets and bugs with occasional moths and spiders. They have been reported to feed on geckos and gecko eggs but the details of this observation are unknown.

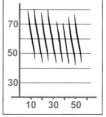

distinguished from other long-eared bats except by analysing the call's peak power frequency (average 50.8 kHz; range 50–52 kHz).

**REFERENCES** Bullen & McKenzie 2002a; Churchill et al. 1984; Johnson 1964; Kitchener 1978; McKenzie, in Strahan 1995; McKenzie et al. 1995; Milne & Burwell (unpubl); Woodside & Long 1984.

● **REPRODUCTION** Males have scrotal testes from May to November. Females are pregnant in September and November, and twins are born from late October to February.

● **NOTES** These bats emit echolocation calls with a wide frequency sweep. They cannot be

# Eastern long-eared bat

## *Nyctophilus bifax* Thomas, 1915

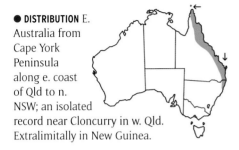

● **DISTRIBUTION** E. Australia from Cape York Peninsula along e. coast of Qld to n. NSW; an isolated record near Cloncurry in w. Qld. Extralimitally in New Guinea.

● **DESCRIPTION** A large species of *Nyctophilus*, with a **forearm length of 37.5–46.8 mm**. The fur colour is usually a rich brown-tan, often with the belly fur a lighter colour. The **ears are long** (19.2–27.1 mm). The **muzzle ridge is poorly developed** with a slight central depression (Type 3). The **glans penis is a square-ended cylinder with a flat circular urethral opening on the underside, near the tip. The baculum is forked at the tip.** The northern long-eared bat, *N. daedalus*, is much paler, usually a light sandy brown. It is superficially similar but differs in the shape of the glans penis, which has a distinctly beaked appearance, and the baculum is unforked. Gould's long-eared bat, *N. gouldi*, differs by usually having longer ears (greater than 24 mm), a better developed muzzle ridge (Type 2), and males have a distinctly beaked glans penis. The south-eastern long-eared bat, *Nyctophilus* species 2, is larger with a broader muzzle and OCW greater than 5.7 mm whereas *N. bifax* is less than 5.3 mm. The lesser long-eared

bat, *N. geoffroyi*, is smaller with a better developed muzzle ridge (Type 1).

● **ROOST HABITS** Eastern long-eared bats are forest dwellers and have been recorded roosting under peeling bark, among epiphytes, in tree hollows and shallow depressions on trunks and branches, in the roots of strangler figs, among the dead fronds of a prickly tree fern and in foliage. They have also been reported to roost in buildings. Tree hollows are used more than foliage when the females are lactating but foliage roosts are more commonly used during the mating season. In northern NSW, eastern long-eared bats shift foliage roosts seasonally to the cooler forest interior in November (late spring) and back to the warmer forest edge in May (late autumn). Roost mobility over seasons may be necessary for foliage-roosting bats as such roosts are not thermally buffered. Colonies of two to seven were recorded (those examined contained only females). These aggregations were loose and females moved between colonies and also roosted alone. Males were usually found roosting alone. These bats changed roost frequently but showed a strong fidelity to one cluster of trees. Most roosts were less than 250 m apart.

● **HABITAT** They favour wetter habitats ranging from rainforest and monsoon forest to riverine forests of paperbark but are also

| | | Wt | Fa | Ear | 3 Met | Tail | HB | WS | OCW | Skull |
|---|---|---|---|---|---|---|---|---|---|---|
| **MEASUREMENTS** | MEAN | 8.6 | 41.8 | 24.0 | 38.5 | 41.7 | 47.1 | 293 | 4.8 | 16.9 |
| | MIN | 5.0 | 37.5 | 19.2 | 36 | 39 | 35 | 280 | 4.4 | 16.1 |
| | MAX | 12.0 | 46.8 | 27.1 | 40.2 | 46 | 55 | 305 | 5.3 | 17.7 |
| | NO | 74 | 124 | 106 | 14 | 14 | 14 | 14 | 68 | 68 |

S. Churchill; Parnaby 2007.

BRUCE THOMSON

found in open woodland, tall open forest and dry sclerophyll woodland. In northern NSW they are restricted to rainforest.

● **DIET AND FORAGING** At Chillagoe they have been observed perch-hunting. The bats typically hang from perches 5–10 m above the ground and pivot their bodies back and forth while echolocating. They periodically make short (less than 3 m) flights from the perch to catch prey. After 3–5 minutes with no foraging flights the bats moved to another perch, usually within 50 m. Dietary analysis has recorded moths, with traces of ants and click-beetles in the stomach and scats. They tend to forage along the edge of the tree canopy rather than within the foliage. They catch prey by aerial capture or gleaning off surfaces. In rainforest they were found to forage in the canopy over 25 m above the ground.

● **REPRODUCTION** Eastern long-eared bats mate in May, give birth to twins in October and lactate in November and December. The twins remain attached to the female for the first few days and are then left at the roost while she forages. Females frequently move their young to different roost sites during lactation; lactating females have been recorded carrying twins whose combined weight was 95% of the mother's weight.

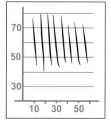

**REFERENCES** Duncan et al. 1999; Churchill et al. 1984; Law 1993; Lunney et al. 1995; H. Parnaby (pers. com.); Parnaby 1987, 2007; Parnaby, in Strahan 1995; Schulz & de Oliveira 1995; Woodside & Taylor 1985.

# Northern long-eared bat

## *Nyctophilus daedalus* Thomas, 1915

● **TAXONOMY** This species had previously been included as a subspecies of *Nyctophilus bifax* but is now regarded as a full species (H. Parnaby pers. com.).

● **DISTRIBUTION** W. Gulf of Carpentaria in Qld through Top End and Kimberley with an isolated population in Pilbara, WA.

● **DESCRIPTION** A **large species** of *Nyctophilus* with a **forearm length of 38.5–45.6 mm**. The fur is a pale sandy brown, with the belly

fur a lighter brown. The **ears are long** (20.5–25.8 mm). The **muzzle ridge is poorly developed** with a slight central depression (Type 3). The **glans penis is divided by a longitudinal groove into two cylinders** with the upper cylinder projecting to give a **distinct beaked appearance**. The baculum is short, tapering and unforked and the upper third molar is reduced and shortened. It is most likely to be confused with the Arnhem leaf-nosed bat, *N. arnhemensis*, which is a smaller build (forearm 33–40 mm; weight 5–10 g), with shorter ears (16–21 mm), a better developed muzzle ridge (Type 2), and glans penis that is a blunt square-ended cylinder, not distinctly beaked. The eastern long-eared bat, *N. bifax*, is superficially similar but is much darker and differs in the shape of the glans penis, which is blunt and not beaked. The baculum is forked. The pygmy long-eared bat, *N. walkeri*, and the lesser long-eared bat, *N. geoffroyi*, are both smaller with better developed muzzle ridges.

● **ROOST HABITS** They are forest dwellers and have been recorded roosting under the soft and peeling bark of *Melaleuca* trees, in tree hollows, at the base of *Pandanus* leaves and in foliage.

● **HABITAT** They favour wetter habitats ranging from monsoon forest to riverine forests of *Melaleuca* but are also found in open woodland and tall open forest.

| MEASUREMENTS | | Wt | Fa | Ear | 3 Met | Tail | HB | WS | Skull | OCW |
|---|---|---|---|---|---|---|---|---|---|---|
| | MEAN | 10.8 | 42.4 | 23.4 | 39.8 | 42.9 | 55.3 | 300 | 17.3 | 5.1 |
| | MIN | 7.6 | 38.3 | 20.5 | 34.7 | 40.0 | 53.0 | 275 | 16.8 | 4.7 |
| | MAX | 14.0 | 45.8 | 25.8 | 43.0 | 45.0 | 57.0 | 323 | 18.3 | 5.5 |
| | NO | 14 | 51 | 39 | 6 | 6 | 6 | 61 | 21 | 22 |

S. Churchill; D. Milne; Parnaby 2007.

● **DIET AND FORAGING** Northern long-eared bats feed on a variety of insects. They are perch-hunters that catch prey by aerial capture or gleaning off surfaces, such as foliage within and below the canopy and along the edges of denser forest types and adjacent woodland. Their flight is faster and more direct than that of other *Nyctophilus*. In the Top End they eat beetles (78%) and cicadas (22%).

● **REPRODUCTION** Little is known of their reproduction. Males with enlarged testes have been recorded in April, September and October. Pregnant females with near-term twins have been captured in late September and lactating females captured in October and November.

● **ECHOLOCATION** The mean peak power frequency is 52.4 kHz; range 50–54 kHz. The linear echolocation call allows these species to detect details of texture in their immediate environment such as a camouflaged moth perched on a leaf. It is less appropriate for detecting the speed and direction of flying insects but is ideally suited for the gleaning mode of foraging used by long-eared bats.

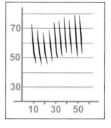

**REFERENCES** Bullen & McKenzie 2002a; Churchill et al. 1984; Duncan et al. 1999; Milne 2002; Milne & Burwell (unpubl.); H. Parnaby (pers. com.); Parnaby 1987, 2007; Parnaby, in Strahan 1995; Tate 1941.

# Lesser long-eared bat
## *Nyctophilus geoffroyi* Leach, 1821

● **DISTRIBUTION** Tas and mainland Australia except the n.e. coast of Qld. Endemic to Australia.

● **DESCRIPTION** This beautiful bat is a **medium-sized species** (forearm length 30.6–41.7 mm) with **very long ears** (17.6–25.3 mm). The **fur is light grey on the back** and **distinctly lighter, often white, on the belly**. The **hairs are bicoloured** being very dark at the base. It has a **high muzzle ridge** (Type 1) that is split and joined by an elastic membrane of skin, giving the ridge a **distinctive 'Y-shaped' groove** that distinguishes it from all other species.

● **ROOST HABITS** These bats are present in large numbers in many areas of Australia. They commonly roost in crevices, under lifting and peeling bark, in tree hollows and in buildings. I have found them roosting inside a rolled-up canvas swag and in fairy martin nests; they also roost under piles of bricks and in old hanging clothing. They roost alone or small groups of two to three, but in some areas maternity colonies of ten to 15 females are formed, often with a single adult male. They shift roost sites regularly within a defined area. A large colony of several hundred bats has been found in a building. Dead specimens have been recorded from caves in the Nullarbor, including one group of 50. A live cave colony is known from the Margaret River caves area in WA. In Vic, maternity roosts were found to be 6–12 km from foraging areas, in patches of extensive woodland.

BRUCE THOMSON

● **HABITAT** Widespread, from deserts to rainforests, wet to dry sclerophyll forests, tropical to alpine woodlands, grasslands, mangroves, agricultural land and urban areas.

● **DIET AND FORAGING** They fly slowly and are highly manoeuvrable, flying close to the vegetation and into the understorey. In forests they forage about 6–10 m above the ground, catching flying insects with sudden gliding changes in direction or by dropping vertically, sometimes to within a few centimetres of the ground. In open areas they fly lower, spiralling around shrubs and bushes. They can land on the ground to capture prey, taking flight again almost vertically. They have been observed to hover and can take off from water. Flight speeds when foraging (4 km/h) were the slowest of all species examined. Commuting flight was up to 20 km/h. Moths, crickets and grasshoppers are the commonest food type but they also eat wingless insects such as ants, cricket nymphs and spiders, as well as beetles, cockroaches, bugs, flies and

lacewings. They have been captured in pit-traps, probably attracted by the sounds of previously captured insects. They use a variety of prey capture methods including echolocation (for gleaning ground and foliage prey, as well as aerial prey), passive listening (for ground and aerial prey) and visual cues (for aerial prey). These bats may exploit seasonally high concentrations of calling tettigoniid crickets, hunting by passively listening for the cricket calls without echolocating or seeing them.

● **REPRODUCTION** Spermatogenesis in males commences in November, peaks in March and ceases by May. Sperm is stored in the epididymides as the testes regress. Mating generally starts in April and females store sperm in the uterine lining and the oviduct for the winter. Ovulation and fertilisation occur in late August or September. Gestation lasts for 72–93 days. Births, usually twins, occur in late October and November but this varies with earlier deliveries occurring at lower latitudes and elevations. By December the young can fly and lactation is usually

| MEASUREMENTS | | Vic | | Northern Australia | | | | | | |
|---|---|---|---|---|---|---|---|---|---|---|
| | | Wt | Fa | Wt | Fa | Ear | 3 met | Tail | HB | WS |
| | MEAN | 8.2 | 37.1 | 5.8 | 34.8 | 20.7 | 32.5 | 35.6 | 45.2 | 245 |
| | MIN | 4.6 | 32.0 | 3.9 | 30.6 | 17.6 | 27.8 | 31.0 | 38.0 | 208 |
| | MAX | 14.5 | 41.7 | 8.5 | 38.6 | 25.3 | 35.4 | 40.5 | 50.2 | 275 |
| | NO | 1122 | 1122 | 46 | 50 | 24 | 22 | 22 | 22 | 22 |

S. Churchill; Lumsden et al. 1994.

completed by early February. A shorter period of lactation has been reported in Tas. Not all females reproduce each year. Sperm competition has been demonstrated in this species.

● **NOTES** Below the thermoneutral zone metabolic rate increases as ambient temperature decreases. At 5°C it has increased almost 500% over the minimum experienced at 35°C. In Tas they enter torpor at temperatures below 15°C. Although metabolic rate remains constant, the ambient temperatures at which they enter torpor changes with latitude. In Tas it is 10°C lower than mainland locations. Echolocation

calls have a peak power frequency average of 47.7 kHz; range 47–48 kHz.

**REFERENCES** Bailey & Haythornthwaite 1998; Brigham et al. 1997; Bullen & McKenzie 2002a; Churchill et al. 1984; Dixon & Rose 2003; Fullard et al. 1991; Geiser & Brigham 2000; Grant 1991; Kincade et al. 2000; Hosken et al. 1994; Hosken 1996, 1997b, 1998a; Hosken & Withers 1999; Lumsden et al. 1994, 2002; Lumsden & Bennett 1995, 1996; Maddock & Tidemann, in Strahan 1995; McKenzie et al. 2002; Menkhorst 1995; Milne & Burwell (unpubl.); O'Neill & Taylor 1986, 1989; Tidemann & Flavel 1987.

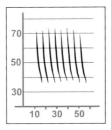

# Gould's long-eared bat
## *Nyctophilus gouldi* Tomes, 1858

● **DISTRIBUTION**
E. Australia from
n. Qld through
NSW and into
Vic; also s.w.
WA. Endemic to
Australia.

● **DESCRIPTION** This well-studied species has **slate grey to grey-brown fur on the back** with an **ash grey belly**. The size varies from north to south, being much larger in the south. The ears are long (24.3–30.1 mm). The **glans penis is divided by a longitudinal groove into two cylinders, with the upper one projecting to give a distinctly beak-like appearance**. The muzzle ridge is moderately developed with a faint vertical groove (Type 2). The eastern long-eared bat, *N. bifax*, differs in having a less developed muzzle ridge (Type 3), usually shorter ears (19.2–27.1 mm),

and the glans penis is not beaked. *N. gouldi* has an OCW of less than 5.1 mm, which separates it from the western long-eared bat, *N. major*, and the south-eastern long-eared bat, *Nyctophilus* species 2, with OCWs of over 5.6 mm.

● **ROOST HABITS** These bats roost in tree hollows, in fissures and under peeling bark. Usually a particular group of trees, often along a creekline, is used for roosting. Within this group they select new roosts frequently. Females form colonies of 20 or more, while males roost alone or in small transient groups of fewer than six. In southern Australia they lay down body fat in late summer and hibernate from April until September. There is a single record of a possible cave roost in north Qld.

● **HABITAT** They are found in a variety of habitats from very wet to semi-arid

BRUCE THOMSON

above the ground, and below the canopy of forest trees. They have been observed landing on the ground to catch prey. Their diet consists of mainly moths and beetles, but crickets, flies, cockroaches, ants, bugs and spiders are taken as well. Insects are caught on the wing or gleaned from surfaces of vegetation or the ground using a variety of techniques, such as passive listening, vision and echolocation. Although their echolocation is highly sophisticated it is not used for orientation except in unfamiliar environments, nor is it used when they approach fluttering prey, as they rely instead on passive listening. This behaviour circumvents the evasive action of sonar-sensitive insects. Visual cues are used to capture flying insects but not substrate prey.

environments. They occur in rainforest, wet and dry sclerophyll forest, *Melaleuca* woodland, river red gum-lined waterways, woodlands and *Acacia* shrubland. In WA they are confined to the more humid forest regions of the temperate zone.

● **DIET AND FORAGING** These bats typically fly slowly in large circles approximately 2–5 m

● **REPRODUCTION** Spermato-genesis commences in summer and sperm is stored in the epididymides from autumn when mating takes place, primarily in April. Sporadic copulation with torpid females continues throughout the winter until the hibernation follicle matures and ovulation, fertilisation and implantation take place in September. One or two young are born in late October, the twinning rate about 50%.

| | | Vic | | Qld | | | | | | | |
|---|---|---|---|---|---|---|---|---|---|---|---|
| | | Wt | Fa | Wt | Fa | Ear | 3 met | Tail | HB | WS | OCW |
| MEASUREMENTS | MEAN | 12.3 | 44.0 | 8.0 | 39.3 | 27.5 | 36.7 | 40.0 | 47.4 | 275.8 | 4.8 |
| | MIN | 9.0 | 40.0 | 5.2 | 36.3 | 24.3 | 36.0 | 39.0 | 44.0 | 270 | 4.5 |
| | MAX | 16.5 | 47.7 | 9.9 | 41.8 | 30.1 | 37.5 | 41.0 | 52.0 | 284 | 5.1 |
| | NO | 146 | 146 | 45 | 149 | 28 | 5 | 5 | 5 | 5 | 19 |

S. Churchill; Lumsden et al. 1994; Parnaby 1987; M. Venz.

By 4 weeks the young are fully furred and make their first attempts at flight accompanied by their mother. The young are weaned at 6 weeks and first appear in the population in January. Novice flyers, probably from the same colony, can be found flying together, often accompanied by one or two adults. Females become sexually mature at 7–9 months, males at 12–15 months. An experimental group kept at a temperature of 22°C throughout the winter gave birth to young 67 days before free-living bats that were hibernating over winter.

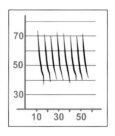

● **NOTES** These bats emit echolocation calls with a wide frequency sweep. They cannot be distinguished from other long-eared bats except by analysing the peak power frequency (average 51.8 kHz; range 50–53 kHz) of the calls.

**REFERENCES** Brigham et al. 1997; Bullen & McKenzie 2002; Campbell 2001; Churchill et al. 1984; Ellis 1989; Fullard et al. 1991; Gee 1999; Grant 1991; Kutt 2003; Lumsden 1994; Lumsden et al. 1994; Lumsden & Wainer (pers. com.); Lunney et al. 1988; Parnaby 1987, 1992; Phillips & Inwards 1985; Schulz 2000; Tidemann & Flavel 1987; Woodside 1984.

# Western long-eared bat

## *Nyctophilus major* Gray, 1844

● **TAXONOMY** This species has previously been considered a subspecies of *N. timoriensis*.

● **DISTRIBUTION** S.w. corner and coast near Cocklebiddy, WA.

● **DESCRIPTION** The fur is dark grey-brown all over. The muzzle ridge is low without a vertical groove (Type 4), with an OCW greater than 5.7 mm. It has a forearm length of 43.2–48.4 mm. It is heavier (13.6 g), with a longer skull (greatest length greater than 18.8 mm) and wider skull (zygomatic width greater than 11.6 mm) than the central long-eared bat (11.0 g; greatest skull length less than 18.8 mm; zygomatic width less than 11.2 mm). Gould's long-eared bat, *N. gouldi*, is smaller, forearm length less than 42 mm in sympatric populations with a proportionally smaller and narrower head, a better developed muzzle ridge (Type 2) and an OCW of less than 5.1 mm. *N. major* has darker fur and is a larger size than the northern long-eared bat, *N. daedalus* (forearm length 38.3–45.8 mm; OCW less than 5.5 mm). The lesser long-eared bat, *N. geoffroyi*, is much smaller with a distinctive, well-developed muzzle ridge (Type 1).

● **ROOST HABITS** They roost alone or in pairs in tree hollows and fissures in tree limbs, often in mature or dead *Eucalyptus rudis* and *Melaleuca rhaphophylla*. Roosts are occupied for 1–2 days with only small distances travelled between roosts. They move at least 1200 m from their roost to foraging areas.

● **HABITAT** They are mostly restricted to the *Banksia* woodlands, *Casuarina* and *Melaleuca* forests and tall eucalypt forests of karri, jarrah, tuart and marri of the high rainfall areas of south-western Australia. They show a preference for habitats with a well-developed shrub understorey. There is an isolated population in woodland at Eyre Bird Observatory on the edge of the Nullarbor Plain.

● **DIET AND FORAGING** In the *Banksia* woodlands their diet is predominantly beetles. As the bat slips in and out of the understorey its flight is slow, fluttery and undulating. They ambush their prey from a perch and can hunt for crickets by passive listening for cricket calls without echolocating or seeing them. They commonly glean insect prey and spend part of their time foraging on the ground. The wing loading is higher than other *Nyctophilus* species implying higher flight speeds. Flight speeds of 6–9 km/h have been recorded while foraging.

● **REPRODUCTION** Testicular activity commences in November and testes size increases to maximum in March and declines until May when no bats have enlarged testes but most have enlarged epididymides. Mating occurs between March and May, although copulation in captive bats occurs as late as June. Most copulations probably occur after spermatogenesis has ceased. Sperm is then stored in the cauda isthmus of the oviduct and in endometrial glands near the utero-tubal junction. Ovulation and fertilisation occur in late August or September and twins are common. Births occur between late

October and November, with volant young first captured during December. Lactation ceases by February, which is when the last detectably juvenile bats are caught. A captive female was observed to give birth to twins in late October: young were born breech first while the female hung by one foot from the wall of the cage. Her head was curled towards her vulva, wings were opened and cupped over her head and around her body and the birth was accompanied by loud vocalisations. The hairless newborn young quickly attached to the nipples and placentas were apparently eaten as no sign of them was found.

● **NOTES** Their body temperature is about 35°C. When they enter torpor they can drop their body temperature to within 1–5°C of air temperature. Torpor provides a metabolic saving of around 95% at air temperatures between 5 and 15°C. They enter into and spontaneously arouse from torpor at air temperatures as low as 5°C and become torpid at air temperatures as high as 23°C. They can only maintain torpor for about 60 days if they rely solely on fat reserves.

● **ECHOLOCATION** These bats emit echolocation calls with a wide frequency sweep. They cannot be identified from other long-eared bats except by analysing the call's peak power frequency (average 44.4 kHz; range 43–47 kHz).

**REFERENCES** Bailey & Haythornthwaite 1998; Bullen & McKenzie 2002; Duncan et al. 1999; Hosken 1996, 1997a, d, e, 1998; Hosken et al. 1994; McKenzie, in Van Dyck & Strahan 2008; H. Parnaby (pers. com.); Parnaby 1987, 2007; Parnaby, in Strahan 1995.

| | | Wt | Fa | Ear | Tail | HB | OCW | Skull |
|---|---|---|---|---|---|---|---|---|
| **MEASUREMENTS** | MEAN | 13.6 | 45.5 | 26.1 | 51.5 | 61.5 | 5.9 | 19.6 |
| | MIN | 11.5 | 43.2 | 24.4 | 51 | 62 | 5.7 | 18.8 |
| | MAX | 17.5 | 48.4 | 28.6 | 52 | 62 | 6.3 | 20.7 |
| | NO | 12 | 20 | 16 | 2 | 2 | 19 | 18 |

Hosken 1997; McKenzie 2008; Parnaby 2007.

# Tasmanian long-eared bat

## *Nyctophilus sherrini* Thomas 1915

● **TAXONOMY** This species has usually been considered a subspecies of *N. timoriensis* but a revision of the genus has shown it to be a valid species (H. Parnaby pers. com.).

● **DISTRIBUTION** Tas except s.w. corner. Endemic to Tas.

● **DESCRIPTION** The fur is **dark brown on the back** and lighter brown on the belly. It is a large bat with a forearm length of 43.9–48.0 mm. The **muzzle ridge** is **poorly developed** being low with only a **shallow central depression** (Type 3 or 4). The lesser long-eared bat, *N. geoffroyi*, is smaller (forearm length less than 42 mm). It is most closely related to the western long-eared bat, *N. major*, but it has a smaller and differently shaped skull and shorter tooth row. Externally it resembles larger examples of Gould's long-eared bat, *N. gouldi*, from high rainfall areas of mainland Australia, but is distinguished from *N. gouldi* by OCW greater than 5.6 mm.

● **ROOST HABITS** Tasmanian long-eared bats have been found in tree hollows, fissures in branches, and under dried sheets of bark still attached to the trunks of dead trees.

● **HABITAT** They occupy blackwood swamps, *Acacia melanoxylon* forest with 20-m canopy and a rainforest-like understorey, dense tea tree to 7 m, coastal mallee, and wet sclerophyll forests. They are most common in wet sclerophyll but do not occur in rainforest, dry sclerophyll or regrowth. They are more commonly associated with tracks than with water.

● **DIET AND FORAGING** They appear to specialise in non-flying insects, eating mainly caterpillars (85%), scorpions (5%) and moths. These are captured by gleaning in the understorey. They spend part of their time foraging on the ground and they have been captured in pitfall traps. They have the broadest wings of all the Tasmanian bats and the slowest flight, which is undulating and agile as the bat slips in and out of the understorey. They are highly manoeuvrable, flying close to vegetation often in the lowest, densest layer of the forest.

● **REPRODUCTION** Spermatogenesis in males occurs in spring and summer. Sperm is stored in the cauda epididymides after the testes regress. Mating generally commences in autumn. The twin young are born in late spring and early summer. Lactation is usually completed by early February.

**REFERENCES** O'Neill & Taylor 1986, 1989; H. Parnaby (pers. com.); Parnaby 1987, 2007; Schulz 1994; Taylor and O'Neill 1986, 1988; Taylor et al. 1987; Thomas 1915.

| MEASUREMENTS | | Wt | Fa | Ear | 3 met | HB | OCW | Skull L | Skull W |
|---|---|---|---|---|---|---|---|---|---|
| | MEAN | 12.9 | 45.9 | 26 | 40 | 55 | 5.3 | 18.85 | 11.4 |
| | MIN | 9.8 | 43.9 | - | - | - | 5.0 | 18.3 | - |
| | MAX | 18.9 | 48.0 | - | - | - | 5.5 | 19.2 | - |
| | NO | 23 | 24 | 1 | 1 | 1 | 11 | 10 | 1 |

O'Neill & Taylor 1986; Parnaby 2007; Thomas 1915 (Type specimen).

# Central long-eared bat

## *Nyctophilus* **species 1** (undescribed)

● **TAXONOMY**
This species
was originally
included
under
*Nyctophilus*
*timoriensis* but
has recently been recognised
as an undescribed species
(H. Parnaby pers. com.).

● **DISTRIBUTION** In WA, across s. and central
wheatbelt, e. goldfields, into Great Victoria
Desert, along Nullarbor coast, e. as far as
Eyre Peninsula, SA. Does not appear to live
on Nullarbor Plain. One specimen from
the radiator grille of a car driven overnight
between Marla Bore, SA, and Alice
Springs, NT.

● **DESCRIPTION** The **central long-eared bat** has
not yet been scientifically described. In
general the **fur is grey-brown all over**. The
**muzzle ridge is low and lacks a vertical
groove** (Type 4). It is smaller (forearm length
37.6–45.3 mm) and lighter (9.5–12.7 g), with
a shorter skull (greatest length less than 18.8
mm) and narrower skull (zygomatic width
less than 11.2 mm) than the western long-
eared bat, *N. major* (forearm length
43.2–48.4 mm; weight 11.5–17.5 g; skull
length more than 18.8 mm and width
greater than 11.6 mm). The south-eastern

long-eared bat, *Nyctophilus* species 2, is
usually larger (forearm length 41.3–49.4 mm)
and heavier (11.8–21.0 g). Gould's long-eared
bat, *N. gouldi*, is usually smaller with a
proportionally narrower snout, a better
developed muzzle ridge (Type 2) and OCW of
less than 5.1 mm. The lesser long-eared bat,
*N. geoffroyi*, is smaller with a well-developed
muzzle ridge (Type 1).

● **ROOST HABITS** They have been found
roosting in tree cavities, in foliage and under
loose bark.

● **HABITAT** Desert habitats include mallee,
open savannah woodland, desert shrublands
and spinifex grasslands, mixed eucalypt
woodlands and tall woodlands; it is less
common in open woodlands. It has been
found on the fringes of the treeless
Nullarbor Plain but not extending any
distance into it.

● **DIET AND FORAGING** Their flight is slow,
fluttery and very manoeuvrable, enabling
them to negotiate obstacles as they forage
within the understorey. They ambush their
prey from a perch, glean from the ground,
from bark and from foliage surfaces, and also
forage aerially within vegetation. They are
thought to spend part of their time foraging
on the ground as they have been captured in
pitfall traps. Flight speeds of 5 km/h when

| MEASUREMENTS | | Wt | Fa | Ear | Tail | HB | OCW | Skull | Skull W |
|---|---|---|---|---|---|---|---|---|---|
| | MEAN | 11.0 | 41.2 | 24.7 | 47.5 | 61 | 5.4 | 18.1 | 11.0 |
| | MIN | 9.5 | 37.6 | 21.3 | 45 | 55 | 5.0 | 17.2 | 10.7 |
| | MAX | 12.7 | 45.3 | 27.5 | 50 | 65 | 5.8 | 18.8 | 11.2 |
| | NO | 15 | 74 | 57 | 15 | 15 | 40 | 40 | 15 |

Bullen & McKenzie 2002; McKenzie & Parnaby 2008; Parnaby 2007.

foraging and up to 24 km/h when commuting have been recorded for this species.

● **REPRODUCTION** Spermatogenesis commences in November with testicular enlargement apparent from March and epididymal distension with sperm noticeable from May to July. By September the testes have regressed. Mating is recorded from March to May, with sperm storage in the oviduct and endometrial glands until ovulation and fertilisation in late August or September. Twins are common. Births occur between late October and November, with independent young first captured during December. Lactation ceases by February.

**REFERENCES** Bullen & McKenzie 2001, 2002; Duncan et al. 1999; Hosken 1996, 1997b, e; McKenzie & Parnaby, in Van Dyck & Strahan 2008; H. Parnaby (pers. com.), Parnaby 1987, 2007; Parnaby, in Strahan 1995; Reardon & Flavel 1991; Thomson 1991; Turbill & Ellis 2006.

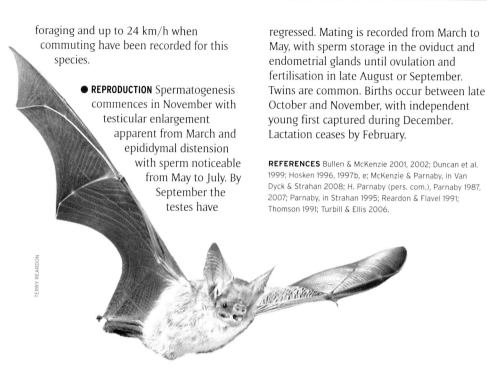

TERRY REARDON

# South-eastern long-eared bat
## *Nyctophilus* species 2 (undescribed)

● **TAXONOMY** Until recently this bat was considered to be *Nyctophilus timoriensis*. A taxonomic revision of the genus by Harry Parnaby (pers. com.) shows that *N. timoriensis* does not occur in Australia and that the Australian form represents a species complex. This species has been refered to in the literature as the 'south-eastern form'.

● **DISTRIBUTION** Largely restricted to Murray-Darling basin and w. slopes of Great Dividing Range, across s.e. Australia from s. central Qld through inland NSW to just s. of Murray River in Vic and n. of Murray River in e. SA.

● **DESCRIPTION** Rarely caught and little known, these bats are often found alone. This species has not yet been formally described. The **fur is dark grey-brown all over** and only slightly lighter brown at the tips. The **muzzle ridge is low** and **lacks a vertical groove** (Type 4) and the OCW is greater than 5.6 mm. It is **larger** (forearm length 41.3–49.4 mm) and **heavier** (11.8–21.0 g) with a broader skull

BRUCE THOMSON

*Eucalyptus gracilis.* Roost hollows are less than 3 m above the ground with multiple small entrances of 5–10 cm. Elsewhere they roost in fissures in branches and under dried sheets of bark still attached to the trunks of ring-barked trees. They forage at least 3 km from the roost. Tree hollows are used as maternity sites.

● **HABITAT** South-eastern long-eared bats are most abundant where the vegetation has a distinct canopy and a dense, cluttered understorey layer. They inhabit a wide variety of vegetation types including river red gum, black box, *Allocasuarina*, belah, mallee, open woodlands, and savannahs. They are most common in box, ironbark and cypress open forests and buloke woodlands of inland northern NSW. In SA they are confined to tall mallee shrublands. In Qld they have been recorded from semi-evergreen vine thicket with *Brachychiton sp.* emergents, inland dry sclerophyll forest with *Corymbia citriodora* and ironbark, open forest with grass trees, *Callitris* forest, mixed eucalypt forest, poplar box open forest, and open forest with midstorey of *Allocasuarina* and *Callitris.*

(greater than 11.8 mm) than the central long-eared bat, *Nyctophilus* species 1 (forearm length 37.6–44.0 mm; weight 9.5–12.7 g), and skull breadth less than 11.8 mm. Gould's long-eared bat, *N. gouldi*, is smaller where the two species occur together (forearm length less than 42 mm), has a proportionally smaller head, with narrower snout, a better developed muzzle ridge with a distinct vertical groove (Type 2), and the OCW is less than 5.1 mm. The lesser long-eared bat, *N. geoffroyi*, is smaller with a well-developed muzzle ridge (Type 1).

● **ROOST HABITS** In SA they roost in hollows of live trees including *Casuarina pauper*, *Myoporum platycarpum* and the mallee

● **DIET AND FORAGING** Highly manoeuvrable, they are able to change direction often and quickly. They fly very close to vegetation,

| | | Wt | Fa | Ear | Tibia | Tail | HB | Skull | OCW |
|---|---|---|---|---|---|---|---|---|---|
| **MEASUREMENTS** | MEAN | 15.3 | 45.6 | 26.4 | 20.4 | 42 | 62 | 19.5 | 6.1 |
| | MIN | 11.8 | 41.3 | 23.9 | 20.0 | 35 | 50 | 18.0 | 5.7 |
| | MAX | 21.0 | 49.4 | 29.3 | 20.6 | 50 | 75 | 20.8 | 6.5 |
| | NO | 32 | 111 | 39 | 3 | 3 | 33 | 33 | 33 |

Dominelli 2000; Lumsden 1994; Parnaby 1995, 2007; M. Pennay; M. Venz; A. Young.

often weaving through the canopy but also flying through gaps. They have been seen catching insects by first flying high and then swooping almost to the ground. They usually fly at canopy height (4–5 m) but this depends on the vegetation through which they are foraging. Their diet has not been examined.

● **REPRODUCTION** In inland Qld males with enlarged testes and epididymides have been caught in February, March, April and November. One male caught in October had enlarged testes and small epididymides. Pregnant females have been captured in early November; a female caught in early November carried a single newborn young. Pregnant and lactating females have been caught in mid December and post-lactating females captured in late December.

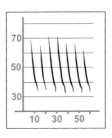

**REFERENCES** Calaby 1966; Dominelli 2000; Ellis & Turbill 2002; G. Ford (pers. com.); Lumsden 1994; Parnaby, in Strahan 1995; H. Parnaby (pers. com.); Parnaby 1987, 2007; Reardon & Flavel 1991; Smales & Koehler 2005; Turbill & Ellis 2006; Turbill et al., in Van Dyck & Strahan 2008; A. Young (pers. com.); M. Venz (pers. com.).

# Pygmy long-eared bat

## *Nyctophilus walkeri* Thomas, 1892

● **DISTRIBUTION** N. Australia from w. Kimberley through Top End to w. Gulf of Carpentaria in Qld. Endemic to Australia.

● **DESCRIPTION** A small and distinctive bat, it is the **smallest species of long-eared bat**. The **fur is pale orange-brown on the back** with a **contrasting cream belly and dark wing membranes**. It is identified by its **small size** (forearm length 30.1–36 mm) and **short ears** (10.7–14.1 mm) when compared to other long-eared bats. There is a **small but distinct muzzle ridge with a distinct central groove** (Type 2).

● **ROOST HABITS** I have found them roosting in the dead fronds of large *Livistonia* palms, 10 m above the ground. They were roosting in such large numbers that they could be heard squabbling with each other throughout the day. I have also seen them emerge at dusk from thickets of *Pandanus* at the water's edge.

● **HABITAT** Usually found in association with water courses and permanent water. They have been caught in riverine *Melaleuca* and *Pandanus* forest, monsoon rainforest patches, open savannah woodland, tall open forest and mixed shrubland. The dominant feature of most of these localities was the presence of *Melaleuca* and *Pandanus*.

● **DIET AND FORAGING** They forage by aerial capture or gleaning off the ground and other surfaces, such as foliage in vegetation thickets low to the ground in denser forest types (e.g. monsoon thickets and riverine forest), above pools, and in adjacent open woodland associated with water courses. At one Qld site I have seen them in hundreds flying over the water surface at night and staying out foraging until well after dawn. They fly low, often within 1–2 m of the ground or water surface and they are capable of flying in complex vegetation such as between the prickly leaves of *Pandanus*. The flight is jerky and irregular, two or three wing flaps followed by a glide, then a couple more flaps. This unpredictable alternation in flight may help them to avoid predators. In the Top End they eat mainly moths and beetles, but also cockroaches, termites, mosquitoes, leaf-hoppers, lacewings and spiders.

BRUCE THOMSON

● **REPRODUCTION** There is little information. In the NT one female was caught in late September in early pregnancy with twins and three females caught in mid October were in advanced pregnancy. In the Kimberley, a female was pregnant with a foetus in each uterine horn in October. Young are probably born in early November.

● **NOTES** They appear to be long-lived as it is common to catch individuals with teeth so worn that they are only small nubbins, virtually flush with the gum.

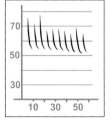

● **ECHOLOCATION** These bats emit echolocation calls with a wide frequency sweep. They cannot be distinguished from other long-eared bats except by analysing the call's peak power frequency (average 56.0 kHz; range 54–58 kHz).

**REFERENCES** Bullen & McKenzie 2002a; Churchill et al. 1984; Kitchener et al. 1981; Milne & Burwell (unpubl.).

| MEASUREMENTS | | Wt | Fa | Ear | Tibia | 3 met | Tail | HB | WS |
|---|---|---|---|---|---|---|---|---|---|
| | MEAN | 4.4 | 33.2 | 12.7 | 15.0 | 32.4 | 32.6 | 41.1 | 236 |
| | MIN | 3.0 | 30.1 | 10.7 | 14.0 | 29.9 | 26 | 38.0 | 215 |
| | MAX | 7.0 | 36.0 | 14.1 | 15.0 | 35.0 | 36 | 44.0 | 254 |
| | NO | 57 | 68 | 55 | 5 | 22 | 22 | 22 | 20 |

S. Churchill; D. Milne.

# Golden-tipped bat

## *Phoniscus papuensis* (Dobson, 1878)

● **TAXONOMY** The genus *Phoniscus* is distinguished from *Kerivoula* by having a longitudinal groove on the front of the upper canine, and by the reduced size of the third lower incisor compared to the second. Although some authors have considered *Phoniscus* to be a subgenus of *Kerivoula*, most researchers in south-east Asia (where there are many species) and New Guinea elevate *Phoniscus* to full genus status.

● **DISTRIBUTION** Along e. coast from Cape York Peninsula in Qld to s. of Eden in s. NSW. Extralimitally in New Guinea.

● **DESCRIPTION** This spider-eating specialist is a distinctively coloured bat with **dark brown curly fur and bright golden tips to each hair**. The fur extends along the wing bones, legs and tail, with abundant hair on the tail membrane. The **ears are distinctly funnel shaped** with a very **long, straight and pointed tragus** with a notch at its base. The **nose is conspicuously pointed** and overhangs the lower jaw. The **long, thin upper canines are grooved** and fit into pockets in the lower lip. The tail is longer than the combined head and body length and the calcaneum is long, strong and curved backwards.

● **ROOST HABITS** Although recorded from tree hollows and among leaves and epiphytes the vast majority of roosts have been in the (mostly) abandoned nests of yellow-throated scrubwrens and brown gerygones. These dome-shaped nests are suspended from thin vines and twigs and made of bark fibre, moss and lichen. All nests used as roosts have an

BRUCE THOMSON

entry hole in the base made by the bat. Many of the roosts are occupied by single bats, mainly solitary males. Males also burrow beneath clumps of hanging epiphytic moss to roost. Bats change roosts every day or two, with a maximum stay of 4 days. The average distance between roosts is 350 m. Maternity colonies of five to 20 bats, made up predominantly of females and young, have been found in birds' nests and tree hollows.

● **HABITAT** Most captures are in rainforest or rainforest with a well-developed overstorey of eucalyptus or brushbox. The remaining records are from tall open forest, dry and wet sclerophyll forest, *Casuarina*-dominated riparian forest and coastal Melaleuca forests. Many of these forests lack a rainforest sub-canopy. Several individuals have been recorded inside houses on the edge of residential areas.

● **DIET AND FORAGING** Orb-weaving spider remains are found in 99% of stomach contents and scat analyses. Small quantities of beetles and moths, traces of flies and bugs, and balls of spider web are also ingested. Typically these bats forage within a 2-km radius inside rainforest gullies or cluttered habitat and up the slope into sclerophyll forest, where orb-weaving spiders are more common. Web-building spiders are present year round but they are more common in the wetter summer months. Spider remains found in the stomach are generally fairly intact, suggesting that the bats may suck the spiders dry before swallowing the soft abdomen.

● **REPRODUCTION** Males have enlarged testes in February to April (one was found in September near Cairns). Most females captured in November are pregnant. A single young is born in November to January, with lactation in December to February. On the south coast of NSW in mid January a bird's nest contained lactating females and two suckling juveniles that were barely furred. Females cease lactating in January or February and volant juveniles enter the population at this time. Approximately 5% of females are non-breeding each year. A maternity colony containing up to 20 lactating females in early December was found in the hollow of a rainforest canopy tree *Flindersia australis*; this was used again the following year.

● **NOTES** The broad wings and large tail membrane of golden-tipped bats allow them to hover and manoeuvre precisely; their broadband frequency sweep calls are

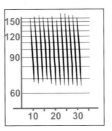

designed to provide fine detail and texture. Both are essential traits for finding spider webs in the dark and plucking out the spiders without getting entangled.

REFERENCES Bonaccorso 1998; Duncan et al. 1999; Flannery 1995b; Hill 1965; Koopman 1984; Law & Chidel 2004; Lunney & Barker 1986; Pennay et al. 2004; Rhodes 1995; Ryan 1965; Schulz 1995b, 1997a, 2000a, b; Schulz & Eyre 2000; Schulz & Wainer 1997; Walton et al. 1992; Woodside & Taylor 1985; Woodside, in Strahan 1995.

| MEASUREMENTS | | Wt | Fa | Ear | Trag | 3 met | 5 met | Tail | WS | Skull |
|---|---|---|---|---|---|---|---|---|---|---|
| | MEAN | 6.9 | 36.7 | 15.2 | 8.9 | 36.7 | 35.3 | 40.1 | 250 | 9.52 |
| | MIN | 5.3 | 34.6 | 13.9 | 8.1 | 35.8 | 33.7 | 36.7 | 220 | 9.1 |
| | MAX | 8.0 | 40.3 | 16.5 | 9.5 | 37.4 | 36.7 | 42.3 | 278 | 9.9 |
| | NO | 46 | 58 | 7 | 7 | 5 | 5 | 7 | 5 | 5 |

S. Churchill; M. Pennay; M. Venz.

# Forest pipistrelle

**_Pipistrellus adamsi_** Kitchener, Caputi and Jones, 1986

● **DISTRIBUTION**
Recorded from
Top End, NT, to
Cape York
Peninsula, Qld.
Several isolated
records in e. Qld,
on Atherton Tableland, at Cape
Hillsborough and near Blackwater.
Endemic to Australia.

● **DESCRIPTION** The fur of this tiny bat shows considerable colour variation **from dark brown to grey-brown or rusty red**. The belly is not noticeably lighter than the back. The skin on the face, ears, forearms and wings varies from light brown to very dark, almost black. The **ear is broadly rounded** with the tragus about half the length of the ear. It has a larger lobe at the base and the rear edge is

more convex than in the mangrove pipistrelle, *P. westralis*. The wings join the foot at the base of the fifth toe. The calcar has a **semicircular lobe**. The head of the **glans penis is slightly flared with small ventral flaps against the shaft**. There is a relatively **long fleshy lobe, projecting from the ventral tip**. The baculum is long with a narrow base; it is **considerably curved with a deeply forked tip (30% of length)**. In the Top End, the forest pipistrelle differs from the mangrove pipistrelle, *P. westralis*, by its **broader outer canine width**; *P. westralis* is 3.4–3.8 mm and *P. adamsi* is 3.9–4.3 mm. This does not hold true in Qld where reliance has to be placed on skull features, baculum, habitat and distribution.

● **ROOST HABITS** Forest pipistrelles probably roost in tree hollows. No roosts have been recorded.

● **HABITAT** Monsoon forest, *Melaleuca* forests, rainforests with surrounding eucalypt forest, and open woodland, and along creek and river systems in savannah woodlands.

● **DIET AND FORAGING** In the Top End they eat mainly beetles, ants and leaf-hopper bugs as well as occasional moths, flies, termites, mosquitoes, cockroaches and spiders. Here their activity pattern differs from other bats in that they become active later in the evening, most commonly after midnight.

LINDY LUMSDEN

| | | Wt | Fa | Ear | Trag | Tibia | Tail | HB | WS | OCW | Skull |
|---|---|---|---|---|---|---|---|---|---|---|---|
| **MEASUREMENTS** | MEAN | 4.3 | 31.3 | 10.7 | 4.8 | 12.3 | 31.2 | 39.2 | 225 | 4.2 | 12.0 |
| | MIN | 3.2 | 29.6 | 8.5 | 4.1 | 10.7 | 26.0 | 36.0 | 212 | 3.9 | 11.7 |
| | MAX | 6.2 | 32.7 | 11.5 | 5.8 | 13.1 | 35.0 | 44.0 | 231 | 4.3 | 12.6 |
| | NO | 52 | 63 | 14 | 14 | 23 | 14 | 14 | 14 | 24 | 18 |

S. Churchill; Kitchener et al. 1986; D. Milne.

This may account for the low capture rate of this species as mist nets are usually closed by this time. On Cape York Peninsula, by contrast, they forage early in the night and can be locally very numerous. I have captured up to 17 individuals in a short period, in one net, just after dark, suggesting they may roost in large colonies. Foraging groups are often predominantly male or predominantly female. They appear to be most common in areas where there are few *Vespadelus* species.

Little is known of the foraging strategy of this species. It is likely to be a continuous flight forager feeding on a variety of small insects captured in flight or gleaned off surfaces, such as foliage within and below the canopy and along the edges of denser forest types such as monsoon thickets, riverine forest and adjacent woodland. Where they emerge late and forage in the cooler part of the night they are thought to rely more heavily on gleaning insects that are resting on vegetation.

● **REPRODUCTION** Pregnant females carrying a single foetus have been recorded in September and October. Lactating and post-lactating females have been captured in early December and late February with almost adult-sized volant young.

● **ECHOLOCATION** The echolocation call is curvilinear with a characteristic frequency of 43.9 kHz (42.5–45.3 kHz) in the Top End. They overlap with *P. westralis* above 43.9 kHz.

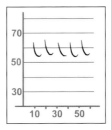

REFERENCES Coles & Lumsden 1993; Hoye, in Strahan 1995; Kitchener et al. 1986; Milne 2002; Milne & Burwell (unpubl.); Milne et al. 2005.

# Christmas Island pipistrelle

## *Pipistrellus murrayi* Andrews, 1900

● **DISTRIBUTION** Endemic to Christmas Island in the Indian Ocean.

● **DESCRIPTION** A small species with a forearm length of 30–33 mm. The fur on the back is brown with yellowish tips and slightly lighter on the belly. The forward upper premolar is visible in a gap between the canine and rear upper premolar. It is the only insectivorous bat on Christmas Island.

● **STATUS** This species has undergone a rapid and dramatic decline in population. It was common from the time of settlement in 1899. Studies in 1984, 1998 and 2004 show declines in both abundance and range of about 75% over 10 years. The reason for this decline is unknown but if these trends continue this species will become extinct within the next few years.

● **ROOST HABITS** A forest-dwelling bat, all roosts have been located within primary plateau rainforest. They mostly roost alone among vegetation 5–20 m above the ground, most commonly under the exfoliating bark of dead canopy trees, but also under flaking fibrous matter on the trunk and under dead fronds of live *Arenga* palms, under dead *Pandanus* fronds, and under the tangled roots of a strangler fig against the trunk of a canopy tree 5 m above the ground. One male was observed to share its roost with six other bats among a mass of epiphytic vegetation in a *Eugenia grandis* tree about 20 m above the ground. A colony of 47 individuals was seen roosting in a tree hollow in a large *Syzygium nervosum* 26 m above the ground. There is no information on maternity roosts or wet season roost patterns.

● **HABITAT** Primary rainforest, terrace rainforest, secondary regrowth and mine rehabilitation areas. One radio-tagged male was caught in a trap having travelled 2 km in 20 minutes since leaving its roost.

● **DIET AND FORAGING** They eat predominantly moths (50%), beetles (25%) and ants (22%), with occasional bugs and flies. Thrips and micro-wasps have also been recorded in their diet. Flight is swift and highly manoeuvrable. They forage mostly below the canopy but also above the canopy, along tracks, forest edges and small clearings in primary and secondary forests.

In the 1980s these bats were commonly observed flying up to 1.5 hours before sunset. They were active until dawn with a peak of activity 45 minutes after sunset, a hiatus of about 2 hours and then renewed activity until midnight. In the last 20 years there has been a shift in their daily activity patterns. In 2004 no bats were observed or recorded anywhere on the island before sunset and post-dusk activity was sustained longer into the night. The shift in daily activity has been gradual and is probably related to the declines in distribution and abundance.

● **REPRODUCTION** Spermatogenesis begins in March, and the epididymides are full of sperm in September. Females with sperm in the uterus and a copulatory plug have been captured in September. Births are synchronised, once a year, towards the end of December when a single young is born. Lactation is expected to last for about 4 weeks into mid or late January. They are likely to form maternity roosts during the wet season.

CHRIS TIDEMANN

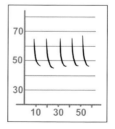

**REFERENCES** Andrews 1900; G. Hoye (pers. com.); James 2005; Kitchener et al. 1986; L. Lumsden (pers. com.); Lumsden & Cherry 1997; Schulz & Lumsden 2004; Tate 1942; Tidemann 1985.

| MEASUREMENTS | | Wt | Fa | Ear | Trag | Foot | Tibia | 3 met | Tail | HB | Skull |
|---|---|---|---|---|---|---|---|---|---|---|---|
| | MEAN | 3.3 | 31.3 | 10.8 | 5.8 | 6.1 | 12.7 | 30.1 | 33.9 | 34.0 | 12.0 |
| | MIN | 3.0 | 30.5 | 10.0 | 5.2 | 5.5 | 12.4 | 29.6 | 30.8 | | |
| | MAX | 4.2 | 32.6 | 11.8 | 6.7 | 6.7 | 13.1 | 31.0 | 35.7 | | |
| | NO | 48 | 48 | 10 | 10 | 10 | 10 | 10 | 10 | 1 | 1 |

G. Hoye; L. Lumsden; Kitchener et al. 1986; Tidemann 1985.

# Mangrove pipistrelle
## *Pipistrellus westralis* Koopman, 1984

● **DISTRIBUTION** Coastal areas of Kimberley, the NT and w. Gulf of Carpentaria. Endemic to Australia.

● **DESCRIPTION** This tiny bat of the mangroves is one of Australia's smallest. The fur is dark grey tipped with light brown on the back and tipped with buff on the belly. The muzzle, ears and forearms are usually brown to light brown and the wings are dark brown. The ear is broadly triangular with a less rounded tip than the forest pipistrelle, *P. adamsi*. The tragus is less than half the length of the ear. It has a smaller lobe at the base and the rear edge is less convex than in *P. adamsi*. The wing joins the foot at the base of the fifth digit. The calcar has an elongated lobe. The head of the glans penis is slightly flared with a central circular depression at the tip, containing many small fleshy spines. The baculum is shorter with a wider base than for *P. adamsi* and the shaft is straight with only the final 10% of the tip forked. In the Top End it differs from *P. adamsi* by its narrower outer canine width; *P. westralis* is 3.4–3.8 mm and *P. adamsi* is 3.9–4.3 mm. This is not always true in Qld where reliance has to be placed on skull features, baculum, habitat and distribution.

● **ROOST HABITS** They are presumed to roost in tree hollows although no roost sites have been reported.

● **HABITAT** In WA they appear to be virtually confined to mangroves. In the Top End they have a broader habitat range, still living primarily in mangroves, but also along associated waterways including *Melaleuca* swamps, *Pandanus*, freshwater mangroves (*Barringtonia*) and along tracks in dense pindan thickets.

● **DIET AND FORAGING** These bats forage along small creeks and tidal waterways in mangrove forests. Using shallow but rapid wing beats and acrobatic flight they follow the irregular contours of the outer foliage

| | | Wt | Fa | Ear | Trag | Tibia | Tail | HB | OCW | Skull |
|---|---|---|---|---|---|---|---|---|---|---|
| MEASUREMENTS | MEAN | 3.9 | 29.1 | 10.0 | 5.0 | 11.9 | 31.5 | 37.0 | 3.6 | 11.4 |
| | MIN | 2.7 | 27.4 | 8.1 | 4.7 | 11.1 | 29.0 | 34.4 | 3.4 | 11.1 |
| | MAX | 4.8 | 31.3 | 11.0 | 6.1 | 12.9 | 37.2 | 42.2 | 3.8 | 11.9 |
| | NO | 12 | 43 | 31 | 30 | 35 | 28 | 29 | 16 | 18 |

Kitchener et al. 1986; D. Milne.

catching flying insects, including moths, small beetles, ants and bugs, with occasional cockroaches and spiders.

● **REPRODUCTION** Births of the single young have been recorded in the dry season, in June and July. It is likely, as with *Pipistrellus papuanus* in New Guinea, that breeding is continuous and young are born throughout the year.

● **ECHOLOCATION** Calls are curvilinear with a characteristic frequency of 46.6 kHz (44.0–49.3 kHz). In the Top End the call overlaps with *P. adamsi* below 45.4 kHz.

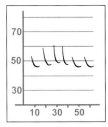

**REFERENCES** Kitchener et al. 1986; McKenzie, in Strahan 1995; McKenzie & Rolfe 1986; D. Milne (pers. com.); Milne 2002; Milne & Burwell (unpubl.).

# Greater broad-nosed bat
## *Scoteanax rueppellii* (Peters, 1866)

● **DISTRIBUTION**
N. Qld from Mount Carbine and Atherton Tablelands s. to Charters Towers; from Rockhampton to s. NSW. Endemic to Australia.

● **DESCRIPTION** A bat with an unusual diet, it is large and robust, with a long forearm (51.0–56.2 mm). The fur on the back is reddish brown to dark brown, slightly paler on the belly. It is distinguished from other broad-nosed bats by its much larger size. The ear is slender and triangular, with a moderately rounded tip and a notch on the rear edge. The tragus is triangular due to a pronounced lobe midway along the rear edge; the front edge is straight or slightly concave. The penis is largely hairless. It is most easily confused with the eastern falsistrelle, *Falsistrellus tasmaniensis*, from which it can be separated by the presence of two, not four, upper incisor teeth; there is no gap between the canines and incisors

BRUCE THOMSON

of *S. rueppellii* and the ears are shorter, only just touching when pressed together above the head.

● **ROOST HABITS** They roost in tree hollows, cracks and fissures in trunks and dead branches, under exfoliating bark, as well as the roofs of old buildings. One female was observed roosting for 4 days in the hollow spout of a *Melaleuca* tree 8 m above the ground.

● **HABITAT** A variety of habitats including moist gullies in mature coastal forest, rainforest, open woodland, *Melaleuca* swamp woodland, wet and dry sclerophyll forests, cleared paddocks with remnant trees and tree-lined creeks in open areas. They are found from sea level to an altitude of 1200 m and they are strongly associated with areas with mild winters and annual rainfall of over 600 mm.

● **DIET AND FORAGING** These large bats have a high wing loading, and intermediate aspect ratio, and their flight is characterised by limited manoeuvrability and moderate speed in open situations. They forage about 5 m from the edge of isolated trees, forest remnants or along forest crowns with a slow direct flight pattern. They also use perch-hunting, echolocating for passing prey before flying out to intercept it. Beetles are the dominant prey type with occasional moths, ants and large flies taken as well. Surprisingly, spiders are quite commonly eaten with up to 20% of samples containing spider remains. This is unexpected, given the bats' wing morphology and loading, and the spiders may be ground-dwelling rather than web-building species.

Of most interest is their propensity for eating other bats in captivity, whenever the opportunity arises. They commonly eat other bats caught with them in bat traps. They have been recorded eating nine species of bats ranging in size from little forest bats, *Vespadelus vulturnus*, to eastern blossom bats, *Syconycteris australis*. They have been observed attacking bats in mist nets, particularly juvenile bats, and breaking into adjoining cages to eat other captive bats. Several researchers have reported them circling closely when they have been handling and measuring bats. They have also been seen chasing chocolate wattled bats, *Chalinolobus morio*, emerging from their roost at dusk. It is very likely that bats form part of their diet in the wild.

● **REPRODUCTION** Females congregate in maternity colonies and a single young is born in January, slightly later than other vespertilionid bats that share its range. Males appear to be excluded from the colony during the birth and rearing of the young.

● **NOTES** I captured two individuals in a bat trap on the Atherton Tablelands along with 190 little bentwing bats, *Miniopterus australis*. In the morning, the greater broad-nosed bats were found deep within the bundles of clustered bats, warm and contented with full bellies after eating at least five little bentwing bats between them, and leaving just the head or the muzzle of their victims at the bottom of the bat trap bag.

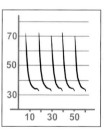

**REFERENCES** Calaby 1966; Campbell 2001; C. Corben (pers. com.); Duncan et al. 1999; Hoye & Richards, in Strahan 1995; Kitchener & Caputi 1985; Kutt 2003; Law et al. 2000; Milledge 1987a; Reinhold et al. 2001; Schulz 2000b; B. Thomson (pers. com.); Wilson 2006; Woodside & Long 1984.

| MEASUREMENTS | | Wt | Fa | Ear | Trag | HB | Tail | Tibia | 3 met | WS | Skull |
|---|---|---|---|---|---|---|---|---|---|---|---|
| | MEAN | 25.4 | 53.2 | 16.6 | 8.3 | 67.8 | 51.6 | 23.5 | 51.8 | 395 | 20.1 |
| | MIN | 20.0 | 50.5 | 15.6 | 7.6 | 63.3 | 44.5 | 22.0 | 49.0 | - | 19.1 |
| | MAX | 39.8 | 56.2 | 17.8 | 8.7 | 72.7 | 58.5 | 24.4 | 54.7 | - | 21.3 |
| | NO | 65 | 83 | 12 | 12 | 12 | 12 | 12 | 12 | 1 | 20 |

S. Churchill; Kitchener & Caputi 1985; M. Pennay; M. Venz.

# Inland broad-nosed bat

**_Scotorepens balstoni_** (Thomas, 1906)

● **DISTRIBUTION**
Widespread
through arid
and semi-arid
regions, s. of
latitude 19°S.
Generally does
not occur e. of Great Dividing
Range. Endemic to Australia.

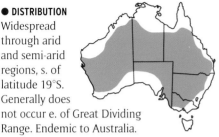

● **DESCRIPTION** A common and pugnacious
species of inland Australia. It is of moderate
size with a slender body shape. The **fur
colour is variable**, ranging from **dark brown
to a pale sandy colour**, most **commonly a
light grey-brown on the back with a pale
brown belly**. The fur is **markedly bicoloured**
(unlike the eastern broad-nosed bat, _S. orion_)
with paler bases. The muzzle is broad and
square-shaped when viewed from above. The
**forearm length is moderate, but varies
geographically** increasing from west to east
and from south to north. A large form of this
species (previously referred to as _Nycticeius
influatus_) is found in northern inland Qld.
The inland broad-nosed bat, _S. balstoni_, is
larger than the little broad-nosed and
northern broad-nosed bats, _S. greyii_ and _S.
sanborni_. The ears are relatively slender, and
longer than the eastern broad-nosed bat, _S.
orion_. The glans penis has up to 22 spines on
the head in two long rows; this also
distinguishes it from the eastern broad-nosed
bat, _S. orion_, which has only eight spines in a
circular cluster.

BRUCE THOMSON

● **ROOST HABITS** Inland broad-nosed bats roost
in tree hollows in colonies of up to 45. They
have been recorded roosting in the roofs of
houses, under the metal caps of power poles
and in a length of water pipe. In Vic, they
have been known to share roosts in houses
and tree hollows with southern freetail bats,
_Mormopterus_ sp. 4.

● **HABITAT** Throughout arid and semi-arid
regions of inland Australia they can be
captured over water and along river red gum-
lined waterways, in open woodland,
shrublands, mallee and grasslands.

| MEASUREMENTS | | Wt | Fa | Ear | Tibia | Tail | HB | WS | OCW | Skull |
|---|---|---|---|---|---|---|---|---|---|---|
| | MEAN | 9.3 | 35.6 | 12.6 | 15.2 | 35.9 | 50.3 | 278 | 5.1 | 15.1 |
| | MIN | 6.3 | 32.0 | 10.7 | 13.0 | 29.0 | 42.2 | 252 | 4.4 | 13.9 |
| | MAX | 12.7 | 40.5 | 14.1 | 17.2 | 41.7 | 59.7 | 295 | 5.6 | 17.0 |
| | NO | 37 | 108 | 108 | 108 | 108 | 108 | 8 | 116 | 117 |

S. Churchill; Kitchener & Caputi 1985.

● **DIET AND FORAGING** Flight is continuous with sudden rapid diversions in pursuit of prey. They often start foraging early and are one of the first species to be caught in mist nets just on dusk. They forage mostly between trees but also at the edges of forests, and out into open areas. They stay within 15 m of the ground and do not forage above the canopy. Flight speeds have been recorded from 12–21 km/h. Stomach contents collected from northern Australia have shown them to eat cockroaches, termites, crickets, cicadas, bugs, beetles, flies, moths and ants (mostly wingless species). In Vic they eat mainly beetles (45%) and ants, bugs, moths and flies as well as a few grasshoppers.

● **REPRODUCTION** In Vic copulation has been observed in captive bats in April. The male mounts the female from behind, grasps her by the nape with his teeth, and wraps his forearms around her chest. The single young is born in mid November. The young bats are well developed at birth although naked. They are vocal when not suckling and capable of walking rapidly with head and chest held high at 1 day old. They remain constantly attached to the female until 10 days of age when they weigh 3–4 g and are left behind when she forages at night. Their eyes open and fur begins to grow by 15 days. At 30 days they are exercising their wings and by January they are foraging independently. In the northern parts of their range mating has been observed in September and twins are usual; one individual caught east of Alice Springs carried three near-term foetuses in October.

● **NOTES** These bats have well-developed jaw muscles and a tenacious nature. Removing them from mist nets can be a painful experience.

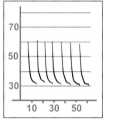

● **ECHOLOCATION** Characteristic frequency is 34.1–38.7 kHz in WA and 28–34 kHz in NSW.

**REFERENCES** Bullen & McKenzie 2002b; Kitchener & Caputi 1985; Lumsden & Bennett 1995; Lumsden & Wainer (pers. com.); Lumsden et al. 1994; McKenzie & Muir 2000; Menkhorst 1995; Parnaby, in Strahan 1995; Pennay et al. 2004; Reardon & Flavel 1991; Ryan 1966b; Thomson 1991.

# Little broad-nosed bat

## *Scotorepens greyii* (Gray, 1843)

● **DISTRIBUTION** N. Australia excluding Cape York Peninsula. Inland areas to s. NSW.

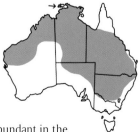

● **DESCRIPTION** Abundant in the north, this species has a small,

slender body shape. The fur is markedly bicoloured. Fur colour is variable from brown to grey-brown on the back with the base of the hairs lighter than the tips; the belly fur is also lighter. The forearm is small (length 27.3–35.0 mm). Ears are relatively broad and the tragus has a narrow and pointed tip. Forearm length increases from east to west and from north to south (the opposite of *S. sanborni*). The

AL YOUNG

glans penis has up to ten spines on the head, mainly in two long rows. It is almost **impossible to separate in the field** from the northern broad-nosed bat, *S. sanborni*, **where their ranges overlap** in the Kimberley and western Top End, although specimens can be separated by examination and measurement of the skull and by plotting braincase width against palatal length (see Kitchener & Caputi 1985). In these areas molecular analysis of wing samples is the only reliable method of identification of live animals. Where their ranges overlap in Qld, the northern broad-nosed bat, *S. sanborni*

(forearm length 33.3 mm; 31–35.8 mm), is usually larger than the little broad-nosed bat, *S. greyii* (forearm length 31.1 mm; 27.3–35 mm).

● **ROOST HABITS** Little broad-nosed bats roost in hollows, usually in trees, but the hollow centres of fence posts and even the space under the metal caps of telegraph poles are accepted. They will also roost in disused buildings. Colonies of two to 20 bats have been found. Although a common species, little has been recorded of its natural history.

| | | Wt | Fa | Ear | Tibia | 3 met | Tail | HB | WS | OCW | Skull |
|---|---|---|---|---|---|---|---|---|---|---|---|
| **MEASUREMENTS** | MEAN | 6.4 | 31.3 | 11.4 | 13.6 | 30.7 | 32.2 | 44.8 | 234 | 4.35 | 13.16 |
| | MIN | 4.0 | 27.3 | 9.7 | 11.5 | 26.7 | 25.2 | 37.2 | 212 | 3.9 | 11 |
| | MAX | 8.5 | 35.0 | 12.9 | 15.8 | 33.8 | 48.5 | 53.0 | 250 | 5.1 | 15.0 |
| | NO | 137 | 139 | 139 | 138 | 138 | 139 | 138 | 37 | 135 | 141 |

S. Churchill; Kitchener & Caputi 1985.

● **HABITAT** Monsoon forest, *Melaleuca* forest, tall open forest, open forest, open woodland, mulga shrublands, mixed shrubland, escarpment, river red gum-lined water courses, *Pandanus* and grasslands. They are commonly caught near water.

● **DIET AND FORAGING** They are continuous flight foragers that use moderately fast, agile flight. They search for insects close to the tree tops but not above them, flying in the open spaces along the contour of the vegetation within 2 m of the foliage. They also forage over water, grasslands and other open habitat. Flight is characterised by abrupt horizontal turns where the bat rolls to near vertical bank angles. They eat large numbers of beetles, bugs and ants with occasional moths, termites, cockroaches, katydids, crickets, flies and lacewings. The high proportion of flightless insects such as ants in the diet indicates that they may glean food from foliage and other surfaces. Michael Pennay has watched these bats near Bourke in NSW dog-fighting and catching moths almost as large as themselves. They are tenacious, with a surprisingly strong bite.

● **REPRODUCTION** Pregnancy lasts from late August to early November. Usually twin young are born in October and November. They are capable of flight, and forage with the females (who are still lactating) in mid December. All males have enlarged testes and epididymides in April, and by November the testes and epididymides have regressed. Not all females breed every year.

● **NOTES** A common species around waterholes where they are often caught early in the evening; I have had groups of up to 15 of these bats hit the mist net within seconds of each other. Interestingly, during a survey near Kununurra in the Kimberley, in May 1999, we captured only one *S. greyii* but in a repeat survey of the same area in November 2004 this was the second most common species captured (116 individuals), suggesting they undergo either seasonal movements or seasonal changes in foraging behaviour.

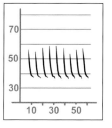

**REFERENCES** Bullen & McKenzie 2002b; Hall & Richards 1979; Kitchener 1978; Kitchener & Caputi 1985; Lumsden & Churchill 1999; Lumsden et al. 2005; McKenzie et al. 2002; Milne & Burwell (unpubl.); M. Pennay (pers. com.); Richards, in Strahan 1995; Young & Ford 2000.

# Eastern broad-nosed bat
## *Scotorepens orion* (Troughton, 1937)

● **DISTRIBUTION** E. Australia from Melbourne to s. Qld along Great Dividing Range to the coastal plain. An isolated population on Atherton Tablelands in n. Qld. Endemic to Australia.

● **DESCRIPTION** This robust bat is of moderate size, **forearm length 32.4–38.8 mm**. The **fur colour is a rich dark brown on the back**, with the **belly fur more drab**. The fur is **not markedly bicoloured**. The bat has a

BRUCE THOMSON

*Scotorepens* species, differs from *S. orion* by its smaller size (forearm less than 32 mm) and weight (6–8 g versus 8–12 g).

● **ROOST HABITS** Eastern broad-nosed bats roost in tree hollows. One roost was found in the hollow of a manna gum, 7 m above the ground. A colony of pregnant females were found sharing a roost in a hollow limb with a colony of chocolate wattled bats, *Chalinolobus morio*, and their young. They have also been reported to roost in buildings.

● **HABITAT** Rainforest, tall wet forest, vine forest, low open forest, cypress pine woodland, stringybark and mixed species woodland.

● **DIET AND FORAGING** Nothing known.

● **REPRODUCTION** Sperm storage occurs in both sexes over winter and ovulation and fertilisation are delayed until spring. The single young is born in late November or early December.

pug nose, the ears are relatively broad and the tragus tip is narrow and pointed. The forearm tends to be longer in the colder areas of this species' range. It is most **likely to be confused with the inland broadnosed bat**, *S. balstoni*, but their ranges do not overlap except in south-eastern Qld and along the west of the Great Dividing Range in NSW. In this area the ratio of tibia to forearm length is less than 41% for *S. orion*. This does not always hold true but is a useful characteristic in many cases. *S. orion* can be separated by the **glans penis that has eight spines on the head** in an almost circular cluster. The central-eastern broad-nosed bat,

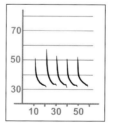

● **NOTES** Their echolocation calls have a characteristic frequency of 34–38 kHz.

**REFERENCES** Hall & Richards 1979; Kitchener & Caputi 1985; Lunney & Barker 1987; Menkhorst 1995; Parnaby 1992; Pennay et al. 2004; Reinhold et al. 2001; Tidemann, in Strahan 1995.

| | | Wt | Fa | Ear | Trag | Tibia | 3 met | Tail | HB | OCW | Skull |
|---|---|---|---|---|---|---|---|---|---|---|---|
| **MEASUREMENTS** | MEAN | 9.3 | 35.1 | 11.9 | 5.6 | 13.7 | 33.2 | 34.5 | 49.3 | 5.1 | 14.7 |
| | MIN | 7.0 | 32.4 | 10.6 | 5.0 | 12.7 | 30.8 | 29.5 | 43.9 | 4.9 | 13.8 |
| | MAX | 14.1 | 38.8 | 13.1 | 6.4 | 14.5 | 36.3 | 37.9 | 53.1 | 5.3 | 15.5 |
| | NO | 57 | 95 | 19 | 19 | 19 | 19 | 19 | 19 | 19 | 19 |

Kitchener & Caputi 1985; M. Pennay.

# Northern broad-nosed bat

## *Scotorepens sanborni* (Troughton, 1937)

● **DISTRIBUTION** Two discrete populations: one in Kimberley and w. Top End; the other in n. Qld from Rockhampton to Cape York Peninsula. Extralimital distribution includes w. Timor in Indonesia, and s. coastal regions of New Guinea.

● **DESCRIPTION** This **small, slender species** is less aggressive than other *Scotorepens*. The **fur is markedly bicoloured**, and **brown with a light reddish tinge on the back** with a dark brown base. Fur on the **belly is slightly lighter**. The muzzle is dark. The **ears are relatively slender** and the tragus is evenly curved upwards. The **small forearm** (27.9–35.8 mm) increases in size from west to east and from south to north (the opposite to *S. greyii*). The glans penis has up to ten spines on the head, mainly in two long rows. It is almost **impossible to separate in the field** from the little broad-nosed bat, *S. greyii*, **where their ranges** **overlap in the Kimberley and western Top End**, although specimens can be separated by examination and measurement of the skull and by plotting braincase width against palatal length (see Kitchener & Caputi 1985). In these areas molecular analysis of wing samples is the only reliable method of identification of live animals. Where their ranges overlap in Qld, *S. sanborni* (forearm length 33.3 mm; 31–35.8 mm) is usually larger than *S. greyii* (forearm length 31.1 mm; 27.3–35 mm).

● **ROOST HABITS** Northern broad-nosed bats usually roost in tree hollows in colonies of ten to 20 bats but they occur in large colonies of several hundred in buildings.

● **HABITAT** In Qld they occur in a broad range of habitats from monsoon forest to open woodland and heathlands. In the Kimberley or the Top End, they prefer mangrove communities and floodplain areas adjacent to paperbark forest.

● **DIET AND FORAGING** In WA they forage in cluttered air spaces within the canopy and

| MEASUREMENTS | North-western Australia | | | | | | | | | |
|---|---|---|---|---|---|---|---|---|---|---|
| | | Wt | Fa | Ear | Tibia | 3 met | Tail | HB | OCW | Skull |
| | MEAN | 6.5 | 31.0 | 10.6 | 13.3 | 30.6 | 31.7 | 42.7 | 4.2 | 12.9 |
| | MIN | 5.7 | 27.9 | 9.1 | 11.9 | 28.4 | 27.5 | 36.8 | 3.9 | 12.1 |
| | MAX | 7.3 | 34.0 | 11.8 | 14.4 | 33.1 | 36.0 | 48.4 | 4.5 | 13.8 |
| | NO | 5 | 23 | 23 | 24 | 24 | 23 | 21 | 22 | 24 |

| | Qld | | | | | | | | | |
|---|---|---|---|---|---|---|---|---|---|---|
| | | Wt | Fa | Ear | Tibia | 3 met | Tail | HB | OCW | Skull | WS |
| MEAN | 7.3 | 33.3 | 11.5 | 14.1 | 32.9 | 34.3 | 44.4 | 4.5 | 13.9 | 253.9 |
| MIN | 5.7 | 31.0 | 10.4 | 12.2 | 30.8 | 29.1 | 39.7 | 4.1 | 13.0 | 230 |
| MAX | 9.1 | 35.8 | 13.1 | 15.6 | 35.2 | 38.9 | 52.3 | 5.0 | 14.8 | 272 |
| NO | 64 | 34 | 34 | 34 | 34 | 34 | 33 | 35 | 35 | 25 |

S. Churchill; Kitchener & Caputi 1985.

BRUCE THOMSON

cockroaches and lacewings. Crane flies, midges, mosquitoes and mayflies have been reported from stomach contents.

● **REPRODUCTION** Pregnant females have been captured in August and September. The single young are born in late September or early December. Females of little broad-nosed bats, *S. greyii*, and northern broad-nosed bats, *S. sanborni*, captured together in the Top End were at the same stage of pregnancy.

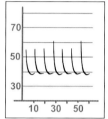

alongside mangroves. In Qld they fly within the forest understorey usually within 4–5 m of the ground. In the Top End beetles (44%), bugs (28%) and ants (18%) are the main prey items with occasional moths, termites,

**REFERENCES** Hall, in Strahan 1995; Hall & Richards 1979; Kitchener & Caputi 1985; Kitchener et al. 1994; McKenzie & Rolfe 1986; Milne & Burwell (unpubl.).

# Central-eastern broad-nosed bat
## *Scotorepens* **species** (undescribed)

● **TAXONOMY** This species has not yet been scientifically described but is well known to researchers in southern Qld. It occurs sympatrically with three other species of *Scotorepens* and all are difficult to identify. Unpublished morphological studies indicate that all Australian species of *Scotorepens* require taxonomic revision to clarify species diagnoses, and that more species exist than are currently recognised (H. Parnaby pers. com.).

● **DISTRIBUTION** Coastal NSW n. of Hunter Valley and w. of Great Dividing Range n. of Coonabarabran into s.e. Qld. Patchily distributed e. of Great Dividing Range in s. Qld; relatively common w. of the range.

● **DESCRIPTION** Fur colour is **brown with a bicoloured pale belly**. The fur is **paler than** *S. orion*, and the **muzzle is less pug-like**. This species is of **intermediate body size** for the genus, with a forearm length of 32.8 mm (31.0–34.6 mm) averaging **larger than** *S. greyii* (31.3 mm; 27.3–35.0 mm) and **smaller than both** *S. orion* (35.1 mm; 32.4–38.8 mm) **and** *S. balstoni* (35.6 mm; 32.0–40.5 mm). Body is less robust, average weight of 7.4 g (6.1–9.0 g), than *S. orion*

AL YOUNG

(9.3 g; 7.0–14.1 g) and *S. balstoni* (9.3 g; 6.3–12.7 g), and slightly larger than *S. greyii*. Ratio of tibia to forearm length is usually greater than 41% in *Scotorepens* sp. compared to less than 41% for *S. orion*, but both *S. greyii* and *S. balstoni* have ratios that range above and below this figure. In some areas of NSW it coexists with both *S. greyii* and *S. orion*. In south-eastern Qld it occurs with *S. greyii* and *S. balstoni*. Although ranges of measurements and weights overlap between these species, live animals from the same area are recognisably distinct.

This species differs on skull, dental and external morphology from *S. balstoni* and *S. orion*, and differs from *S. greyii* on skull morphology. The details are yet to be published.

● **ROOST HABITS** An individual was captured and radio-tracked in dry sclerophyll forest on the NSW coast. The roost was found in a mature swamp mahogany tree (*Eucalyptus robusta*) over 100 cm in diameter. The bat was roosting in a hollow branch about 20 m above the ground. They have also been found roosting in buildings, in wall cavities, between floor joists and in an attic.

● **HABITAT** Occurs in drier forest types east of the Great Dividing Range south to the Hunter Valley. It is relatively common west of the Great Dividing Range in dry open eucalypt woodland and forest, and brigalow-belah forests. It has been recorded from *Eucalyptus pilligaensis* woodland with open *Allocasuarina* and *Callitris*; and open forest of *Corymbia citriodora* and ironbark with scattered *Callitris*.

● **DIET AND FORAGING** The central-eastern broad-nosed bat has a relatively fast flight and forages by aerial pursuit above the canopy or within the sub-canopy. Nothing is known of its diet.

● **REPRODUCTION** In Qld, males have been recorded with regressed testes and enlarged epididymides in December and January and with enlarged testes in February. Pregnant females have been captured in mid October, November and December and lactating females have been captured in December and January. Twins have been recorded. Post-lactation females and volant juveniles have been caught in late January and February.

● **NOTES** Echolocation calls cannot be distinguished from the little broad-nosed bat, *S. greyii*.

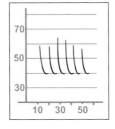

REFERENCES Campbell 2001; Duncan et al. 1999; G. Ford (pers. com.); H. Parnaby (pers. com.); Parnaby 1992; Parnaby & Ford, in Strahan & Van Dyck 2008; Pennay et al. 2004; M. Venz (pers. com.); A. Young (pers. com.).

| MEASUREMENTS | | Wt | Fa | Ear | Trag | Tibia | 3 met | HB |
|---|---|---|---|---|---|---|---|---|
| | MEAN | 7.4 | 32.8 | 7.9 | 3.6 | 13.8 | 29.8 | 47.9 |
| | MIN | 6.1 | 31.0 | 7.8 | 3.5 | 12.4 | 28.0 | 47.9 |
| | MAX | 9.0 | 34.6 | 8.0 | 3.7 | 14.8 | 30.3 | 48 |
| | NO | 26 | 76 | 2 | 2 | 55 | 8 | 2 |

G. Ford; M. Venz.

# Inland forest bat

## *Vespadelus baverstocki* (Kitchener, Jones and Caputi, 1987)

● **DISTRIBUTION**
Widely distributed
in inland arid
and semi-arid
parts of
Australia.
Endemic to
Australia.

● **DESCRIPTION** A **very small bat** with
a forearm length of 28.6 mm (26.5–31.4 mm).
The **fur on the back is light sandy brown to**
brownish grey with the base of the hairs
grey. The **belly fur is much lighter**, the base
of each hair is dark brown and the **tip
creamy white**. The bare skin on the face is
a greyish pink, with the ears and wing
membranes pale grey. The **tragus is**
sometimes white. The **penis is pendulous**
and the **end of the penis is clearly swollen**.
The **head of the glans penis is funnel-
shaped**. At the southern limit of its
distribution (in north-western Vic)
*V. baverstocki* is significantly larger than
elsewhere in its range.
Southern forest bats,
*V. regulus*, are usually larger
with a forearm length greater
than 30.5 mm (versus usually
less than 30.5 mm in
*V. baverstocki*); males have
lateral folds on the glans
penis. Little forest bats,
*V. vulturnus*, are generally
smaller in the same area and
males have a bulbous glans
penis. Large forest bats,
*V. darlingtoni*, inland cave
bats, *V. finlaysoni*, and the
eastern cave bat,
*V. troughtoni*, have longer
forearms (greater than
32.0 mm).

BRUCE THOMSON

| | Wt | Fa | Ear | Tibia | 3 met | P1 | P2 | P3 | Tail | HB | Skull |
|---|---|---|---|---|---|---|---|---|---|---|---|
| MEAN | 4.6 | 28.6 | 10.6 | 11.8 | 28.0 | 10.1 | 8.6 | 6.6 | 29.7 | 39.6 | 12.1 |
| MIN | 3.6 | 26.5 | 9.1 | 10.8 | 26.0 | 9.4 | 7.9 | 4.8 | 26.5 | 35.4 | 11.6 |
| MAX | 5.6 | 31.4 | 11.4 | 13.0 | 31.2 | 10.9 | 9.7 | 7.8 | 33.8 | 43.5 | 12.5 |
| NO | 174 | 25 | 25 | 25 | 25 | 25 | 25 | 25 | 24 | 25 | 25 |

MEASUREMENTS

Kitchener et al. 1987; L. Lumsden.

● **ROOST HABITS** Inland forest bats roost in tree hollows and abandoned buildings. There are no large trees over much of their distribution and they roost in extremely small tree hollows in stunted trees only a few metres high. One large colony, of over 60, was found living in the crack around a door frame in an abandoned railway building.

● **HABITAT** *Acacia, Callitris* and *Casuarina* woodlands, mallee, open eucalypt woodland, river red gum woodland, shrub and grassland communities across inland Australia.

● **DIET AND FORAGING** These are very manoeuvrable bats that fly with rapid wing beats. They forage over a wide area. Their diet has not been studied.

● **REPRODUCTION** Males have enlarged testes between December and April. The females are pregnant in November and congregate in maternity colonies. They are lactating in December and the single young is carried by the female for the first week. The young are flying and independent in January. Sub-adult males exhibit partial testicular enlargement in January and February indicating they may become reproductively active by April in their first year.

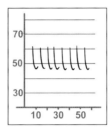

REFERENCES Kitchener et al. 1987; Lumsden & Bennett 1995; Queale 1997; Reardon & Flavel 1991; Thomson 1982.

# Northern cave bat
## *Vespadelus caurinus* (Thomas, 1914)

● **DISTRIBUTION**
The more rugged rocky terrain of Kimberley, WA, and Top End of NT along w. Gulf of Carpentaria into w. Qld.

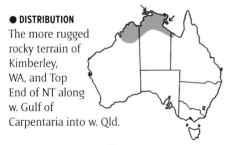

● **DESCRIPTION** A small cave-dwelling species (forearm length 26.6–31.7 mm) with brown fur on back and belly, only slightly paler on belly. The fur has a dark brown, almost black, base; just the tips are brown. The skin on the face, wings and forearms is dark, almost black. The glans penis is cylindrical and laterally compressed; the urethra is covered by an upward projecting narrow tongue of skin from the ventral tip. The dorsal surface has a deep longitudinal groove. The Kimberley cave bat, *V. douglasorum*, differs in its larger size (forearm length of over 32.0 mm). The inland cave bat, *V. finlaysoni*, is generally larger (forearm length averages 32.8 mm; 29.8–36.7 mm), but identification may be difficult in the Top End except by examination of tooth characteristics. In *V. caurinus*, in the upper first molar ($M^1$) the metacone-hypocone crista is moderate-sized whereas in *V. finlaysoni* it is absent.

● **ROOST HABITS** These are cave bats that tend to roost in small cracks and crevices, near the entrances of caves and mines. Colony size averages eight to 12 but ranges from solitary animals to groups of 45. Their roost microclimate reflects the ambient conditions and is very variable with temperatures ranging from 20–34.5°C and 23–98%

relative humidity. Females with young have a more restricted microclimate with temperatures of 28.5–34.5°C and 25–62% humidity. They are found in a variety of roosts including volcanic, sandstone and limestone caves, boulder piles and crevices, disused mines, road culverts and fairy martin nests. They will also use buildings.

LINDY LUMSDEN

● **HABITAT** In or adjacent to rocky outcrops in a range of habitats including *Melaleuca* forest, monsoon forest, tall open forest, open woodland, savannah, spinifex hill woodland, mixed shrubland, floodplain and deciduous vine thickets.

● **DIET AND FORAGING** They are a continuous flight forager that primarily searches for insects within and below the canopy of woodland and other forest types. In the Kimberley stomach contents were found to contain the remains of moths, bugs and caddis flies. In the Top End they eat mainly ants and beetles with a few flies, moths, mayflies and leaf-hoppers. They are most active in the first 3 hours after sunset.

● **REPRODUCTION** The timing of reproduction in this species is quite variable; like the inland cave bat, *V. finlaysoni*, they may produce two or more litters a year. Males have enlarged testes in May to July. Pregnant females have been recorded in June, September, October and November. Usually

they have twins but some have a single young. Most females caught in November are lactating. Volant young have been captured in mist nets in mid November, while in January a cave colony comprised of one lactating female and four sub-adults. Colonies contain roughly equal numbers of males and females.

● **ECHOLOCATION** They have a frequency modulated echolocation call of 59.6 kHz (57.5–61.7 kHz).

REFERENCES Churchill 1991; Kitchener et al. 1987; McKenzie et al. 1975; Milne 2002; Milne et al. 2005; Milne & Burwell (unpubl.).

| | Wt | Fa | Ear | Tibia | 3 met | P1 | P2 | P3 | Tail | HB | Skull |
|---|---|---|---|---|---|---|---|---|---|---|---|
| MEAN | 3.1 | 29.5 | 10.1 | 11.4 | 28.6 | 10.6 | 10.1 | 5.5 | 30.2 | 36.7 | 11.2 |
| MIN | 2.3 | 26.6 | 8.3 | 10.7 | 25.9 | 9.8 | 7.9 | 4.4 | 24.4 | 32.1 | 10.6 |
| MAX | 4.2 | 31.7 | 12.3 | 12.4 | 31.9 | 12.0 | 12.1 | 6.8 | 34.8 | 40.0 | 12.0 |
| NO | 24 | 39 | 38 | 39 | 39 | 39 | 39 | 39 | 39 | 36 | 41 |

S. Churchill; Kitchener et al. 1987.

# Large forest bat
## *Vespadelus darlingtoni* (Allen, 1933)

● **DISTRIBUTION**
Along Great
Dividing Range
of s.e. Australia
from s. Qld to
Adelaide Hills in
SA. Also Tas and
Kangaroo Is. Inland
distribution limit in Vic
corresponds with the 500-mm rainfall
isohyet. Recently captured on Lord Howe Is
although for many years it was thought to be
extinct there. Endemic to Australia and Lord
Howe Is.

● **DESCRIPTION** A distinctive *Vespadelus* with
its **long fur** and **large size** (forearm length
35.1 mm; 32.5–37.2 mm). It has **dark brown
to rusty brown fur all over**. The hairs are
only mildly bicoloured with dark brown
bases and slightly lighter brown tips. The
skin on the **ears and wings is very dark**, the
skin of the arm is the same colour as the
wing membrane. The **penis is small and has
a distinctively angular shape**, and the **tip is
not swollen**. It can be distinguished from
all other species except the eastern forest
bat, *V. pumilus*, by its short angled penis.
*V. pumilus* is smaller with a forearm length of
less than 33 mm (30.9 mm; 28.4–33.0 mm).
A bat with a forearm length greater than
33.5 mm is most likely to be of this species
in south-eastern Australia. By running a
finger lightly from the nose along the

forehead to the ears a distinct bump or rise
can be felt on the bridge of the nose. This
helps to distinguish small female *V.
darlingtoni* from large *V. regulus*.

● **ROOST HABITS** Colonies of up to 80 large
forest bats have been found in tree hollows
but they are more commonly found in small
groups of five to six females or as solitary
males. These bats usually select large live
trees for roosts, 20–40 m high and
commonly smooth-barked. Roost entrances
are 15–20 m above ground. They use
multiple roosts, changing most days to a new
roost less than 1 km away. They are also
found in buildings in colonies of up to 20.
Males and females do not share roosts but
both sexes will roost in association with
other bat species.

● **HABITAT** Rainforest, wet and dry sclerophyll
forest, blackwood swamps, open forest, sub-
alpine woodland and alpine moors,
sclerophyll regrowth and coastal mallee.

● **DIET AND FORAGING** These bats are less
manoeuvrable than most *Vespadelus*. They fly
fast and avoid cluttered regrowth and
rainforest by foraging mainly within the
spaces among trees and between the canopy
and the understorey. Their flight is
characterised by rapid wing beats that are
interrupted by gliding changes of direction
to catch insects. Adapted to cool climates,

| | | Wt | Fa | Ear | Tibia | 3 met | P1 | P2 | P3 | Tail | HB | Skull |
|---|---|---|---|---|---|---|---|---|---|---|---|---|
| MEASUREMENTS | MEAN | 7.2 | 35.1 | 11.8 | 13.7 | 32.9 | 13.0 | 9.6 | 8.8 | 33.5 | 44.1 | 13.4 |
| | MIN | 6.0 | 32.5 | 10.1 | 12.3 | 30.9 | 11.8 | 8.7 | 7.6 | 29.2 | 38.1 | 12.7 |
| | MAX | 8.3 | 37.2 | 13.1 | 14.4 | 35.1 | 14.2 | 10.8 | 10.0 | 38.0 | 48.9 | 14.1 |
| | NO | 16 | 48 | 31 | 31 | 32 | 33 | 33 | 31 | 29 | 30 | 34 |

S. Churchill; Kitchener et al. 1987.

BRUCE THOMSON

they are able to forage during mild winters. In Vic they eat ants, flies, bugs and beetles in equal quantities, with occasional moths and spiders. In Tas they eat predominantly moths, but also take beetles, flies, bugs, lacewings and termites. They can be distinguished from the little forest bat, *V. vulturnus*, and the southern forest bat, *V. regulus*, by their more direct flight and less agile attacking manoeuvres. Foraging areas range from 10 ha to over 300 ha, individuals foraging for distances of up to 6 km during the night.

● **REPRODUCTION** Spermatogenesis commences in summer and the bats mate in March. Over winter a hibernation follicle is present in either ovary but ovulation is delayed until spring when the egg is fertilised by the sperm stored in the female over winter. The males also store sperm and remain reproductively active throughout the winter, arousing from hibernation to mate.

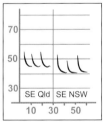

Implantation occurs only in the right uterine horn. Single young are born in late November or December and breech births are usual. Females lactate during December and January. Juveniles are free-flying by late January or early February. Females become sexually mature in their first year and males in their second.

**REFERENCES** Herr & Klomp 1999; Hoye, in Strahan 1995; Kitchener et al. 1987; Law & Chidel 2002; Lumsden & Wainer (pers. com.); Lumsden et al. 1994; O'Neill & Taylor 1986, 1989; Taylor & O'Neill 1986; Tidemann 1993a; Tidemann & Flavel 1987.

# Kimberley cave bat

## *Vespadelus douglasorum* (Kitchener, 1976)

● **DISTRIBUTION**
W. Kimberley, WA.
Mostly caught
in areas that
receive more
than 800-mm
rainfall per year.
Endemic to Australia.

● **DESCRIPTION** A large species of
*Vespadelus* about which little is known, it
has a forearm length of 34.3–37.8 mm. **Fur
colour is a pale grey with slightly paler
belly.** There is often **a deep yellow to
orange tinge to the fur** around the mouth,
head and shoulders, also on the feet and
forearm. This appears to vary at different
times of the year. The head of the **glans
penis is laterally compressed and rod-
shaped**; the urethra is covered by an upward
projecting narrow tongue of skin from the
ventral tip. The dorsal surface has a deep
longitudinal groove, and the ventral surface
is covered with numerous small spines. It
differs from the northern cave bat, *V.
caurinus*, by its much larger size and grey
instead of brown fur. Glandular pads on each
side of the face give it a less pointed
appearance than *V. caurinus*. The inland cave
bat, *V. finlaysoni*, has darker skin on the face,
ears and forearms and the 3 met to P1 ratio
is greater than 0.35 (average of 0.38 versus
0.32 for *V. douglasorum*).

● **ROOST HABITS** They are cave-dwelling bats
forming mixed-sex colonies of up to 200.
I have found torpid individuals roosting in
small clusters of four to six in cool and dry
conditions (20°C and 33% humidity) in July,
not far from the cave entrance. Alert (non-
torpid) individuals were found deeper in the
same cave in conditions of 27°C and 48%
humidity. Even further into the cave where
the temperature and humidity were very
high there was a colony of orange leaf-nosed
bats, *Rhinonicteris aurantia*. Kimberley cave
bats occasionally share caves with northern
cave bats, *V. caurinus*, but roost in different
areas. In May a colony of 36 was found
roosting in a small limestone cave
overhanging a large pool of water. They
shared this cave with dusky horseshoe bats,
*Hipposideros ater*, and common sheathtail
bats, *Taphozous georgianus*. A colony of 12
bats was found roosting in an abandoned
building at Mt Hart.

● **HABITAT** Kimberley cave bats have been
caught in tropical woodlands, usually netted
along *Melaleuca*- and *Pandanus*-lined
waterways and adjacent open woodland.
They use both sandstone and limestone
caves, usually near water.

● **DIET AND FORAGING** The diet of this species
has not been studied.

| | Wt | Fa | Ear | Tibia | 3 met | P1 | P2 | P3 | Tail | HB | Skull |
|---|---|---|---|---|---|---|---|---|---|---|---|
| **MEAN** | 5.2 | 36.3 | 11.9 | 14.4 | 35.0 | 11.1 | 11.5 | 6.1 | 36.8 | 39.7 | 12.8 |
| **MIN** | 4.5 | 34.3 | 11.3 | 13.6 | 32.7 | 10.0 | 10.8 | 5.3 | 35.2 | 35.3 | 12.3 |
| **MAX** | 6.1 | 37.8 | 12.5 | 15.5 | 37.0 | 11.7 | 12.2 | 7.0 | 42.1 | 43.5 | 13.2 |
| **NO** | 22 | 29 | 13 | 14 | 13 | 13 | 13 | 12 | 14 | 13 | 12 |

MEASUREMENTS

K. Armstrong; S. Churchill; Kitchener et al. 1987.

● **REPRODUCTION** Pregnant females have been caught in June, August, October and November. The birth of the single young has been recorded in November and December. A group of eight post-lactating females was caught in a cave in March with a juvenile male, suggesting they form maternity colonies.

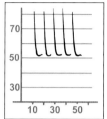

● **ECHOLOCATION** Their echolocation call has a peak frequency of 52.8 kHz.

REFERENCES K. Armstrong (pers. com.); Armstrong & Kitchener, in Van Dyck & Strahan 2008; S. Churchill (pers. obs.); Kitchener 1976b; Kitchener et al. 1987; McKenzie et al. 1975.

# Inland cave bat

## *Vespadelus finlaysoni* (Kitchener, Jones and Caputi, 1987)

● **DISTRIBUTION** Widely distributed in arid and semi-arid areas of inland Australia extending into wet-dry tropics in Top End. Endemic to Australia.

● **DESCRIPTION** A bat of the arid interior, the fur is almost black with just the tips coloured either dark rust-brown or yellow-brown. The belly is only slightly paler. The skin on the ears, face and wings is very dark. The fur is long and on the head it extends well onto the muzzle. The head of the glans penis is laterally compressed and rod-shaped with an upward projecting narrow tongue of skin from the ventral tip. The dorsal surface has a deep longitudinal groove. The ventral surface has a slight ventral keel. The forearm length averages 32.8 mm (29.8–37.6 mm). The northern cave bat, *V. caurinus*, is smaller (26.6–31.7 mm), with *V. finlaysoni* within this size range only in the Pilbara region where *V. caurinus* does not occur. The inland forest bat, *V. baverstocki*, has paler fur and a funnel-shaped glans penis. The eastern cave bat, *V. troughtoni*, is difficult to distinguish in central Qld where they overlap in size. *V. troughtoni* differs by the ratios of tibia to forearm length being less than 0.39, and P2 to forearm length less than 0.32. The glans penis differs in having a deep ventral groove and is blunt at the tip.

● **ROOST HABITS** Inland cave bats roost in the twilight area of caves and rock crevices and will readily roost in disused mines. Colony sizes of two to 20 are common but colonies of up to 500 are recorded. The sexes differ in their roosting behaviour. Females tend to roost in large clusters whereas males tend to roost in smaller groups, often in hard-to-reach crevices. They roost typically near the cave entrance. Preferred roosts tend to have very low humidity (less than 30% relative humidity) and although the temperature fluctuates widely from 16–35°C the bats rarely move between roost sites.

TERRY REARDON

I have found a colony of over 200 young, roosting separately from the adult bats, in a mine in western Qld. They were roosting in a tightly clumped group in a warm area of the mine. When disturbed, they flew off and separated to join the small clusters of adults scattered throughout the mine.

● **HABITAT** Grasslands, spinifex grasslands, savannah woodlands, open forest, mulga and other shrub communities. They usually live close to rocky outcrops or cavernous areas.

● **DIET AND FORAGING** They are aerial foragers but their diet has not been studied. They begin to hunt at dusk, foraging in cluttered air spaces within vegetation stands or while close-contouring vegetation canopies, escarpments, scree slopes and other surfaces. During straight and level flight they reach speeds of 19.5 km/h. Flight is often zigzagged, being a rapid, alternating series of near vertical rolls in opposite directions. They are commonly observed foraging over waterholes.

● **REPRODUCTION** There is considerable variation in the timing of breeding in this species. In the northern part of its range the young are born throughout year, with peaks in March and September to October. Single young are usual but up to 20% of births are

| | | Wt | Fa | Ear | Tibia | 3 met | P1 | P2 | P3 | Tail | HB | Skull |
|---|---|---|---|---|---|---|---|---|---|---|---|---|
| **MEASUREMENTS** | MEAN | 4.3 | 32.8 | 11.1 | 13.6 | 32.3 | 12.3 | 11.2 | 6.7 | 35.2 | 40.1 | 12.4 |
| | MIN | 2.8 | 29.8 | 9.3 | 11.1 | 29.3 | 11.0 | 9.2 | 5.0 | 30.7 | 34.3 | 11.3 |
| | MAX | 6.3 | 37.6 | 13.2 | 16.2 | 36.1 | 13.8 | 13.0 | 7.9 | 42.0 | 46.4 | 13.5 |
| | NO | 28 | 84 | 84 | 82 | 84 | 84 | 83 | 82 | 79 | 83 | 89 |

S. Churchill; Kitchener et al. 1987.

twins. In southern regions there is a single breeding season with mostly twins born in November or December. Mating has been observed in late June. The male couples with the female from the rear while hanging from the ceiling. Females carry the young for the first week and then leave them at the roost at night. On return they accept their own, but will reject other young. Nursing females are found further into mines where the temperature is more constant. The young develop rapidly, and commence trial flights at 2–3 weeks, and fly 3–4 weeks after birth,

when females and weaned young are often caught together.

**REFERENCES** Bullen & McKenzie 2001; G. Ford (pers. com.); Kitchener et al. 1987; Maddock & McLeod 1974, 1976; McKenzie et al. 2002; McKenzie & Muir 2000; Metcalf 2002; Milne 2002; Milne et al. 2005, 2006; Reardon & Flavel 1991; Reardon, in Strahan 1995; Young & Ford 2000.

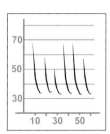

# Eastern forest bat

## *Vespadelus pumilus* (Gray, 1841)

● **DISTRIBUTION** Scattered e. of Great Dividing Range, from Atherton Tablelands, Kirrama and Kroombit Tops to just n. of Sydney, but probably occurs in isolated populations over a wider range. Endemic to Australia.

● **DESCRIPTION** The original little brown bat, its **fur is dark chocolate brown on the back** with an almost black base to the hairs. Forearm length is 30.9 mm; 28.4–33.0 mm. The fur is lighter on the belly, very long and thick and extends onto the dorsal surface of the tail membrane. The wing membrane, face and ears are dark brown. The **penis is small and has a distinctively angular shape**; the **tip is not swollen**. The **glans penis is a blunt rod shape** and **dorsoventrally compressed**. It can be

BRUCE THOMSON

distinguished from all other species except the large forest bat, *V. darlingtoni*, by its short angled penis. *V. darlingtoni* is larger with a forearm length greater than 32.5 mm (35.1 mm; 32.5–37.2 mm).

● **ROOST HABITS** Eastern forest bats roost primarily in tree hollows ranging from large cavities in hollow trunks to small hollows in the extremities of branches. They mostly use large mature trees, both dead and alive, which possess a diversity of hollows. Most females form maternity roosts in tree hollows in November and colonies containing at least 54 bats have been recorded. Males generally roost alone although they share roosts with females during the mating season in April. Solitary males have been recorded roosting in dead *Acacia melanoxylon* trees with small hollows and within epiphytic elkhorn ferns. They use many different roosts that they usually change daily, although they may stay at the same site for up to 6 days. Roosts are usually only 100 m apart and are reused regularly. Maternity roosts are always close to creeks but with the onset of winter, roosts are more commonly found in dead trees further up slope away from the water.

● **HABITAT** Known from sea level to the top of the Great Dividing Range, generally in moister forest, from tropical and subtropical rainforest, wet sclerophyll forest with rainforest gullies, and bunya pine plantations. They are found in regrowth forest but prefer to roost in mature forests.

● **DIET AND FORAGING** In northern NSW their diet consists of moths, beetles, flies, ants/wasps and bugs. Their foraging ranges are small, only 4 ha during the mating season in April and 6 ha when females are lactating in November. Foraging ranges overlap. They forage mainly within the spaces among trees and between the canopy and the understorey. Their flight is more manoeuvrable than the large forest bat, *V. darlingtoni*. They prefer to forage within mature forest rather than along flyways such as tracks. They avoid dense regrowth and in regrowth forest will favour riparian zones.

● **REPRODUCTION** Little is known. In NSW they mate in April. Births, usually of twins, occur in October. Lactation has been recorded in October and November.

● **NOTES** We normally think of torpor as being an adaptation for cold stress and food limitation. A population of these bats in northern NSW has been studied in summer when temperatures and food availability were high. Surprisingly, they were found to enter torpor twice a day. One bout was in the early morning and another in late afternoon, each for 4 hours. Body temperature was normal for only 3 hours, during the warmest part of the day. Torpor reduces energy expenditure substantially and this habit may be common in many small microbats whose day roosts are poorly insulated, even in subtropical climates.

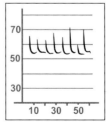

REFERENCES Kitchener et al. 1987; Law & Anderson 2000; Law & Chidel 2002; Parnaby, in Strahan 1995; M. Pennay (pers. com.); Schulz 2000a; Turbill et al. 2003.

| | | Wt | Fa | Ear | Tibia | 3 met | P1 | P2 | P3 | Tail | HB | Skull |
|---|---|---|---|---|---|---|---|---|---|---|---|---|
| **MEASUREMENTS** | MEAN | 4.4 | 30.9 | 10.5 | 12.6 | 29.4 | 11.5 | 8.9 | 7.7 | 30.7 | 39.1 | 12.1 |
| | MIN | 3.5 | 28.4 | 9.0 | 11.6 | 27.3 | 10.5 | 7.6 | 6.6 | 27.6 | 35.0 | 11.3 |
| | MAX | 5.5 | 33.0 | 11.9 | 13.8 | 32.2 | 12.4 | 9.8 | 8.6 | 33.7 | 44.2 | 12.7 |
| | NO | 196 | 225 | 25 | 25 | 25 | 25 | 25 | 25 | 25 | 25 | 25 |

Kitchener et al. 1987; M. Pennay.

# Southern forest bat

### *Vespadelus regulus* (Thomas, 1906)

● **DISTRIBUTION** From Qld near NSW border along Great Dividing Range to Vic and s. SA to s.w. Australia. Also Tas and Kangaroo Is. Endemic to Australia.

● **DESCRIPTION** A small species with a forearm length of 28.0–34.4 mm. The **fur on the back is a warm reddish brown to grey** with a **pale belly**. The fur is **distinctly bicoloured** with a **dark base**. The **ears and wings are grey**. The penis is pendulous and clearly swollen. The glans penis has a deep furrow on the underside and is enclosed by **large** lateral folds. The **distal end is smooth and round** with a slightly raised dorsal hump. The **tragus is usually dark**. By running a finger lightly from the nose along the forehead to the ears the skull can be felt to be flat with no rise at the bridge of the nose. This distinguishes small *V. regulus* from large *V. vulturnus* and large *V. regulus* from *V. darlingtoni*. *V. baverstocki* and *V. vulturnus* are usually slightly smaller in forearm length. *V. darlingtoni* differs by its angular penis. *V. baverstocki* has a funnel-shaped glans penis, and lacks the secondary lateral folds. The glans penis of *V. vulturnus* is bulbous at the tip.

● **ROOST HABITS** These bats are found in colonies of up to 100 in tree hollows. They

LINDY LUMSDEN

commonly roost in houses around Adelaide. Males tend to roost separately from females except during the mating period. Roosts have been reported to contain either large numbers of females or small groups of males.

● **HABITAT** Rainforest, wet and dry sclerophyll forest, shrubland and low shrub woodland, mixed temperate woodland, mallee and open woodland. They are sensitive to extreme forest fragmentation and avoid small forest remnants, corridors and open areas.

● **DIET AND FORAGING** Southern forest bats are highly manoeuvrable, moderately fast aerial insectivores with flight speeds of 5–25 km/h. Their diet in Tas consists predominantly of moths and beetles, with some flies, bugs and termites. In Vic they eat mainly flies and moths, with occasional beetles, bugs and ants. They fly with great aerial agility, with rapid wing beats broken frequently by spiralling, gliding arcs as they change direction to attack flying insects. They tend to fly very close to vegetation and readily enter gaps in the understorey, usually foraging at less than half the canopy height. They are capable of taking off from the ground with ease. They are more active on tracks in mature forests and they have a small foraging range of less than 10 ha. In Tas they hibernate but presumably wake and forage regularly as they do not lose body weight over winter.

● **REPRODUCTION** Spermatogenesis peaks in January. Mating begins in April about 2–3 months after peak testicular development and continues through winter with sperm stored in the epididymides. A copulatory plug is formed in the females after mating, and ovulation and fertilisation are deferred until spring. Gestation takes about 3 months with a single young born in late November or early December. Young are weaned 6 weeks later. Sub-adults first appear in the trappable population in January. Sub-adult males exhibit partial testicular enlargement in January and February. In southern Tas births occur a month later in late December to early January.

● **ECHOLOCATION** This bat shows abrupt and sizeable regional changes in echolocation call frequencies. In north-eastern NSW these are 45–46 kHz and in south-eastern NSW their calls are 40–43 kHz. In the Riverina district of south NSW their calls are 54–55 kHz. The significance of this is currently unknown but it has been suggested that these phonotypes may represent cryptic species.

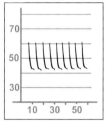

**REFERENCES** Bullen & McKenzie 2001; Herr 1998; Hosken et al. 1998; Kincade et al. 2000; Kitchener et al. 1987; Law et al. 1999, 2002; Law & Chidel 2002; Lumsden & Bennett 1995; Lumsden & Wainer (pers. com.); O'Neill & Taylor 1986, 1989; Taylor & O'Neill 1986, 1988; Taylor & Savva 1990; Tidemann 1993a; Tidemann, in Strahan 1995; Tidemann & Flavel 1987.

| | | Wt | Fa | Ear | Tibia | 3 met | P1 | P2 | P3 | Tail | HB | Skull |
|---|---|---|---|---|---|---|---|---|---|---|---|---|
| **MEASUREMENTS** | MEAN | 5.2 | 31.2 | 11.1 | 12.7 | 30.2 | 11.2 | 9.0 | 7.2 | 31.7 | 41.4 | 12.7 |
| | MIN | 3.6 | 28.0 | 9.0 | 11.4 | 27.0 | 9.8 | 7.5 | 6.0 | 28.5 | 36.2 | 11.9 |
| | MAX | 7.0 | 34.4 | 12.9 | 13.9 | 32.7 | 12.4 | 10.3 | 9.0 | 39.0 | 46.6 | 13.4 |
| | NO | 369 | 77 | 77 | 77 | 77 | 77 | 77 | 75 | 72 | 75 | 84 |

Kitchener et al. 1987; Lumsden & Bennett 1995; O'Neill & Taylor 1986.

# Eastern cave bat

## *Vespadelus troughtoni* (Kitchener, Jones and Caputi, 1987)

● **DISTRIBUTION** E. Australia, from Cape Melville in n. Qld to n. NSW. Several isolated records from further inland Qld and s. coast of NSW. Endemic to Australia.

● **DESCRIPTION** An uncommon bat, the **fur on the back is light brown** with ginger tips mainly around the head. The fur on the belly is dark at the base with light fawn tips. The **penis is pendulous and swollen at the tip**.

The head of the **glans penis is laterally compressed** with a **deep furrow on the ventral surface** and **a blunt tip**. The large forest bat, *V. darlingtoni*, is a similar size but differs in its much smaller, angular penis. The southern forest bat, *V. regulus*, the little forest bat, *V. vulturnus*, and the eastern forest bat, *V. pumilus*, have smaller forearms (shorter than 33.0 mm). The inland cave bat, *V. finlaysoni*, is difficult to differentiate in central Qld where they overlap in size. *V. finlaysoni* can be distinguished by the ratios of tibia to forearm length being greater than 0.39, P2 to forearm greater than 0.32, and the glans penis having a pointed tip.

MICHAEL PENNAY & TERRY REARDON

● **ROOST HABITS** Eastern cave bats have been found roosting in small groups in sandstone overhang caves, boulder piles, mines and occasionally in buildings. They roost near the entrance in reasonably well-lit areas, often in small avons or domes in the roof of caves as well as in cracks and crevices. Roost fidelity is low. They roost individually wedged into cracks or in colonies of six to 100 packed closely together in avons. The smaller colonies tend to be single sex. Maternity colonies of up to 240 adults have been found in shallow sandstone caves. A smaller maternity colony of 50 adults was found under the corrugated roof of a dairy shed. Roost microclimate stability appears to be of low importance in maternity roost selection. They are commonly found in abandoned fairy martin nests under bridges and in culverts. Usually two to three bats roost together in unbroken nests.

● **HABITAT** All records are in close proximity to sandstone or volcanic escarpments. They inhabit tropical mixed woodland, wet and dry sclerophyll forest along the coast and the Great Dividing Range, extending into the drier forest of the western slopes and inland areas. This species has not been recorded during extensive surveys of forests in north-eastern NSW, suggesting that forests without natural roosting sites (caves or large rock overhangs) do not provide habitat for this species.

● **DIET AND FORAGING** They forage over a small area. One male was observed foraging for 5 consecutive nights in an area of only 33 ha. Another male foraged along a creek,

remaining less than 10 m above the surface and staying above the water rather than the surrounding vegetation. It used a circular back-and-forth flight along 20-m sections of the creek, changing frequently to new sections along a 200-m length. They are capable of flying 500 m over cleared paddocks. They have been observed hawking mosquitoes.

● **REPRODUCTION** Pregnant females have been captured in October near Cooktown, lactating females in early December on the Atherton Tablelands and in January at Cape Melville in north Qld. This indicates that births occur at the same time as in NSW where births occur in mid to late November. One female was observed giving birth to twins but seven female bats found at another roost had only single young attached. The young are left alone at the roost, clustered in groups of more than ten, while the females foraged at dusk. Females returned to the young at least once during the night. The females shifted roosts with their young every few days, in one case to a new roost 3.5 km away.

**REFERENCES** Calaby 1966; Ellis 2001; Kitchener et al. 1987; Law et al. 2002, 2005; Parnaby 1992; Parnaby, in Strahan 1995; Pennay et al. 2004; Schulz 1998; Schulz & de Oliveira 1995.

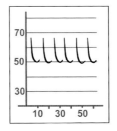

| | | Wt | Fa | Ear | Tibia | 3 met | P1 | P2 | P3 | Tail | HB | Skull |
|---|---|---|---|---|---|---|---|---|---|---|---|---|
| **MEASUREMENTS** | MEAN | 5.4 | 34.6 | 11.4 | 13.6 | 34.0 | 12.6 | 11.0 | 7.4 | 35.3 | 41.5 | 12.7 |
| | MIN | 4.5 | 32.3 | 10.4 | 12.7 | 32.6 | 11.5 | 9.3 | 6.5 | 31.4 | 37.5 | 12.2 |
| | MAX | 6.7 | 36.4 | 12.5 | 14.2 | 35.1 | 13.5 | 12.6 | 8.3 | 37.9 | 44.2 | 13.2 |
| | NO | 11 | 30 | 17 | 17 | 17 | 17 | 17 | 17 | 16 | 17 | 24 |

S. Churchill; Kitchener et al. 1987.

# Little forest bat

## *Vespadelus vulturnus* (Thomas, 1914)

● **DISTRIBUTION** E. Australia s. of latitude 24°S. S. Qld, most of NSW and Vic, s.e. SA, and Tas. Endemic to Australia.

● **DESCRIPTION** One of Australia's smallest bats, the forearm length is 26.2–32.8 mm. The **fur colour is variable** from brown to pale grey with a lighter belly. The **hairs are bicoloured**, being darker at the base, and vary from creamy white to brown or grey for the top one-third. The **tragus is usually white or pale grey**, and the ears and wings are pale. The skin on the forearm is paler than the wing membrane. The **penis is pendulous** and the end of the **glans penis is distinctly round and bulbous**. It is most likely to be confused at the same locality with the inland forest bat, *V. baverstocki*, which has a longer forearm and a funnel-shaped glans penis. There is considerable regional variation, with individuals from arid or northern areas being smaller than those from mesic or southern areas. By running a finger lightly from the nose along the forehead to the ears a distinct bump or rise can be felt on the bridge of the nose. This distinguishes large *V. vulturnus* from small southern forest bats, *V. regulus*.

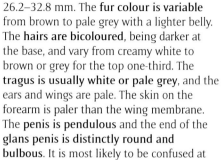

BRUCE THOMSON

● **ROOST HABITS** Little forest bats roost in hollows, usually in dead trees or dead branches of live trees, often with multiple entrances. Hollow entrances are usually very small, only slightly larger than the bats. They also roost in buildings. Colony sizes vary from solitary to 120, and are usually sexually segregated although juveniles and an occasional adult male may be found in a female colony. Roosts are usually near water, often in large trees along creeks and rivers.

● **HABITAT** Wet and dry sclerophyll forest, river red gum forest, montane and dry woodland, blackwood swamp, brigalow, mulga and mallee. In more arid areas they are mostly found in riverine habitats.

● **DIET AND FORAGING** They forage within the upper levels of the forest understorey or in the spaces between trees, often very close to the foliage and below the canopy. They fly with great aerial agility, with spiralling, gliding arcs as they change direction to catch flying insects. They forage up to 1.5 km from their roost sites. They take only flying prey and do not normally take food from the ground or from foliage. Larger prey may be caught and taken to a feeding roost to be eaten. These bats feed opportunistically, the diet reflecting local and seasonal variation in insect abundance and diversity. They eat predominantly moths, bugs and beetles with some flies, wasps, termites, ants, cockroaches and occasional spiders, grasshoppers and lacewings.

● **REPRODUCTION** Females become sexually mature in their first year and males in their second. Spermatogenesis occurs in summer and mating in autumn. Females store sperm in the uterus and a copulatory plug forms in the vagina. Males also store sperm and remain reproductively active throughout the winter, arousing from hibernation to mate. During winter a hibernation follicle is present but ovulation is delayed until spring when the egg is fertilised by the sperm stored in the female's uterus over winter. Single young (occasionally twins) are born in late November or December and breech births are usual. Females lactate during December and January and the dependent young is left at the roost when the female forages at night. Juveniles are free-flying and can be caught foraging with the females in the forest by mid January. In southern Tas, births occur approximately 1 month later than on the mainland and lactation is completed in only 5–6 weeks.

● **ECHOLOCATION** This bat shows abrupt and sizeable regional changes in echolocation call frequencies. In south-east and central Qld the calls range from 43–47 kHz, in coastal NSW 44–49 kHz, and in southern NSW 49–53 kHz. It has been suggested that these phonotypes may represent cryptic species.

**REFERENCES** Campbell et al. 2005; Herr 1998; Kincade et al. 2000; Kitchener et al. 1987; Law & Chidel 2000; Law et al. 2002; Lumsden & Bennett 1995; Lumsden & Wainer (pers. com.); Lumsden et al. 1994; Menkhorst 1995; O'Neill & Taylor 1986, 1989; Parnaby 1992; Reardon & Flavel 1991; Rounsevell et al. 1991; Taylor & O'Neill 1986, 1988; Taylor et al. 1987; Tidemann 1993a; Tidemann & Flavel 1987; Young & Ford 1998.

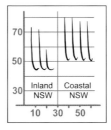

| | Wt | Fa | Ear | Tibia | 3 met | P1 | P2 | P3 | Tail | HB | Skull |
|---|---|---|---|---|---|---|---|---|---|---|---|
| MEAN | 3.9 | 28.4 | 10.6 | 11.8 | 27.6 | 11.5 | 8.9 | 6.7 | 30.9 | 40.2 | 12.2 |
| MIN | 3.0 | 23.5 | 9.1 | 10.8 | 24.6 | 10.5 | 7.8 | 4.8 | 27.5 | 34.7 | 11.8 |
| MAX | 6.5 | 32.8 | 12.2 | 13.0 | 31.1 | 12.4 | 10.8 | 7.8 | 34.2 | 48.0 | 12.7 |
| NO | 850 | 34 | 34 | 22 | 34 | 34 | 34 | 34 | 32 | 33 | 34 |

MEASUREMENTS

Kitchener et al. 1987; M. Pennay.

# Bentwing Bats

## Family MINIOPTERIDAE: Key to Species

The terminal phalanx of the third finger is at least three times the length of the second phalanx. The muzzle is short and the forehead rises abruptly to the rounded crown of the head. The ears are short and broad. There is only a single genus in the family.

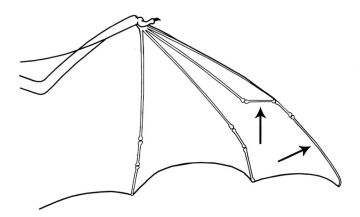

### GENUS *Miniopterus*

**1a** Forearm length less than 42 mm.
→ *M. australis* (page 180)

**1b** Forearm length greater than 42 mm.
→ **2**

**2a** Occurs in south-eastern SA and south-western Vic only. Skull length greater than 15.8 mm; males 16.2–16.67 mm; females 15.82–16.5 mm.
→ *M. orianae bassanii* (page 182)

**2b** Occurs in eastern Australia from southern Vic to Cape York Peninsula. Skull length intermediate; males 15.62–16.55 mm; females 15.1–16.35 mm.
→ *M. orianae oceanensis* (page 184)

**2c** Occurs in the Top End and Kimberley regions of northern Australia. Skull length less than 14.9 mm; males 14.81; females 14.4 mm.
→ *M. orianae orianae* (page 186)

# Little bentwing bat

## *Miniopterus australis* (Tomes, 1858)

● **DISTRIBUTION** E. coast of Australia from Cape York to n. NSW as far s. as Sydney. Confined to subtropical coastal belt in s. part of its range. Extralimital distribution in New Caledonia, New Guinea, Indonesia, Solomon Is and Vanuatu.

● **DESCRIPTION** The little bentwing bat has uniform **dark chocolate-brown fur on back**, slightly **lighter on belly**. Distinctly **short muzzle and domed head**. The ears are short, rounded and roughly triangular. This is the smallest bentwing bat, with a forearm length of 37.3–40.8 mm.

● **ROOST HABITS** These are cave-dwelling bats that congregate in the summer months into maternity colonies and disperse during the winter. In the southern part of their range they hibernate during the winter but only go into a shallow hibernation, arousing frequently throughout the winter to hunt for food. In the north they remain active throughout the year. The few documented maternity sites are normally situated in limestone cave systems. There is a huge maternity colony of 100 000 adult bats at Mt Etna caves, in central Qld. They are known to roost in caves, abandoned mines, tunnels,

stormwater drains, and occasionally buildings, and they have even been reported to roost in banana trees within a plantation. In November a colony of 30 bats was found roosting in a crevice in a hollow of a large rainforest tree *Citronella moorei* in northern NSW. Conditions inside the tree hollow were 21°C and 81% humidity (cooler and more humid than outside). It appeared to be used only as an occasional roost and the three bats captured were males.

● **HABITAT** Well-timbered areas including rainforest, vine thicket, wet and dry sclerophyll forests, *Melaleuca* swamps and coastal forests.

● **DIET AND FORAGING** These bats fly rapidly and with considerable manoeuvrability between shrub and canopy layers of densely wooded areas. In the Richmond Range in NSW, analysis showed their diet contained mostly beetles, moths and flies but also a surprisingly high proportion of spiders (30% of scats contained spiders). Elsewhere they have also been reported to eat crane flies, ants and wasps.

● **REPRODUCTION** These are essentially tropical bats whose range extends into subtropical northern NSW. Here the reproductive pattern is modified by winter hibernation. At this latitude (30°S) spermatogenesis commences in late December or early January, with

| | | Wt | Fa | Ear | Foot | 3 met | 5 met | Tail | HB | WS |
|---|---|---|---|---|---|---|---|---|---|---|
| MEASUREMENTS | MEAN | 6.7 | 39.3 | 9.2 | 7.2 | 36.0 | 32.8 | 43.0 | 43.1 | 288 |
| | MIN | 5.2 | 37.3 | 7.2 | 5.7 | 34.0 | 31.3 | 39 | 40 | 278 |
| | MAX | 8.3 | 40.8 | 11.1 | 8.4 | 38.3 | 34.5 | 47 | 45 | 300 |
| | NO | 79 | 84 | 21 | 21 | 21 | 21 | 18 | 21 | 18 |

S. Churchill.

BRUCE THOMSON

the 3000 little bentwing bats to join the 13 000 larger-bodied eastern bentwing bats. This may be the main reason that these bats have been able to extend their range into northern NSW. Up to two-thirds of the colony is male when it forms in September, but by December when the young are born there are only 2% adult males, the rest having moved away to other caves. Little is known of their reproductive patterns in the tropics although the timing of births in December is the same throughout their range.

● **NOTES** At Mt Etna the large number of bats leaving the cave each evening to forage attracts predators such as pythons, ghost bats, *Macroderma gigas*, green tree frogs and cane toads. They catch bats at the cave entrance and are most successful when the young are learning to fly.

maximum testis size in May and maximal epididymal volume in July. Copulation occurs in July and August and implantation occurs, after a delay, in September. They congregate in maternity caves with the eastern bentwing bat, *M. o. oceanensis*, from August, and the young are born in December. The warm conditions of this maternity cave (as high as 39°C) are the result of the heat generated by the dense aggregation of a large number of pregnant bats. It is clearly advantageous for

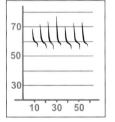

**REFERENCES** Dwyer 1965, 1968; Dwyer, in Strahan 1995; Flannery 1995a, b; Hall & Richards 1979; Reinhold 1997; Reinhold et al. 2001; B. Law (pers. com.); Richardson 1977; Vestjens & Hall 1977; Schulz 1997b, 2000.

# Southern bentwing bat

## *Miniopterus orianae bassanii* Cardinal and Christidis, 2000

● **TAXONOMY** There is further taxonomic assessment underway. This subspecies is likely to be upgraded to full species status.

● **DISTRIBUTION** S.e. SA from Robe to Naracoorte, s. to Port MacDonnell and into s.w. Vic to Heywood, Portland, Hamilton and Warrnambool. Easternmost site found at Pomborneit near Camperdown. Two known maternity sites, one at Warrnambool and the other at Naracoorte.

● **DESCRIPTION** This bat has **grey-brown to dark brown fur on its back**, slightly lighter on the belly. It has a distinctly **short muzzle and domed head**. The ears are short, rounded and roughly triangular. The three subspecies of *M. orianae* are very similar but differ genetically and form separate maternity colonies. The southern bentwing bat is usually slightly larger with a larger skull than the eastern bentwing bat and distinctly larger than the northern bentwing bat. Southern bentwing bats have a **forearm length of 45.4–49.6 mm**. The little bentwing bat, *M. australis*, is much smaller with a forearm length of 37–41 mm.

● **ROOST HABITS** Southern bentwing bats roost in caves but also use manmade constructions such as mine adits and road culverts. They form discrete populations centred on a maternity cave that is used annually for the birth and development of young. Only two maternity caves are known for the southern bentwing bat. Both males and females congregate in many thousands in a dome-shaped chamber of the cave. The large numbers of bats in close proximity produce a lot of body heat which is trapped in the dome roof. It is in these pockets of warm and humid air that the young are born and reared. The bats' combined body heat can raise the cave temperature by up to 12°C. Each population disperses to other caves from April to August. Movement between territories is unusual. Over 50 caves are known to be used as wintering sites. Winter caves need to be cold enough to allow bats to keep their body temperature low to reduce their metabolic rate.

● **HABITAT** Woodlands near large natural wetlands, river basins and agricultural areas.

● **DIET AND FORAGING** Moths make up the majority of the diet. Where there are trees this species flies high, from just above the canopy to many times canopy height. In more open areas such as grasslands, flight may be within 6 m of the ground. Flight is very fast and typically relatively level with

| | Wt | Fa | Tibia | Tail | HB | Skull-Male | Skull-Female |
|---|---|---|---|---|---|---|---|
| **MEAN** | 15.7 | 47.6 | 19.7 | 54.2 | 51.7 | 16.2-16.67 | 15.82-16.5 |
| **MIN** | 14.2 | 45.4 | 18.6 | 52 | 52 | | |
| **MAX** | 18.5 | 49.6 | 20.7 | 58 | 58 | | |
| **NO** | 33 | 33 | 29 | 20 | 20 | | |

MEASUREMENTS

B. Appleton; Cardinal & Christidis 2000; Reardon & Lumsden, in Van Dyck & Strahan 2008.

TERRY REARDON

swift shallow dives. They can forage long distances from the roost site.

● **REPRODUCTION** In late August bats commence their annual migration to one of only two maternity caves, using transition caves along the way. Almost the entire population (both males and females) moves into the caves by October. Births occur from late October to late November at Naracoorte and early December at Warrnambool. After 4–5 weeks the young are fully furred and capable of flight. They are weaned when 3 months old and at the end of April they disperse. Females do not become sexually mature until their second year.

● **NOTES** The longevity record for an Australian bat is from a pregnant female southern bentwing bat that was banded as an adult and recaptured 22 years later (she was still healthy and had recently given birth!). These bats commonly carry large numbers of small orange bat-flies (*Streblidae*) in their fur and on their wings.

● **ECHOLOCATION** Calls for the three subspecies of *M. orianae* differ from each other. The southern bentwing bat, *M. o. bassanii*, has a mean frequency of 47.7 kHz.

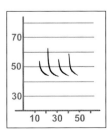

**REFERENCES** B. Appleton (pers. com.); Baudinette et al. 2000; Cardinal & Christidis 2000; Codd et al. 2003; Conole 2000; Duncan et al. 1999; Dwyer 1963, 1966c; Grant (unpubl.); Reardon & Lumsden, in Van Dyck & Strahan 2008; Richardson 1977.

# Eastern bentwing bat
## *Miniopterus orianae oceanensis* Maeda, 1982

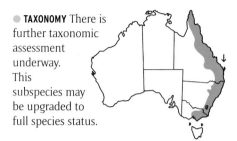

● **TAXONOMY** There is further taxonomic assessment underway. This subspecies may be upgraded to full species status.

● **DISTRIBUTION** E. coast of Australia from Cape York, n. Qld, to Castlemaine, Vic, predominantly e. of Great Dividing Range.

● **DESCRIPTION** This bat has **dark reddish brown to dark brown fur on its back**, slightly lighter on its belly. A red colour form is known from Qld. It has a distinctly **short muzzle and domed head**. The ears are short, rounded and roughly triangular. The three subspecies of *M. orianae* are very similar but differ genetically and form separate maternity colonies. The eastern bentwing bat is slightly smaller with a smaller skull than the southern bentwing bat and larger than the northern bentwing bat. Eastern bentwing bats have a forearm length of 45.2–50.0 mm. The little bentwing bat, *M. australis*, is much smaller with a forearm length of 37–41 mm.

● **ROOST HABITS** Eastern bentwing bats are cave dwellers but also use man-made constructions such as abandoned mines and road culverts. Populations are centred on a maternity cave that is used annually for the birth and development of young. Each population disperses to other caves during the year but only within its own territorial range. Movement between territories is unusual, although one bat is recorded to have moved 1300 km. In the southern Australian winter these bats select hibernation caves that are cold enough to keep their body temperature low, to reduce their metabolic rate and prolong fat reserves built up during the summer. In the tropical 'winter' they remain active and forage nightly, selecting roost caves of moderate temperatures. I have found several colonies of over 1000 bats in northern Cape York Peninsula during this time.

● **HABITAT** Rainforest, wet and dry sclerophyll forest, monsoon forest, open woodland, *Melaleuca* forests and open grasslands.

● **DIET AND FORAGING** At Richmond Range in NSW moths were found to be the dominant prey item with a few flies, cockroaches and beetles. In forested areas this species flies high, from just above the canopy to many times canopy height. In more open areas such as grasslands, flight may be within a few metres of the ground. Flight is very fast and typically relatively level with swift shallow dives. They can forage long distances from the roost site and several marked females have travelled up to 65 km in one night.

| | Wt | Fa | Ear | 3 met | Tail | HB | WS | Skull-Male | Skull-Female |
|---|---|---|---|---|---|---|---|---|---|
| MEAN | 14.1 | 47.9 | 10.7 | 44.3 | 52.7 | 55.9 | 341.2 | 15.62-16.55 | 15.1-16.35 |
| MIN | 10.6 | 45.2 | 9.3 | 43.2 | 47 | 50 | 330 | | |
| MAX | 20.0 | 50.0 | 13.5 | 45.7 | 57.4 | 65.3 | 350 | | |
| NO | 120 | 141 | 16 | 16 | 9 | 16 | 9 | | |

Cardinal & Christidis 2000; S. Churchill; M. Pennay.

LINDY LUMSDEN

The mothers then leave the cave to disperse to their winter roosts in March. A few weeks later there is a mass exodus of juveniles and the maternity colony is deserted by April. In tropical areas at latitude 22°S, copulation occurs in September and pregnancy proceeds to birth of the single young in December with no delay in implantation. On Cape York Peninsula (latitude 15°S) a maternity colony of over 2000 bats has been recorded in late February to March. The young had been born in mid to late January, and adult males roosted with the adult females and clusters of young in the twilight area of two small sea caves. Neither females nor males become sexually mature in their first year.

**REFERENCES** Cardinal & Christidis 2000; Coles & Lumsden 1993; Conole 2000; Duncan et al. 1999; Dwyer 1963, 1965, 1966c; Dwyer, in Strahan 1995; Parnaby 1996; Purchase 1982; Reinhold 1997; Richardson 1977; Schulz 2000a.

● **REPRODUCTION** Spermatogenesis starts in late November and the testes reach maximum development in April. In temperate regions mating takes place during May to June and conception occurs but implantation is delayed until late August. Up to 100 000 adult females from the surrounding area congregate in October into maternity colonies and give birth to their single young in December to mid January. The young are left in crèches while the mother forages. They can fly by 7 weeks and reach adult size and are weaned by 10 weeks.

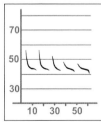

# Northern bentwing bat
## *Miniopterus orianae orianae* Thomas, 1922

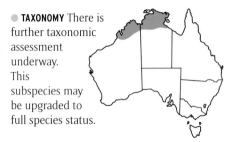

● **TAXONOMY** There is further taxonomic assessment underway. This subspecies may be upgraded to full species status.

● **DISTRIBUTION** N. Australia from Kimberley through Top End.

● **DESCRIPTION** This bat has **dark brown fur on its back**, slightly lighter on the belly. It has a distinctly **short muzzle and domed head**. The ears are short, rounded and roughly triangular. The three subspecies of *M. orianae* are very similar but differ genetically and form separate maternity colonies. The northern bentwing bat is smaller than the southern and eastern bentwing bats. Northern bentwing bats have a forearm length of 42.1–49.7 mm. The little bentwing bat, *M. australis*, is much smaller with a forearm length of 37–41 mm.

● **ROOST HABITS** Northern bentwing bats roost in a variety of caves and mines from shallow sandstone overhangs to complex limestone labyrinths, abandoned mines, road culverts and bridges as well as buildings. From April to August in the tropical 'winter' bats do not hibernate; instead they remain active and forage nightly, selecting roost caves of moderate temperatures (26.5°C) and high humidity (95%). This choice of roost microclimate enables them to maintain water balance at minimum metabolic cost. They usually roost clinging to the walls in large clusters in close contact with each other.

● **HABITAT** Rainforest, wet and dry sclerophyll forest, monsoon forest, mangroves, open woodland, *Melaleuca* forests and open grasslands.

● **DIET AND FORAGING** Moths are the major dietary item. In the Kimberley, analysis showed their stomachs also contained grasshoppers; in the Top End they also eat leaf-hoppers, ants, occasional beetles, flies and spiders. In forested areas this species flies high, from just above the canopy to many times canopy height. In more open areas, such as grasslands and over water, they fly lower, within a couple of metres of the ground. Flight is very fast and typically relatively level with swift shallow dives. Flight speeds of 20–32 km/hr have been recorded. When exiting from a cave their flight is sharply zigzagged, presumably to reduce predation. They are often predated upon by ghost bats, *Macroderma gigas*, as they exit the cave.

● **REPRODUCTION** Females are pregnant in October and November with the single

| | Wt | Fa | Ear | 3 met | Tail | HB | WS | Skull-Male | Skull-Female |
|---|---|---|---|---|---|---|---|---|---|
| MEAN | 10.8 | 44.9 | 9.3 | 41.3 | 49 | 52.2 | 324.3 | 14.81 | 14.4 |
| MIN | 8.6 | 42.1 | 7.2 | 39.6 | 43 | 47 | 313 | | |
| MAX | 14.1 | 49.7 | 11.4 | 42.8 | 56 | 63 | 332 | | |
| NO | 99 | 109 | 16 | 16 | 10 | 16 | 10 | | |

Cardinal & Christidis (2000); S. Churchill.

LINDY LUMSDEN

young born in early December. By March the young are adult size and hard to tell from adults. At Tolmer Falls, in the Top End, bats move from their regular dry season roosts in September and do not return until the following April. A maternity colony of over 4000 bats roosts in an old grain silo inside a shed near Darwin during the wet season. The bats cluster on the walls and domed ceiling of the silo with the young. The conditions in the steel silo were hot and humid (30°C and 80% relative humidity), and both adult males and females use the roost.

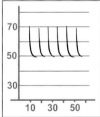

**REFERENCES** Baudinette et al. 2000; Bullen & McKenzie 2002; Cardinal & Christidis 2000; Churchill 1991; Conole 2000; Duncan et al. 1999; Dwyer, in Strahan 1995; Milne & Burwell (unpubl.); Reinhold 1997; Richardson 1977.

# Freetail Bats
## Family MOLOSSIDAE: Key to Species

The tail membrane is relatively narrow, only partially enclosing the stout tail that extends a considerable distance beyond the rear edge of the membrane. The legs are short and strong, and the toes are hairy, glandular and carry long bristles. The flight membranes are thick and leathery. The muzzle is broad, sharply cut off at the front and the lips are often wrinkled. They have no nose-leaf. The ears are thick, and a small tragus is present.

**1a** Forearm length greater than 46 mm; ears large and rounded; upper lip heavily wrinkled. → **2**

PAUL BARDEN

**1b** Forearm length less than 41 mm; ears triangular; upper lip not heavily wrinkled. → **3**

BRUCE THOMSON

**2a** Throat pouch present; white stripe of fur along the junction of the belly and the wings; ears not joined above head; forearm length averages 60.6 mm (57.2–64.5 mm).
→ *Austronomus australis* (page 190)

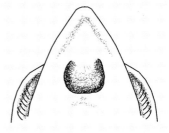

**2b** Throat pouch absent; fur uniform dark brown, no white stripe; ears joined above head by a band of skin across the forehead; forearm length averages 49.2 mm (46.5–51.5 mm).
→ *Chaerephon jobensis* (page 192)

**3a** Size larger; forearm length usually greater than 36 mm. → **4**

**3b** Size smaller; forearm length usually less than 36 mm. → **5**

**4a** Heavy thickset species, weight greater than 11.0 g (12–18 g); the upper first premolar is vestigial; widespread in northern Australia; fur shorter, brown to grey; forearm length averages 38.7 mm (37.4–40.5 mm); ears rounded at tip, thick and leathery, not translucent.
→ *Mormopterus beccarii* (page 195)

**4b** Lighter build, weight less than 11.0 g (6.8–10.5 g); the upper first premolar is well developed; restricted to coastal NSW and southern Qld; fur longer, dark brown to reddish brown; forearm length averages 37.3 mm (36.0–38.3 mm); ears pointed.
→ *Micronomus norfolkensis* (page 193)

**5a** Very small build, weight less than 6.0 g; the muzzle is narrow; OCW less than 3.7 mm; forearm length 31.9–35.3 mm; distinctive bristles on face.
→ *Mormopterus* **species 6** (page 203)

**5b** Larger build, weight greater than 6.0 g; muzzle broader, OCW greater than 3.7 mm; no bristles on face.     → **6**

MICHAEL PENNAY

**6a** Distribution eastern Australia; penis short, less than 5 mm; fur a light to rich brown colour; ears thin and translucent.
→ *Mormopterus ridei* (page 198)

**6b** Coastal WA from Derby to Exmouth and coastal NT and Gulf of Carpentaria; restricted to mangrove forests or adjacent areas.
→ *Mormopterus cobourgiana* (page 197)

**6c** Inland Australia; penis short, less than 5 mm long; fur light grey-brown with pale bases to hairs.
→ *Mormopterus* **species 3** (page 200)

**6d** South-western and south-eastern Australia; penis long, greater than 9 mm; fur longer, shaggier and slightly darker.
→ *Mormopterus* **species 4** (page 201)

# White-striped freetail bat
## *Austronomus australis* (Gray, 1838)

● **TAXONOMY** A revision of Australian molossids by Terry Reardon has found that *Nyctinomus* is an invalid name and *Tadarida* does not occur in Australia. He has reinstated the genus name *Austronomus* for this species.

● **DISTRIBUTION** S. Australia, except Tas, primarily s. of Tropic of Capricorn. Migrates seasonally. From November to February range restricted to s. of about 30°S; from April to September it is found up to 1200 km further n. and predominantly n. of 30°S. March and October are migration months. Endemic to Australia.

● **DESCRIPTION** A large distinctive species. Dark brown to black fur with two distinctive bright white stripes along the sides of the belly and onto the wings. This varies, with some individuals having all black chests and some having large patches of white fur on the chest. The ears are large and rounded but not joined across the top of the head. A prominent throat pouch is present in both sexes. The lips are thick with many short vertical wrinkles. The baculum is trifid.

● **ROOST HABITS** White-striped freetail bats are tree dwellers. They roost either solitarily or in groups of up to 25, most commonly less than ten. Maternity colonies are larger with up to 300 individuals. They roost in hollows in old eucalypt trees with large trunk cavities and multiple entrances, usually hollow branches. They have been observed sharing roosts with common brushtail possums, but rarely with other bats. White-striped freetail bats make loud chirping audible calls (which can be heard up to 5 m away) from the late afternoon until the colony leaves the roost 30–40 minutes after sunset. These social roost calls are distinctly different from the audible echolocation calls produced during flight. If ambient light is sufficient they do not echolocate but leave the roost relying on vision. They launch by dropping about 4 m to gain speed before circling slowly upwards using search calls.

● **HABITAT** Urban areas, forests, woodland, shrubland, open agricultural landscapes with scattered stands of trees, grasslands and deserts, including the Nullarbor. Migration appears to be driven by the average minimum temperature of an area. Temperatures of less than 21°C are needed for these bats to dissipate the heat they generate by flying. In summer the bats move south to cooler areas; they also tend to forage later in the night along the northern parts of their range.

| MEASUREMENTS | | Wt | Fa | Ear | Tibia | 3 met | Tail | Body |
|---|---|---|---|---|---|---|---|---|
| | MEAN | 37.6 | 60.6 | 25.9 | 21.6 | 35.1 | 46.2 | 80.1 |
| | MIN | 30.5 | 57.2 | 22.9 | 20.4 | 33.2 | 39.1 | 75.2 |
| | MAX | 47.5 | 64.5 | 27.7 | 23.7 | 36.9 | 52 | 86.5 |
| | NO | 172 | 180 | 9 | 9 | 9 | 9 | 9 |

Bullen & McKenzie 2002; S. Churchill; L. Lumsden; M. Pennay; M. Rhodes.

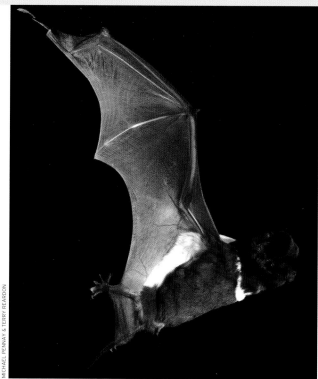

MICHAEL PENNAY & TERRY REARDON

● **REPRODUCTION**
Copulation, ovulation
and fertilisation occur in
late August. The single
young is born between
mid December and late
January. The female
reproductive tract is
asymmetrical and only
the right uterine horn
and ovary are functional.
Most young are weaned
by May and the females
are sexually mature by
August. The timing of
reproduction appears to
be very similar
throughout their range.

● **NOTES** This bat has a
distinctive audible,
constant frequency
search mode
echolocation call ranging
from 11–13 kHz. This

● **DIET AND FORAGING** They are a fast-flying
species capable of speeds of up to 61 km/h.
They are not designed for manoeuvrability
and intercept their prey 50 m or more above
the ground, catching large numbers of
moths, beetles and grasshoppers. Their diet
also includes large numbers of ants and non-
flying beetles which they presumably catch
on the ground. They are surprisingly agile on
the ground and have an unusual gait,
scurrying along with their thumbs and hind
feet, their wings folded away to free the
forearms and the tail membrane retracted
along the tail to free the hind legs. It is
difficult to launch themselves from the
ground, and they prefer to climb anything
available to gain height first. They may leave
their roosts before full dark and forage for
several hours even on cool and moonlit
nights. They are known to become torpid but
not to hibernate.

frequency range is lower than any other bat
call in Australia. The search mode call is
powerful, audible to humans and carries for
hundreds of metres so its presence or
absence is very obvious. It can be heard

distinctly at night as
a regular metallic
ting...... ting......
ting...... ting.

REFERENCES Bullen &
McKenzie 2002b, 2004,
2005; Hall & Richards 1972;
Kitchener & Hudson 1982;
Kristo 1987; Lumsden et al.
1994; Lumsden 1999;
McKenzie & Bullen 2003; Menkhorst 1995; Milne & Nash
2003; Reardon & Flavel 1991; Reardon 1999; M. Rhodes (pers.
com.); Rhodes 2001; Rhodes et al. 2005; Rhodes & Wardell-
Johnson 2006; Vestjens & Hall 1977.

# Northern freetail bat

## *Chaerephon jobensis* (Miller, 1902)

● **DISTRIBUTION** N. Australia, from Pilbara to Kimberley, across Top End, through n. Qld. Extralimital distribution in Indonesia and New Guinea.

● **DESCRIPTION** The **fur on the back is short and a rich dark reddish brown to smoky black**. The fur on the **belly is a lighter grey-brown**. There is no white stripe. The **lips are thick and fleshy with** large numbers of **vertical wrinkles. The ears are large, round and joined across the top of the head by a low band of skin.** The skull is sinuate in profile with a sagittal crest; there is **no throat pouch in either sex.** The third molar is slightly reduced. There is no baculum.

● **ROOST HABITS** Northern freetail bats usually roost in tree hollows in colonies of ten to 15, but they have also been found in caves and buildings in colonies of up to 300. An interesting roost was found in cracks in the wooden pylons of Derby Jetty, in the Kimberley. The bats were discovered because during the day their social calls could be heard. Up to 40 roosts were found with colonies of mostly one to three, but up to seven, bats. The cracks were narrow, about 2–3 cm wide, but quite long and the roosts were vertical, hanging directly over the water. The bats left the roosts in the evening by dropping from the bridge towards the water up to 10 m below and making their way to shore under the bridge. Recently a large colony was found in a horizontal split in a sandstone cliff in the Kimberley. The bats were calling during the day, making loud chirping sounds that could be heard 30 m away. They shared the roost with the northern bentwing bat, *Miniopterus o. orianae*. In the Top End a small colony roosting in a large tree hollow was found sharing its roost with several yellow-bellied sheathtail bats, *Saccolaimus flaviventris*.

PAUL BARDEN

| | | Wt | Fa | Ear | 3 met | 5 met | Tail | HB | WS |
|---|---|---|---|---|---|---|---|---|---|
| **MEASUREMENTS** | MEAN | 20.4 | 49.2 | 19.5 | 49.1 | 29.4 | 34.2 | 61.2 | 355 |
| | MIN | 16.0 | 46.5 | 16.2 | 42.5 | 27.5 | 32.0 | 58.0 | 337 |
| | MAX | 28.0 | 51.5 | 21.7 | 51.3 | 31.4 | 37.0 | 65.0 | 375 |
| | NO | 26 | 26 | 10 | 10 | 10 | 10 | 10 | 10 |

S. Churchill.

**HABITAT** Mangroves, monsoon forests, paperbark-lined creeks, tall open forest, savannah, riverine forest, open *Bauhinia* shrubland, rocky hillsides, eucalypt woodlands, monsoon thickets and frequently along the narrow bands of river gums that fringe the dry beds of ephemeral river systems. They also forage over cane fields and other croplands in irrigated farmland.

**DIET AND FORAGING** They hunt insects in the unobstructed air-spaces from just above to well above the canopy of woodland and other forested habitat, along forest edges as well as over grasslands and above the ground in large clearings. When foraging, their flight is fast to very fast with an average speed of 24 km/h, and they use a straight or gently curved flight rather than tight or abrupt turns. They travel widely from roosts to foraging areas, and eat large numbers of cockroaches, moths, beetles and crickets with smaller numbers of bugs, ants, mosquitoes, lacewings, sawflies and earwigs.

**REPRODUCTION** Pregnant females have been caught in October and November and lactating females in November and March.

Young have been found in colonies in December and January. Volant suckling young have been caught in early March. A volant (13-g) juvenile was caught in mid August as it left its cave roost in the Kimberley.

**NOTES** They are very placid when captured in mist nets, unlike the small molossids that tend to struggle. I have often caught them over water in mist nets. Their echolocation calls have a characteristic frequency of 19.8 kHz (16.1–23.6 kHz). This is within the range of human hearing and they are often heard foraging for insects around streetlights. They usually fly in pairs and this tends to produce paired echolocation calls at alternating frequencies.

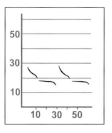

**REFERENCES** Begg & McKean 1982; de Lestang 1929; Ingleby & Colgan 2003; Flannery 1995a, b; Kitchener et al. 1981; Lumsden et al. 1993, 2005; D. Milne (pers. com.); Milne & Burwell (unpubl.); McKenzie & Rolfe 1986; McKenzie et al. 2002; J. Reside (pers. com.); Richards, in Strahan 1995.

# East-coast freetail bat
## *Micronomus norfolkensis* (Gray, 1839)

**TAXONOMY** A taxonomic revision of Australian molossids by Terry Reardon has shown that the genus *Mormopterus* does not occur in Australia. He has reinstated the generic name *Micronomus* (Troughton 1944) for this species.

**DISTRIBUTION** E. coast of NSW from s. of Sydney into s.e. Qld near Brisbane, e. of Great Dividing Range. Not known from Norfolk Is;

the original specimen location was in error and was most likely collected near Sydney. Endemic to Australia.

GLENN HOYE

● **DESCRIPTION** The **fur is dark brown to reddish brown on the back, slightly lighter on belly**, with pale bases to the hairs. The ears are triangular, not joined together and shorter than the head. The **forearm length is 36–38.3 mm with a weight of 6.8–10.5 g**. There is no throat pouch (previous reports are incorrect). The skull is sinuate in profile with the first upper premolar well developed and the first molar with a characteristically zigzagged edge. Both males and females possess a **long finger-like genital projection**. The baculum is small and arrow-shaped. Beccari's freetail bat, *Mormopterus beccarii*, has shorter fur and a heavier build (12–18 g). The eastern freetail bat, *Mormopterus ridei*, usually has a shorter forearm (30.6–34.5 mm). It differs from both *M. ridei* and the

southern freetail bat, *Mormopterus* species 4, by its more upright ears and less robust head and body. The bristle-faced freetail bat, *Mormopterus* species 6, is less robust, weighing less than 6.0 g.

● **ROOST HABITS** They roost in tree hollows, usually in hollow spouts of large mature trees, but there are also several records from buildings. Two males were collected from the wall cavity of a house, a roost they shared with eastern horseshoe bats, *Rhinolophus megaphyllus*, and a broad-nosed bat, *Scotorepens* sp. Another was found roosting in the roof of a hut with an eastern broad-nosed bat, *Scotorepens orion*, and several Gould's wattled bats, *Chalinolobus gouldii*. They have been collected from under the metal cap on the top of telegraph poles and under exfoliating bark on trees. They will also roost in bat boxes, and a colony in NSW has used the same boxes for over 5 years.

● **HABITAT** Most records are from dry eucalypt forest and woodland on the coastal side of the Great Dividing Range. Usually only solitary bats are captured, but one group was caught flying low over a rocky river in rainforest and wet sclerophyll forest. They show a preference for open spaces in woodland or forest, and are more active in

| | | Wt | Fa | Ear | Tibia | 3 met | Tail | HB |
|---|---|---|---|---|---|---|---|---|
| MEASUREMENTS | MEAN | 7.8 | 37.3 | 14.5 | 12.0 | 27.8 | 34.1 | 49.2 |
| | MIN | 6.8 | 36.0 | 12.7 | 11.0 | 27.2 | 30.9 | 47.0 |
| | MAX | 10.5 | 38.3 | 16.5 | 14.0 | 28.6 | 36.3 | 53.8 |
| | NO | 5 | 8 | 6 | 5 | 5 | 6 | 5 |

S. Churchill; M. Pennay.

the upper slopes of forest areas rather than in riparian zones. They forage more commonly over larger rather than small waterways.

● **DIET** They forage in openings and gaps in the forest usually within a few kilometres of their roost but one female was observed foraging up to 6 km away. They are more active on upper slopes where flyways are large than along creeks. Their diet has not been studied.

● **REPRODUCTION** Females give birth in late November or early December. Lactation lasts until late January. Juveniles are flying by late January.

REFERENCES Allison 1989; Allison & Hoye, in Strahan (1995); Dobson (1876); Hall & Richards (1979); G. Hoye (pers. com.); Hoye et al., in Van Dyck & Strahan 2008; Law et al. 2000; Lloyd et al. 2006; T. Reardon (pers. com.); A. Young (pers. com.).

# Beccari's freetail bat

## *Mormopterus beccarii* (Peters, 1881)

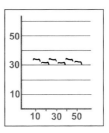

● **TAXONOMY** A taxonomic revision of Australian molossids by Terry Reardon has shown that the genus *Mormopterus* does not occur in Australia. He is in the process of describing a new genus for the Australian species.

● **DISTRIBUTION** Widely distributed across n. Australia from WA to Qld, extending s. to n.e. corner of NSW. Extralimital distribution in Indonesia and New Guinea.

● **DESCRIPTION** A thick, muscular and **robust body shape. The fur is short and bicoloured.** On the **back, the bases of the hairs are pale** and the **tips darker, ranging from dark brown to grey.** The fur is **distinctly paler on the belly.** The skin on the face, ears and wings is brown to dark grey. The ears are triangular, rounded at the tip and not joined together. This is the **largest**

species of *Mormopterus*, **based on weight (12–18 g)**, which distinguishes it from all other species. The **forearm length is 38.7 mm (37.4–40.5 mm)**, which overlaps slightly with the inland freetail bat, *Mormopterus* species 3 (forearm length 34.2 mm; 32.2–37.9 mm; weight 6.2–11.3 g). The skull is dorsoventrally flattened and the **first upper premolar is minute.**

● **ROOST HABITS** Beccari's freetail bats roost commonly in tree hollows but have also been found in caves in New Guinea. They often roost in the roofs of houses in Qld. The only confirmed record in NSW is of a colony found in the roof of a house in Murwillumbah. Colonies of up to 50 have been recorded. Several of these bats were found roosting in an old horse blanket in a shed and another one was under the topping cap of a telegraph pole. A survey near Kununurra in the Kimberley found this species to be widespread in low numbers in all natural habitats but it was not detected in agricultural areas.

● **HABITAT** Rainforest, river flood plains, tall open forest, savannah woodlands, arid shrublands and grasslands. They are commonly caught along water courses, lined with river red gums, in arid areas.

● **DIET AND FORAGING** Their diet is predominantly aerial moths and beetles that they capture above the canopy, but they also eat bugs, lacewings, flies and grasshoppers. In the Top End stomachs were found to contain predominantly flightless ants (54%). The presence of flightless insects in its diet suggests that it captures some prey by scurrying on the ground. They are certainly very agile on the ground and can run surprisingly fast. They have short, narrow, pointed wings and fly with very rapid wing beats. Flight is fast but not very manoeuvrable so they prefer to forage in areas relatively free of obstructions above the canopy, along water courses and over water where they are often caught in mist nets. Flight speeds of 28 km/h have been reported. They favour semi-open conditions and when foraging fly fast and straight with gentle curves but no tight or abrupt turns. Horizontal turns are frequent when foraging along a canopy edge.

BRUCE THOMSON

● **NOTES** A strong species that is impatient in a mist net. They can become quite horribly tangled and take considerable time to extract. They also have the habit of screaming loudly at a nerve-racking frequency during these proceedings, further trying one's patience. Fortunately they are usually reluctant to bite. Their screams often attract other individuals into the net, which can be a mixed blessing.

● **REPRODUCTION** They give birth to a single young during the summer wet season. Females in advanced pregnancy have been recorded in early October to January and lactating females from November to January. Males with scrotal testes have been captured in November.

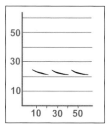

REFERENCES Adams et al. 1988; Flannery 1995a; Lumsden et al. 2005; McKenzie, in Strahan 1995; McKenzie et al. 2002; Milne & Burwell (unpubl.); T. Reardon (pers. com.); Vestjens & Hall 1977; A. Young (pers. com.).

| MEASUREMENTS | | Wt | Fa | Ear | 3 met | 5 met | Tail | HB | WS |
|---|---|---|---|---|---|---|---|---|---|
| | MEAN | 14.6 | 38.7 | 14.9 | 40.6 | 26.9 | 30 | 60.7 | 285 |
| | MIN | 12.0 | 37.4 | 11.6 | 38.5 | 26.0 | 26 | 54 | 278 |
| | MAX | 18.0 | 40.5 | 16.8 | 41.5 | 28.4 | 37 | 67.5 | 290 |
| | NO | 16 | 22 | 8 | 9 | 8 | 12 | 12 | 7 |

S. Churchill.

# Mangrove freetail bat

## *Mormopterus cobourgiana* (Johnson, 1959)

● **TAXONOMY** A taxonomic revision of Australian molossids by Terry Reardon has shown that the genus *Mormopterus* does not occur in Australia. He is in the process of describing a new genus for the Australian species. This species was previously regarded as *Mormopterus loriae cobourgiana* and *Mormopterus* species 5 (Population U and V) in Adams et al. 1988.

● **DISTRIBUTION** WA coastal areas from Exmouth Gulf to Broome, not recorded in Kimberley, but present along the n. and e. coast of NT and just reaching Qld border in Gulf of Carpentaria. Also occur on Tiwi Is near Darwin. Endemic to Australia.

● **DESCRIPTION** The fur on the head and back is brown to grey-brown and the belly is a distinctly paler greyish lemon to greyish buff, with lemon on the throat and chin. Hairs are white at the base. Skin of the muzzle and wings is dark brown. They are smaller than Beccari's freetail bat, *M. beccarii*, which has a forearm length of more than 37 mm.

● **ROOST HABITS** Mangrove freetail bats have been found roosting in small spouts and crevices in dead upper branches of the grey mangrove *Avicennia marina*. They emerge early and swarms of up to 100 individuals may be seen flying above the mangrove canopy soon after sunset, later dispersing to forage alone or in pairs.

● **HABITAT** They are primarily restricted to mangrove forests, adjacent areas of monsoon forest along larger waterways, and semi-deciduous vine thickets.

● **DIET AND FORAGING** The wings are short, narrow and pointed and the flight is fast, direct and agile. They prey upon flying

| | Wt | Fa | Tibia | Tail | HB |
|---|---|---|---|---|---|
| **MEAN** | 7.3 | 34.0 | 11.4 | 33.0 | 50.5 |
| **MIN** | 6.2 | 32.5 | 11.3 | 30.0 | 47.0 |
| **MAX** | 10.3 | 35.0 | 11.4 | 36.0 | 55.0 |

MEASUREMENTS

McKenzie, in Strahan 1995; D. Milne.

insects above and beside the forest canopy. They can be seen flying through gaps in the forest formed by roads or creeks and providing unobstructed corridors. Like other molossid species they are agile on the ground. In the Top End they were found to eat large numbers of beetles (74%), wingless ants (22%) and leaf-hoppers. A specimen collected in the NT was taken from a group of about ten bats seen flying about a meadow-like opening in the monsoon forest shortly after sunset. The group dispersed soon after.

● **REPRODUCTION** They give birth to a single young during the summer wet season and most females are still lactating in March.

Juveniles have been captured in mist nets from March to May and have body weights of 3.7–5.3 g. By early June the juveniles can no longer be distinguished, as most individuals weigh more than 7 g.

● **NOTES** They emerge at dusk and can be captured at first dark in mist nets set across shadowed glades at the edge of a forest or in mangroves.

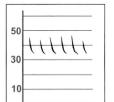

REFERENCES Adams et al. 1988; McKenzie, in Strahan 1995; D Milne (pers. com.); Milne et al. 2006; Milne & Burwell (unpubl.).

# Eastern freetail bat
## *Mormopterus ridei* (Felten 1964)

● **TAXONOMY** A taxonomic revision of Australian molossids by Terry Reardon has shown that the genus *Mormopterus* does not occur in Australia. He is in the process of describing a new genus for the Australian species. This species combines bats previously referred to as the little northern freetail bat, *Mormopterus* species 5 (S,T), as well as the eastern freetail bat, *Mormopterus* species 2 of Adams et al. 1988.

● **DISTRIBUTION** E. Australia from n. Cape York Peninsula, Qld, to Geelong, Vic. Mainly along and e. of Great Dividing Range, extending

inland in s. Qld. Found throughout e. half of Vic. Endemic to Australia.

● **DESCRIPTION** A **medium-sized species** with a forearm length of 30.6–34.5 mm. The **fur on the back is usually a rich brown colour with a light creamy brown base to the hairs. The belly fur is only slightly paler** than the back. The **skin of the face, ears and wings is dark grey.**

| | | Wt | Fa | Ear | Tibia | 3 met | Tail | HB | Wing | OCW | Penis |
|---|---|---|---|---|---|---|---|---|---|---|---|
| MEASUREMENTS | MEAN | 9.0 | 33.0 | 10.2 | 7.0 | 34.2 | 26.9 | 47.7 | 246 | 4.2 | 3.4 |
| | MIN | 6.3 | 30.6 | 8.0 | 4.0 | 32.6 | 18.1 | 42.0 | 235 | 3.6 | 2.6 |
| | MAX | 11.2 | 34.5 | 15.0 | 12.9 | 36.3 | 31.0 | 55.0 | 256 | 4.6 | 4.5 |
| | NO | 72 | 84 | 36 | 3 | 11 | 36 | 11 | 11 | 32 | 13 |

S. Churchill; L. Lumsden; M. Pennay; A. Reside; M. Venz.

LINDY LUMSDEN

woodland of *Eucalyptus microcarpa* and *E. crebra* with sparse sub-canopy of *Allocasuarina luehmannii* and *Melaleuca decora*.

● **DIET AND FORAGING** In Vic the diet was found to include a large proportion of bugs (60%), flies (18%) and beetles (15%), and a few moths, ants and occasional spiders. The bats fly predominantly in the spaces between trees. In Vic they have a higher level of activity in riparian habitats than the southern freetail bat, *Mormopterus* species 4.

The **fur tends to be longer, shaggier and generally much darker** than the inland freetail bat. Southern freetail bats differ in having a much longer penis (over 9 mm), but are otherwise identical. Beccari's freetail bat, *M. beccarii*, and the east-coast freetail bat, *Micronomus norfolkensis*, have longer forearms, over 36.0 mm. Bristle-faced freetail bats, *Mormopterus* species 6, are of a lighter build, weighing less than 6.0 g.

● **ROOST HABITS** Eastern freetail bats roost mainly in tree hollows but will also roost under bark, in buildings and cracks in posts. Colonies of several hundred have been recorded. They have been reported to share roosts with Gould's wattled bats, *Chalinolobus gouldii*, and the eastern broad-nosed bat, *Scotorepens orion*.

● **HABITAT** Rainforest, *Melaleuca* forest, monsoon forest, tall open forest, river red gum and yellow box woodlands, riparian open forest and dry sclerophyll forest. Spotted gum/grey gum/ironbark woodland, inland dry sclerophyll forest of *Corymbia citriodora*, open forest of *C. citriodora* and ironbark with scattered *Callitris*, open

● **REPRODUCTION** A group of 15 females captured in late November in north Qld were either heavily pregnant or lactating. Several lactating females had stretch marks around the vagina, indicating they had given birth very recently, but none of the females was carrying their single, newborn young. Lactation occurs until mid to late January and free-flying young have been caught at this time. Post-lactating females have been caught in late March. In Vic considerably more females are trapped than males.

**REFERENCES** Adams et al. 1988; Lumsden & Bennett 2005; Lumsden & Wainer (pers. com.); McKenzie (pers. com.); Menkhorst 1995; A. Reside (pers. com.); Reside 2004; M. Venz (pers. com.).

# Inland freetail bat

## *Mormopterus* **species 3** (undescribed)

● **TAXONOMY** A taxonomic revision of Australian molossids by Terry Reardon has shown that the genus *Mormopterus* does not occur in Australia. He is in the process of describing a new genus for the Australian species. Previously referred to as *Mormopterus planiceps* (small penis form) and *Mormopterus* species 3 in Adams et al. 1988.

● **DISTRIBUTION** Inland Australia s. of Tropic of Capricorn. Inland s.w. WA to coast at Eyre Peninsula, SA, and into w. NSW and s.w. Qld. Restricted to arid and semi-arid areas. Endemic to Australia.

● **DESCRIPTION** The **fur on the back is bicoloured, with a creamy white base** and **light grey to light grey-brown tips**. The fur on the belly is notably paler, with creamy bases and very light brown tips. The skin on the ears, muzzle and wings is pink to pale grey. **Males have a short penis (less than 5 mm)**. The ears are triangular and not joined across the top of the head. The upper lip overhangs the lower lip and bears a fringe of stiff hairs. There is considerable variation in size in this species with the largest individuals occurring in central Australia. Both the southern freetail bat, *Mormopterus* species 4, and the eastern freetail bat, *M. ridei*, tend to have longer, darker and more shaggy fur. Southern freetail bats have a distinctly larger penis (over 9 mm). Beccari's freetail bat, *M. beccarii*, is heavier (12–18 g). The bristle-faced freetail bat, *Mormopterus* species 6, is lighter, weighing less than 6.0 g.

● **ROOST HABITS** Their flat head and body enable them to squeeze into small roost sites such as cracks and fissures in trees and posts, between roof beams and corrugated iron roofs, and in lengths of water pipe. They most often roost in tree hollows, preferring roosts with very small entrances. Colonies are usually small, less than ten. They often roost in association with the inland broad-nosed bat, *Scotorepens balstoni*. Colonies usually have several roosts in an area and move between them every few days.

● **HABITAT** They are common in the more arid parts of Australia, generally associated with open woodland or shrubland and are often caught along water courses lined with river red gums in inland areas. They live in cypress pine woodlands, mallee, myall and mulga woodlands, chenopod shrublands and grasslands. They tend to be more common in areas of taller vegetation associated with creeklines and drainage areas.

● **DIET AND FORAGING** Stomach contents have been found to include flies, and winged and

| | | Wt | Fa | Ear | Tibia | 3 met | Tail | HB | OCW | WS |
|---|---|---|---|---|---|---|---|---|---|---|
| MEASUREMENTS | MEAN | 9.1 | 34.2 | 13.2 | 11.8 | 32.5 | 30.6 | 51.6 | 4.3 | 247.0 |
| | MIN | 6.9 | 32.2 | 12.7 | 10.9 | 29.9 | 24.0 | 45 | 4.3 | - |
| | MAX | 11.3 | 37.9 | 13.9 | 12.9 | 36.2 | 34.4 | 56.8 | 4.3 | - |
| | NO | 55 | 95 | 7 | 10 | 7 | 19 | 16 | 2 | 1 |

S. Churchill; L. Lumsden; M. Pennay; M. Venz; A. Young.

● **REPRODUCTION** The single young are born in November and December and volant young have been captured in mid December.

● **NOTES** Inland freetail bats are quiet and gentle to handle but are extremely aggressive towards bats of other species both in captivity and in the wild. They have been observed aggressively chasing each other and other bat species while aerially foraging, indicating that they may establish and defend foraging territories.

wingless ants. They tend to forage in open unobstructed areas. When foraging over water they were observed to fly 3–5 m above the surface and then drop rapidly for a few metres to scoop up water before rising again to their previous height. They fly fast above the canopy, over water or along tree-lined creeks where they catch and eat insects on the wing. They are not very manoeuvrable in flight. They will sometimes land and crawl rapidly over the ground and on tree trunks to chase and eat prey.

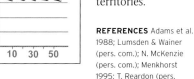

REFERENCES Adams et al. 1988; Lumsden & Wainer (pers. com.); N. McKenzie (pers. com.); Menkhorst 1995; T. Reardon (pers. com.); Reardon & Flavel 1991; Thomson 1991; Young & Ford 2000.

# Southern freetail bat
## *Mormopterus* **species 4** (undescribed)

● **TAXONOMY** This species was previously referred to as *Mormopterus planiceps* (long penis form) and *Mormopterus* species 4 in Adams et al. 1988. There are two populations, the south-eastern and south-western, and these may prove to be separate subspecies.

● **DISTRIBUTION** In WA restricted primarily to the wheatbelt; in s.e. Australia it occurs inland of Great Dividing Range. Ranges from s.e. SA into w. and central Vic, as well as w. and central NSW.

● **DESCRIPTION** This is a **medium-sized species** with a forearm length of 30.6–35.7 mm. The **fur on the back is usually dark grey-brown with a light creamy brown base to**

LINDY LUMSDEN

● **ROOST HABITS** They roost in tree hollows and in the roofs of houses. One colony was found under the metal cap of a power pole. A study of roosts showed that colonies of females are fairly large and average 30–40 bats, whereas males form smaller colonies of three or four. Colonies of several hundred have been recorded in buildings. They select roosts with entrances and cavities that are narrow and not much larger than themselves. They often share these roosts with several other species including the inland broad-nosed bat, chocolate wattled bat, large forest bat and the southern forest bat.

● **HABITAT** Tall forests, dry open forest and river red gum, box-ironwood, and cypress pine woodlands, mallee, grassland, coastal heathlands and chenopod shrublands. They have adapted well to city life and colonies of up to 100 have been found in houses and sheds around Adelaide in SA.

the hairs. The **belly is paler brown** also with a lighter base. The most obvious identifying characteristic of this species is only found in males; the **penis is long (9 mm)** (it is slightly shorter in the south-western population). The eastern freetail bat, *Mormopterus ridei*, has a smaller penis (5 mm) but is otherwise difficult to distinguish. The **fur tends to be longer, shaggier and generally much darker** than the inland freetail bat, *Mormopterus* species 3, which also has a shorter penis (5 mm). Beccari's freetail bat, *M. beccarii*, and the east-coast freetail bat, *Micronomus norfolkensis*, have longer forearms, over 36.0 mm.

● **DIET AND FORAGING** They typically forage at or above the canopy height in the spaces between the trees, along roadways, at the outer edge of remnant vegetation and above the forest canopy. They have also been recorded foraging on the ground, where they are extremely agile. They have difficulty taking off from the ground and will usually climb 1–2 m above the ground before launching. Radio-tracking studies have shown that they forage up to 12 km from their roost. In rural Vic up to 80% of the diet was found to be composed of bugs, predominantly the Rutherglen bug, an agricultural pest species, as well as flies, beetles, moths, ants and termites.

| MEASUREMENTS | | Wt | Fa | Ear | Foot | 3 met | Tail | HB | WS |
|---|---|---|---|---|---|---|---|---|---|
| | MEAN | 9.0 | 33.6 | 9.5 | 7.8 | 32.7 | 28.6 | 54.5 | 246.5 |
| | MIN | 6.8 | 30.6 | 7.3 | 6.4 | 32.0 | 22.0 | 54.0 | 240 |
| | MAX | 13.0 | 35.7 | 11.7 | 9.2 | 33.4 | 33.0 | 55.0 | 253 |
| | NO | 317 | 323 | 95 | 2 | 2 | 99 | 2 | 2 |

S. Churchill; L. Lumsden; M. Pennay; A. Reside.

● **REPRODUCTION** Spermatogenesis starts in September and is established from February to May. The males then store sperm in the epididymides. Mating has been observed as early as March in captive bats and continues until about September. Sperm is present in the uterus and oviduct for at least 2 months before ovulation, fertilisation and implantation in August or September. The single young is born in December or January. Growth of the young is slow but females attain sexual maturity during their first year. In March, when all young bats are independent fliers, a high proportion of them leave the roost. There is an influx of new adult males into the colony at this time. This is the only species where both male and female molossids store sperm.

Individuals have been captured 10 years after they were initially banded at a colony of 30 near Adelaide, indicating that they are very long-lived. During trapping surveys in Vic more than three-quarters of the individuals captured were males.

**REFERENCES** Adams et al. 1988; Bullen & McKenzie 2001; Crichton & Krutzsch 1987; Fullard et al. 1991; Holsworth 1986; Krutzsch & Crichton 1987; Law & Chidel 2006; Lumsden & Wainer (pers. com.); Lumsden et al. 1994; Lumsden & Bennett 2005; N. McKenzie (pers. com.); Menkhorst 1995; A. Reside (pers. com.); Reside (2004); Sanderson 2000; Tidemann & Flavel 1987.

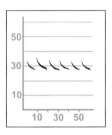

# Bristle-faced freetail bat
## *Mormopterus* **species 6** (undescribed)

● **TAXONOMY** Currently undergoing taxonomic revision by Terry Reardon, it represents a new genus and species. Regarded as *Mormopterus* species 6 in Adams et al. 1988.

● **DISTRIBUTION** Few records available: specimens have been collected from s. NT and just into n. SA. They occur in central and w. Qld. Recently recorded from central NSW.

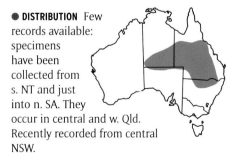

● **DESCRIPTION** A distinctly small bat with a comparatively long forearm. One female I caught in central Australia had **light sandy**

fur on the back and slightly paler underneath. The three museum specimens I examined were pale grey to reddish brown. It has a **long thin face with scattered dark bristles** and a **fringe of fur around the top lip**. The ears are triangular and not joined across the forehead. The skin around the nostrils is distinctly darker than the face. The **outer canine width is less than 3.7 mm**. Forearm length is 31.9–35.3 mm. It **differs from** all other freetail bats by its **light build** (weight less than 6.0 g) **and narrow muzzle**. In NSW the skin around the nostrils is much darker than the skin on the muzzle. Females are slightly larger than males. Both males and females have a long fleshy **finger-like projection arising from the genitals**. In males it arises from the tip of the dorsal surface or prepuce of the penis and is almost as long as the penis. There are hairs along

BRUCE THOMSON

the projection with several hairs extending well beyond the tip.

● **ROOST HABITS** A radio-tracking study by Michael Pennay in NSW found several roosts in eucalypts among the fringing vegetation of a dry creek. The roosts were in trunk and branch hollows with entrances only just big enough for one bat to squeeze through (1.3–2 cm) at a height of 3–6 m above the ground. One roost contained a maternity colony of 15 lactating females. Adults took turns babysitting the young while the others foraged. The two males roosted in different colonies of four and 20 bats. Roosts were up to 4 km from the capture sites and two roosts were used on consecutive nights.

● **HABITAT** Open forests of bimbil box (*Eucalyptus populnea*), belah (*Casuarina pauper*) and coolibah (*Eucalyptus coolibah*), open woodland, river red gum-lined water courses, mulga and hummock grasslands. Several individuals have been captured in mist nets over dams and waterholes, and one was found drowned in a swimming pool.

● **DIET AND FORAGING** The bristle-faced freetail bat has a distinctive flight pattern. Their relatively long, narrow wings suggest straight, high-speed flight but the bats have been observed to use a more agile foraging strategy with most foraging relatively close to the ground and near vegetation. Flight was relatively slow, fluttery and below canopy height at around 3–4 m elevation. They flew in loose circles with occasional rapid changes in height and direction in pursuit of prey. Almost all foraging activity occurred along the open creek channel, not in the surrounding mulga shrublands. Their diet has not been recorded.

● **REPRODUCTION** One NT female was found in advanced pregnancy with a single young in early October. In NSW two lactating females were captured in late October. A maternity colony of lactating females was located in NSW in November. Males with abdominal testes have been captured in January and October.

● **NOTES** The average echolocation call frequency is 36 kHz. The pulse shape is unusual in that it is a 'J' shape more typical of vespertilionid bats than the usually flatter profile calls of molossids. The call shape supports the foraging observations that the species forages in semi-cluttered spaces close to vegetation rather than in open air above the canopy like other molossid bats.

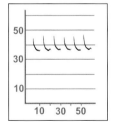

**REFERENCES** Adams et al. 1988; Ellis 2001; McKenzie, in Strahan 1995; M. Pennay (pers. com.); Pennay 2006; T. Reardon (pers. com.); Reardon 2001; Young & Ford 2000.

| MEASUREMENTS | | Wt | Fa | Ear | Tibia | 3 met | HB | Tail | OCW |
|---|---|---|---|---|---|---|---|---|---|
| | MEAN | 5.2 | 33.4 | 12.9 | 10.6 | 37.9 | 46.3 | 30.8 | 3.41 |
| | MIN | 4.5 | 31.9 | 12.5 | 9.7 | 36.5 | 41.0 | 27.8 | 3.2 |
| | MAX | 6.0 | 35.3 | 13.3 | 11.4 | 39.7 | 50.0 | 34.2 | 3.6 |
| | NO | 15 | 26 | 3 | 10 | 4 | 4 | 4 | 7 |

S. Churchill; Ellis 2001; M. Pennay; M. Venz; A. Young.

# Sheathtail Bats

## Family EMBALLONURIDAE: Key to Species

The tail is partially enclosed in a tail membrane, with the tip projecting into a sheath in the upper surface. Some species have a glandular throat pouch, and some have a wing pouch near the wrist. Ears are often joined over the forehead.

**1a** Wing pouch absent. → **2**

**1b** Wing pouch present. → **3**

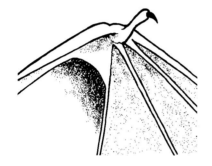

**2a** Fur on back is rich glossy black with white to yellow belly; rump not naked; forearm length averages 75.0 mm (65.7–82.1 mm); OCW averages 6.4 mm (5.9–7.1 mm).
→ ***Saccolaimus flaviventris*** (page 207)

**2b** Fur is variable; dark reddish brown to dark brown usually with irregular white flecks on the head and shoulders; belly fur from dirty white to grey-brown; rump may be almost naked with fur ending in a distinct line between the tops of the legs; forearm length averages 75.3 mm (72.3–80.0 mm); OCW averages 5.5 mm (5.0–5.6 mm).
→ ***S. saccolaimus*** (page 210)

**3a** Throat pouch present in males and represented by a rudimentary edge in females. → **4**

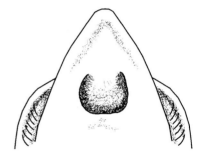

**3b** Throat pouch absent in both sexes. → **7**

**4a** Areas of white fur on belly. → **5**

**4b** No areas of white fur on belly. Fur a uniform grey-brown. → **6**

**5a** Fur is pale orange-brown with two broad white stripes along the sides of the belly in adults (can be lacking in juveniles); forearm length averages 59.8 mm (58.0–64.1 mm).
→ ***Taphozous kapalgensis*** (page 218)

**5b** Fur on back is dark grizzled grey with white belly; forearm length averages 64.4 mm (61.5–68 mm).
→ ***S. mixtus*** (page 209)

**6a** Coastal species not found more than 30 km from the sea; restricted to the east coast of Qld; forearm length averages 64.5 mm (61.3–67.6 mm).

→ **T. australis** (page 212)

**6b** Inland species found in areas more than 100 km from the coast; forearm length averages 67.7 mm (60.4–71.7 mm).

→ **T. hilli** (page 216)

**7a** Generally smaller (forearm length averages 67.9 mm; 61.7–73.1 mm) and narrower (OCW averages 4.17 mm; 3.95–4.46 mm); common and widespread species across northern WA and NT (differences in size are greatest where they overlap in range near Mt Isa in western Qld); can be separated reliably on skull characters; sagittal and lambdoidal crests relatively weak.

→ **T. georgianus** (page 214)

**7b** Generally larger (forearm length averages 72.3 mm; 67.2–75.9 mm) and wider (OCW averages 4.34 mm; 3.95–4.68 mm); Qld only; sagittal and lambdoidal crests sharply edged.

→ **T. troughtoni** (page 220)

# Yellow-bellied sheathtail bat
## *Saccolaimus flaviventris* (Peters, 1867)

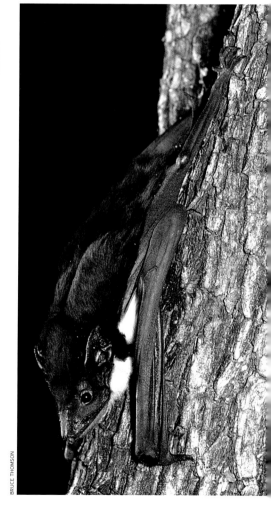

BRUCE THOMSON

● **DISTRIBUTION** Wide-ranging through tropical Australia. Migrates into s. Australia in summer: the only sheathtail bat to extend so far into temperate areas. Extralimitally in New Guinea.

● **DESCRIPTION** A striking looking bat that is very gentle in the hand. It is **large**, with rich **shiny black fur on the bac**k and contrasting bright **white, cream or yellow fur on the belly**. Males have a **large throat pouch**, with a small secondary pouch. There is no pouch in females: instead there is a naked area and a ridge of skin. There is **no wing pouch** in either sex. Outer canine width is larger (5.9–7.1 mm) than *S. saccolaimus* (5.0–5.6 mm) and *S. mixtus* (4.5–4.8 mm).

● **ROOST HABITS** Yellow-bellied sheathtail bats roost in large tree hollows and are usually found in mixed-sex groups of two to six and occasionally up to 30. A colony of six found roosting inside the trunk of a large hollow tree were clinging to the walls, hanging head down and propped up by their forearms. They were well separated from each other but tended to cluster around the entrance hole. They have been found sharing hollows with northern freetail bats, *Chaerephon*

| | Wt | Fa | Ear | Tibia | Tail | HB | OCW | Skull |
|---|---|---|---|---|---|---|---|---|
| **MEAN** | 44.0 | 75.0 | 19.6 | 30.3 | 27.0 | 81.8 | 6.4 | 25.2 |
| **MIN** | 27.8 | 65.7 | 16.5 | 26.7 | 21.3 | 72.3 | 5.9 | 23.8 |
| **MAX** | 60.0 | 82.1 | 23.0 | 32.9 | 33.3 | 91.9 | 7.1 | 27.0 |
| **NO** | 38 | 106 | 104 | 106 | 100 | 101 | 107 | 106 |

MEASUREMENTS

Chimimba & Kitchener 1991; D. Milne; Rhodes & Hall 1997; M. Venz.

*jobensis*, and in the abandoned nests of sugar gliders, *Petaurus breviceps*. Solitary animals have also been found roosting in animal burrows, in cracks in dry clay and under slabs of rock in the Top End.

● **HABITAT** Almost all habitats, from wet and dry sclerophyll forest, to open woodland, *Acacia* shrubland, mallee, grasslands and desert. They are only reported in southern Australia between January and April when they migrate during the summer. Sick or apparently exhausted animals have occasionally been found hanging from the outside walls of buildings in broad daylight in Vic and SA.

BRUCE THOMSON

● **DIET AND FORAGING** They fly fast and straight usually above the canopy, but lower over open spaces and at the forest edge. In pursuit they are capable of tight lateral turns. They eat predominantly beetles but also grasshoppers, crickets, leafhoppers, shield bugs, wasps and a few flying ants. In the Top End they are usually only active until midnight but they have been recorded foraging all night on Cape York Peninsula during the wet season.

● **REPRODUCTION** Mating occurs in August and pregnancy is always restricted to the right uterine horn. A single young is born between December and March. Volant young, 75% of adult weight, have been captured with a post-lactating female in early March. Sub-adults have been collected in January, February and April. Male reproductive condition cannot be determined from testicular size or examination of the throat pouch.

● **NOTES** They are easily seen with a spotlight. I have frequently observed them flying high above the ground but have only ever mist-netted two over water and have never seen them drinking. They are more commonly caught in mist nets set on high poles at canopy level. They may be territorial as it is common to see and hear these bats having aerial 'dogfights'. The bats chase each other and often spiral down towards the ground vocalising loudly as the air rushes past their wings with a ripping sound. They veer off only at the last second when they are very close to the ground. In normal flight they have an audible low frequency component to their call sounding like a repetitive, high-pitched, bird-like chirp.

A strain of Australian Bat Lyssavirus has been isolated from this bat. Sick individuals should not be handled (see **Bats and emerging viral diseases**).

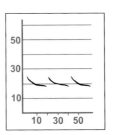

**REFERENCES** Aitken 1975; Bullen & McKenzie 2004; Chimimba & Kitchener 1987, 1991; Coles & Lumsden 1993; Hall & Gordon 1982; Hall & Richards 1979; D. Milne (pers. com.); Milne et al. 2005; Milne & Burwell (unpubl.); Reardon & Flavel 1991; Rhodes & Hall 1997b; Richards, in Strahan 1995; Thomson 1991; Troughton 1925.

# Papuan sheathtail bat

## *Saccolaimus mixtus* Troughton, 1925

● **DISTRIBUTION** Cape York Peninsula, near Iron Range and Weipa. Extralimitally in New Guinea.

● **DESCRIPTION** An elusive species that is rarely caught. The fur on the back is a mixture of dark brown and white hairs (60% brown and 40% white) giving an overall grizzled grey appearance. The belly fur varies from white to pale buffy brown with a very small scattering of brown hairs. This species is distinctly smaller (forearm length 62.0–68.0 mm) than the other two *Saccolaimus* species. There is a well-developed wing pouch filled with white hairs. There is a strongly developed throat pouch in males, only slightly less developed in females. The rump is well furred. Outer canine width is smaller (4.5–4.8 mm) than *S. saccolaimus* (5.0–5.6 mm) and much smaller than *S. flaviventris* (5.7–7.1 mm).

● **ROOST HABITS** In Australia, Papuan sheathtail bats are most likely to roost in tree hollows as they have all been found in areas that are a long way from caves or mines. One specimen was captured in a limestone cave in New Guinea.

LINDY LUMSDEN

● **HABITAT** Tall open forests, low open woodlands, along creeklines and in heathlands.

● **DIET AND FORAGING** They have been shown to eat mainly beetles (71%) and large numbers of flying ants (17%), as well as grasshoppers (6%), bugs (4%) and occasional moths (2%) during the wet season. One animal kept in captivity for 4 days was fed insects collected at a light trap. It ate between 60 and 110 insects each day, readily eating small beetles and flying ants, and showing some preference for the ants. It ate a few small moths but would not eat large moths. It also ate a large grasshopper and one large beetle

| | | Wt | Fa | Ear | Tibia | 3 met | Tail | OCW | Skull |
|---|---|---|---|---|---|---|---|---|---|
| **MEASUREMENTS** | MEAN | 23.3 | 64.4 | 18.3 | 24.2 | 63.4 | 24.7 | 4.6 | 21.8 |
| | MIN | 21.3 | 61.5 | 16.5 | 22.2 | 61.6 | 22 | 4.5 | 21.7 |
| | MAX | 26.5 | 68 | 21.3 | 25.5 | 64.9 | 28 | 4.8 | 21.9 |
| | NO | 4 | 15 | 8 | 6 | 7 | 15 | 2 | 2 |

Bonaccorso 1998; Chimimba & Kitchener 1991; Coles & Lumsden 1993.

that took considerable effort to open. Little is known of their flight and foraging habits. They were seen foraging with yellow-bellied sheathtail bats high above an isolated homestead where they were feeding on the large numbers of insects attracted by the lights. When the lights were turned off at midnight these bats foraged lower and were caught in a mist net set 10 m above the ground at canopy height. They have also been shot while foraging along a creekline in semi-open heathland. Other specimens have been captured in low open eucalypt woodland in bat traps set along tracks at ground level.

Although they have been seen foraging with yellow-bellied sheathtail bats there is a difference in their flight morphology. The aspect ratio of *S. mixtus* is 9.25 compared to 8.25 for *S. flaviventris*, with a wing loading of

13.6 compared to 15.85. This indicates that Papuan sheathtail bats probably fly faster and are slightly more manoeuvrable than yellow-bellied sheathtail bats.

● **REPRODUCTION** Nothing known.

● **NOTES** They can be seen, with a spotlight, flying with the yellow-bellied sheathtail bat, *S. flaviventris*, near Weipa and may be identified by their smaller size. *S. flaviventris* has an echolocation call that is audible for some humans but *S. mixtus* does not. This may be a useful guide to identification in the field.

**REFERENCES** Bonaccorso 1998; Chimimba & Kitchener 1991; Coles & Lumsden 1993; Flannery 1995b; Lumsden & Coles 1993; Richards & Thomson, in Strahan 1995; Troughton 1925; Winter & Atherton 1982.

# Bare-rumped sheathtail bat
## *Saccolaimus saccolaimus* (Temminck, 1838)

● **DISTRIBUTION** Two populations: one in Top End of NT; the other in n.e. Qld, in coastal areas from Bowen to Cape York Peninsula. Extralimitally from the Solomon Is to India.

● **DESCRIPTION** A **large** high-flying bat that is rarely caught. Forearm length 72.3–80.0 mm. The **fur colour varies** between individuals. On the back, fur may be **brown or dark reddish brown or almost black**, usually with **white flecks or speckles, at least on the head and shoulders**, although these are absent in juveniles and some adults. The belly fur is also variable from white to grey-brown. In most individuals the rump, hind legs and feet are hairless, with

| | | Wt | Fa | Ear | Tibia | Tail | HB | OCW | Skull |
|---|---|---|---|---|---|---|---|---|---|
| MEASUREMENTS | MEAN | 48.9 | 75.3 | 18.4 | 30.1 | 26.5 | 91.5 | 5.5 | 24.7 |
| | MIN | 31 | 72.3 | 16.2 | 28.6 | 22.5 | 81.2 | 5.0 | 22.7 |
| | MAX | 61 | 80 | 22.5 | 32 | 40.2 | 99.3 | 5.6 | 26.6 |
| | NO | 8 | 19 | 20 | 20 | 20 | 18 | 10 | 2 |

Chimimba & Kitchener 1991; Compton & Johnson 1983; McKean et al. 1981; D. Milne.

BRUCE TAUBERT

a colony of about 40, containing adults and large suckling young, was found in a hollow of a large Darwin woolly butt (*E. miniata*) when it was cut down. In December 2006, 130 bats were found in a large hollow (25 cm wide) in a Darwin stringybark tree that was blown down in a storm. The colony contained adults, sub-adults, large juveniles and very young juveniles.

● **HABITAT** Tropical woodland and tall open forests. They are mostly found in poplar gum and Darwin stringybark in savannah woodland in Qld. In the NT they are recorded from tall open eucalypt forest of Darwin woolly butt and Darwin stringybark, *Pandanus* woodland fringing the South Alligator River and in grassy beach dunes with *Melaleuca* and *Acacia* adjacent to open eucalypt forest.

the fur stopping abruptly in a distinct line between the hips. There is a **throat pouch in males**, and **females have a well-defined naked area** encircled with a crescent-shaped rudimentary pouch ridge. There is **no wing pouch**. Some individuals appear very similar to the yellow-bellied sheathtail bat, *S. flaviventris*, but can be reliably separated by outer canine width. OCW of *S. saccolaimus* is smaller (5.0–5.65 mm) than *S. flaviventris* (5.7–7.1 mm) and larger than the Papuan sheathtail bat, *S. mixtus* (4.5–4.8 mm).

● **ROOST HABITS** In Qld they have been found in the hollow trunks and branches of poplar gums (*Eucalyptus platyphylla*) in colonies of three to four bats. A colony of ten to 15 was found roosting in the large hollow trunk of a dead Darwin stringybark (*E. tetradonta*), near Iron Range. The cavity was 3 m deep, 25 cm wide, and open above where the top of the tree had fallen off. They remained at this roost for the wet season, and used it to rear their young, although the hollow provided no shelter from rain. In the NT, in April 1996

● **DIET AND FORAGING** They feed above the canopy on aerial insects. They have been observed flying from 80 m above the canopy to within 2 m of the ground while swooping down to chase prey. They are fast fliers and surprisingly manoeuvrable. In Sarawak I have watched them leave their roost in a thatched roof before dark. They dropped from the top of the roof for a distance of 3 m, before fully opening their wings and swooping up into the sky.

● **REPRODUCTION** In Qld females give birth to a single young in late December and early January, and lactate during the tropical wet season. The young are large and well developed at birth. In the Top End there is more variation in the timing of births although within colonies the young are of a similar age. In January a female was found in the early stages of pregnancy, while in March another had a half-term embryo. In late December one colony contained many large juveniles, as well as newborn young, while another colony contained well-developed juveniles in April.

● **NOTES** In Qld they were found to make high-pitched calls at the roost that could be heard over 8 m away. In New Guinea they have been noted to make high-pitched audible clicks during echolocation calls while in flight.

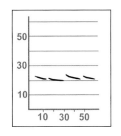

Their echolocation calls cannot be distinguished from those of the yellow-bellied sheathtail bat, *S. flaviventris*.

**REFERENCES** Bonaccorso 1998; Chimimba & Kitchener 1991; Churchill & Zborowski 1987; Compton & Johnson 1983; Hall, in Strahan 1995; McKean et al. 1981; D. Milne (pers. com.); Milne & Nash 2003; Milne et al. 2008; Murphy 2002; Woinarski & Milne 2002c.

# Coastal sheathtail bat
## *Taphozous australis* Gould, 1854

● **DISTRIBUTION** E. coast and many coastal islands off Qld from Shoalwater Bay to Cape York and Torres Strait. Rarely found roosting more than a few kilometres from the sea. Extralimitally known from a few records from s. New Guinea.

● **DESCRIPTION** A bat of coastal caves, its **fur is greyish brown all over**, and **slightly lighter on the belly**. The bases of the hairs are whitish. Both light brown and grey-brown colour forms have been noted within the one colony. This is a **smaller species** with a forearm length of 61.3–67.6 mm. **Males have**

a **distinct throat pouch**, and this is represented by a **rudimentary pouch ridge in females**. A **wing pouch is present** near the wrist. Troughton's sheathtail bat, *T. troughtoni*, which occurs further inland, is larger (forearm length 67.2–75.9 mm) and lacks the throat pouch or throat ridge.

● **ROOST HABITS** Coastal sheathtail bats roost in disused mines, sea caves, boulder piles, rock fissures, old Second World War concrete bunkers, even occasionally in buildings. They are usually in colonies of two to 25, but up to 100 have been recorded. They generally roost in shallow caves, within the twilight zone, but will sometimes move to the darker parts of larger caves and mines.

In the cave they are alert and usually hang against the wall, head down and

| MEASUREMENTS | | Wt | Fa | Ear | Tibia | 3 met | Tail | HB | WS | OCW | Skull |
|---|---|---|---|---|---|---|---|---|---|---|---|
| | MEAN | 21.0 | 64.5 | 22.2 | 25.7 | 59.1 | 27.6 | 70.1 | 413 | 4.0 | 21.6 |
| | MIN | 19.0 | 61.3 | 18.9 | 24.5 | 57.2 | 22.0 | 61.0 | 405 | 3.9 | 21.4 |
| | MAX | 23.0 | 67.6 | 24.3 | 27.1 | 60.9 | 30.6 | 75.0 | 425 | 4.1 | 22.0 |
| | NO | 14 | 28 | 17 | 13 | 17 | 17 | 17 | 6 | 9 | 9 |

Chimimba & Kitchener 1991; S. Churchill.

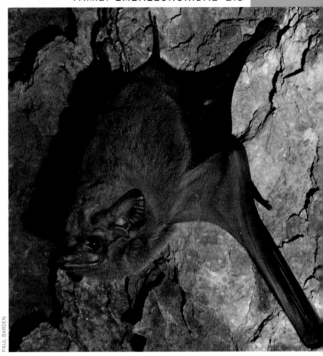

PAUL BARDEN

propped out on their forearms. Their very long wings are neatly folded away at the elbows, giving them mobility on the rock surface. They scurry into smaller cracks and crevices when disturbed. They roost on near-vertical rock faces, usually where they can drop several metres before flying and they often give an audible chirp before leaving their roost. When disturbed in small roost caves, the bats will fly out in daylight to another cave nearby.

In the northern part of their range they roost in conditions of moderate temperature and relatively high humidity (26.5–28°C and 84–92% humidity) and the bats space themselves about 20 cm apart. At the southern end of their range they are more commonly encountered in sea caves, which have entrances at or slightly above the high water mark. These are characteristically airy with numerous openings at roof level resulting in cave conditions that are considerably cooler than outside ambient temperature. Within these caves the bats roost either in clusters of up to five bats or individuals separated by a distance of approximately 10 cm. During the autumn these bats have noticeable yellow fat deposits around their rump. During winter they often have cold body temperatures and are sluggish, requiring at least 10 minutes to warm up before being able to fly.

● **HABITAT** Open eucalypt forest, grasslands, coastal heathlands, sand dune scrub, monsoon forests, mangroves and paperbark swamps, all within a short distance of the sea.

● **DIET AND FORAGING** They feed on beetles and other insects, sometimes returning to the roost to eat their prey and leaving telltale remains. They forage above the canopy. Their flight is fast and direct with rapid changes in direction to capture prey. They are found on many of the Qld coastal islands and I have seen them fly across to the mainland at dusk to forage.

● **REPRODUCTION** In males the testes are scrotal in April and abdominal in September. Groups of pregnant females have been found in September, and it is thought that most births occur from September to November. Colonies contain large young in January.

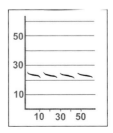

**REFERENCES** Bonaccorso 1998; Chimimba & Kitchener 1991; Flannery 1995b; Hall & Richards 1979; Hoye 1985; Little & Hall 1996; Richards, in Strahan 1995; Troughton 1925.

# Common sheathtail bat
## *Taphozous georgianus* Thomas, 1915

● **DISTRIBUTION** N. Australia: Pilbara, Kimberley, Top End and n.w. Qld. Range extends to s. of Tropic of Capricorn in WA. Endemic to Australia.

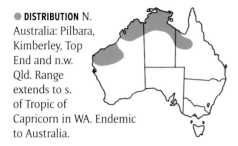

● **DESCRIPTION** This sheathtail bat is a **medium-sized** species with an average **forearm length of 67.9 mm** (61.7–73.1 mm). The **throat pouch is absent** in both sexes. A **wing pouch is present.** The **fur is light charcoal grey on the back** but slightly brownish on the rump. The **fur on the belly is brownish.** The grey wings have a translucent quality and a sticky feel. The outer margin of the tragus is concave on the upper half. They are **very similar to Hill's sheathtail bat**, *T. hilli*, which has a shallow throat pouch in males. *T. georgianus* has longer and thicker canines that lack the small anterobasal cusp of *T. hilli*. **Troughton's sheathtail bat**, *T. troughtoni*, generally has a **larger forearm** of 72.3 mm (67.2–75.9 mm), a **wider outer canine width** of 4.34 mm (3.95–4.68 mm), as opposed to 4.14 mm (3.90–4.46 mm), and more strongly defined sagittal and lambdoidal crests on the skull. Both *T. hilli* and *T. troughtoni* will share roosts with *T. georgianus* where their ranges overlap.

● **ROOST HABITS** Common sheathtail bats are cave dwellers, usually found in the twilight zone near the cave entrance. They prefer to roost fairly high above the ground on vertical walls so they can gain more speed as they drop to become airborne. They show a preference for boulder piles and split caves but are also found in abandoned mines and caverns (preferring those with multiple entrances). Colony size varies from one to 50 (one colony of 260 was reported) but is most commonly four to ten. Individuals may use several caves, regularly moving from one to another. Their roost microclimate varies considerably in the Top End ranging from 21–33°C with 20–100% humidity. Clusters of pregnant females (maternity colonies) have been found roosting deeper in caves and mines, beyond the twilight zone, in areas where conditions are more humid and generally warmer.

● **HABITAT** Monsoon forest, paperbark forest, tall open forest, open woodland, deciduous vine forest, spinifex and hummock grasslands. Distribution is related to the availability of rocky outcrops and caves for roost sites.

● **DIET AND FORAGING** Common sheathtail bats use fast semi-agile flight with steep turns to catch insects in open airspaces more than 5 m from tree canopies. They frequently use tight lateral turns, rolling to steep bank

| MEASUREMENTS | | Wt | Fa | Ear | Tibia | Tail | HB | WS | OCW | Skull |
|---|---|---|---|---|---|---|---|---|---|---|
| | MEAN | 25.8 | 67.9 | 20.5 | 27.5 | 30.5 | 72.8 | 413 | 4.17 | 23.1 |
| | MIN | 16.5 | 61.7 | 19 | 26.2 | 28.7 | 61.6 | 402 | 3.95 | 22.1 |
| | MAX | 41 | 73.1 | 22.1 | 29.7 | 34.1 | 80.0 | 423 | 4.46 | 24.1 |
| | NO | 35 | 80 | 24 | 20 | 20 | 20 | 4 | 55 | 20 |

S. Churchill; Kitchener 1980; Reardon & Thomson 2002.

BRUCE THOMSON

● **REPRODUCTION**
Reproduction has not been studied in this species. I have seen newborn young in early to mid November at Kununurra in WA. At this time the females had congregated in the larger caves in the area in colonies of seven to 40 animals and were roosting in the darker, more humid areas of the caves. Other small colonies of one to five were present in more open splits and overhangs. These were presumed to be males or non-breeding females but this was not confirmed. Microclimate conditions were warm to hot (27–37°C) in all caves.

● **NOTES** Like all *Taphozous* species they are very hard to catch in mist nets and traps (except at the cave entrance) and they are most commonly collected at the roost with a hand net. In the cave they often give a single loud audible chirp before flying from their roost.

angles (more than 60°) to catch prey. They often forage along the tops of escarpments and along gullies in hill country. Level open air speeds of 26 km/h, and up to 36 km/h in a descent, have been recorded. Speeds are as low as 16 km/h during abrupt manoeuvres to catch insects. They are frequently seen foraging above a wide variety of vegetation types and over pools and creeks. In the Top End they eat mainly beetles, but also bugs, grasshoppers and ants as well as occasional moths, lacewings and spiders.

**REFERENCES** Chimimba & Kitchener 1991; Churchill 1987, 1991; Kitchener 1980; Kitchener et al. 1981; McKenzie & Bullen 2003; Reardon & Thomson 2002; Schulz & Menkhorst 1986.

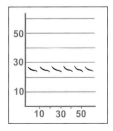

# Hill's sheathtail bat

## *Taphozous hilli* Kitchener, 1980

● **DISTRIBUTION** Inland Australia including Pilbara and Murchison regions and Gibson Desert of WA; through central Australia to Tennant Creek, NT; n. SA and Simpson Desert in w. Qld. Endemic to Australia.

● **DESCRIPTION** A widespread species of the inland areas. The **fur on the back is grey-brown, belly fur not distinctly lighter** but bicoloured, being lighter at the base. **Medium size** (forearm length 60.4–71.7 mm). A **throat pouch is present in males** and represented by a **rudimentary edge and bare patch in females**. A **wing pouch is present** near the wrist. It is **very similar to the common sheathtail bat**, *T. georgianus*, which lacks the throat pouch. The two species are known to roost together where their ranges overlap. The canines are shorter and more slender than those in *T. georgianus*, with a small anterobasal cusp about one-third the length of the tooth.

● **ROOST HABITS** Hill's sheathtail bats are cave-dwelling, usually living in groups of two to ten in the twilight zones of open caves, rock splits, disused mines and boulder piles. These sites offer little constancy of microclimate with humidities of 8–25% being common. They normally roost well-separated from each other. I have found them forming maternity colonies in September. These were located in the dark part of the caves and had conditions of 20–24°C and 40–78% relative humidity. The heavily pregnant females were extremely reluctant or possibly unable to fly. All these bats were placid, with slow movements, although they were alert and warm to touch (they were not torpid). Many of the pregnant females were roosting in tiny crevices and some were seen to burrow between loose stones on the floor of the cave. Males were also roosting in these caves but closer to the entrance and would readily fly when approached.

● **HABITAT** Common in arid areas. They can be found in eucalypt woodlands, open plains, spinifex grasslands and *Acacia* shrublands. They are restricted by the availability of rocky habitat with crevices and caves or areas with abandoned mines. They may be found a considerable distance from permanant water. In the Simpson Desert they were found to forage mostly around rocky outcrops, over open plains and dry creek beds. They did not forage at either the temporary or permanent waterholes. I think it is probable that these bats do not need to drink: certainly I have never seen any species of *Taphozous* drinking nor caught them over water.

| | | Wt | Fa | Ear | Tibia | 3 met | Tail | HB | WS | Skull |
|---|---|---|---|---|---|---|---|---|---|---|
| **MEASUREMENTS** | MEAN | 24.3 | 67.7 | 21.1 | 26.8 | 59.9 | 30.3 | 72.6 | 418 | 20.0 |
| | MIN | 20.0 | 60.4 | 18.5 | 25.0 | 56.0 | 23.9 | 64.7 | 412 | 19.1 |
| | MAX | 29.0 | 71.7 | 23.7 | 31.3 | 64.2 | 37.7 | 81.1 | 421 | 21.1 |
| | NO | 12 | 102 | 102 | 102 | 102 | 101 | 102 | 8 | 75 |

Chimimba & Kitchener 1991; S. Churchill; Kitchener 1980.

BRUCE THOMSON

caves. Colonies of 50–120 bats of both sexes were found with all the females either in advanced pregnancy or with newborn young. The young are well furred and very large when born, with a forearm length of 21 mm, and are almost one-quarter of the female's weight.

● **NOTES** This species is quite common and its range has probably been extended by mining operations throughout inland Australia. They will move into mines and adits within months of these being abandoned. These bats overlap in range with the common sheathtail bat, *T. georgianus*, in WA and will roost together. As they overlap in size it would be interesting to know how they differ from each other ecologically.

● **DIET AND FORAGING** Their diet has not been examined. Their flight is similar to other *Taphozous*, being relatively fast and direct.

● **REPRODUCTION** Males have active spermatogenesis throughout the year, but the testes only become scrotal in summer. At this time the throat pouch becomes deeper. In southern WA, the single young is born between late November and late April. In central Australia near Alice Springs I have found females with newborn young in early September. At this time these bats were not in their usual rock splits and cave entrances, although many were searched, but were roosting deep within the dark zone of larger

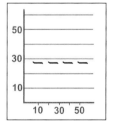

**REFERENCES** Chimimba & Kitchener 1991; Churchill 1987; Kitchener 1976a, 1980; Kitchener, in Strahan 1995; Williams & Dickman 2004.

# Arnhem sheathtail bat

## *Taphozous kapalgensis* McKean and Friend, 1979

● **DISTRIBUTION** Very few records exist. Originally collected from Alligator River floodplains in Kakadu National Park. Subsequent specimens are from coastal areas closer to Darwin, NT. Echolocation calls attributed to this species have been reported from upper South Alligator River valley, lower Victoria River, Muldiva Creek near Daly River, Cobourg Peninsula and more recently from near Kununurra, WA. Endemic to Australia.

● **DESCRIPTION** This rare and little known species is a **small** *Taphozous* with a **forearm length of 58–64.1 mm**. There is a **throat pouch in males**, which is represented by a rudimentary ridge in females. A **wing pouch is present**. The fur is a beautiful **pale orange-brown on the back** and paler grey on the belly. A band of long white hair extends over the ventral surface of the wings along the sides of the body forming **two distinct white lateral stripes** that are visible in flight. These lateral white stripes were not present on an 18.5-g sub-adult male collected at the same time as an adult male and female that possessed well-developed stripes.

● **ROOST HABITS** Not recorded but Arnhem sheathtail bats are most likely to roost in tree hollows as most of the records have been a long distance from caves or rocky areas.

● **HABITAT** They have been collected, mostly by shooting, in sedge land and coastal floodplain adjacent to *Pandanus spiralis* woodland with nearby small patches of monsoon forests, in tall open forests, in paperbark swamps and open woodland. Habitat details based on echolocation calls include cleared areas, mangroves, tall coastal eucalypt woodland of *Eucalyptus tectifera* and *E. miniata*, *Pandanus spiralis* mixed woodland adjacent to floodplain, open woodland, open floodplain grassland with scattered *Bauhinia*, and grassy coastal dunes with patchy monsoon forest and *Acacia* regrowth.

● **DIET AND FORAGING** They fly above the canopy in forests, but come lower when feeding over open areas or along unobstructed flyways usually between 10 and 20 m above the ground. These bats fly rapidly with abrupt changes in direction and emit a succession of loud shrill calls. The stomach contents of three specimens contained almost entirely (96%) field crickets (Gryllidae), with traces of beetles and moths.

● **REPRODUCTION** Little is known of their reproductive patterns. A lactating female was

| MEASUREMENTS | | Wt | Fa | Ear | Tibia | 3 met | Tail | HB | Skull |
|---|---|---|---|---|---|---|---|---|---|
| | MEAN | 27.2 | 59.8 | 18.3 | 24.0 | 59.2 | 21.1 | 75.2 | 20.3 |
| | MIN | 26.0 | 58.0 | 16.5 | 22.7 | 57.8 | 17.6 | 68.8 | 20.0 |
| | MAX | 29.5 | 64.1 | 19.7 | 25.8 | 60.2 | 24.2 | 81.2 | 20.7 |
| | NO | 5 | 9 | 8 | 8 | 3 | 8 | 8 | 3 |

Chimimba & Kitchener 1991; McKean & Friend 1979; D. Milne; Milne et al. 2003.

caught in early January and a sub-adult male collected in early November. Extrapolation from *T. troughtoni* growth rates (the only species well enough studied) suggests that the sub-adult male was about 4 weeks old and born in early October. Lactation in *T. troughtoni* lasts only 4 weeks so it is likely that the lactating female gave birth during December. Births are therefore not synchronised but occur from at least early October to December.

● **NOTES** Only a few specimens have ever been collected. One was captured in a mist net while flying along an enclosed road corridor in dense paperbark forest. The mist net was set high at canopy level on very long poles. At Kununurra, echolocation call analysis has shown that where they occur they are in low densities, representing less than 0.05% of calls recorded.

● **ECHOLOCATION** Their distinctive echolocation call has been used to help define the distribution of the species. The echolocation call is 23–25.5 kHz with short duration calls of 3–7 milliseconds.

REFERENCES Chimimba & Kitchener 1991; Lumsden et al. 2005; McKean & Friend 1979; McKean & Thomson, in Strahan 1995; D. Matthews (pers. com.); D. Milne (pers. com.); Milne et al. 2003; Milne & Burwell (unpubl.); Milne & McKean, in Van Dyck & Strahan 2008; Thomson 1991; Woinarski & Milne 2002a.

DENNIS MATTHEWS

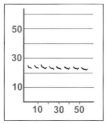

# Troughton's sheathtail bat
## *Taphozous troughtoni* Tate, 1952

● **TAXONOMY** Although described in 1952, this species was largely overlooked until a revision of Australian Emballonuridae in 1991. Recent taxonomic work by Terry Reardon and Bruce Thomson has shown that this is actually a widespread species that was misidentified as *Taphozous georgianus* in Qld.

● **DISTRIBUTION** Throughout Qld from Mt Isa to n. of Cooktown and s. to at least Taroom. Endemic to Australia.

● **DESCRIPTION** A **large species**: average **forearm length 72.3 mm** (67.2–75.9 mm). The **throat pouch is absent** in both sexes. **Wing pouch present. Fur is brown with pale grey guard hairs**; no difference between back and belly fur colour. The large skull is distinctive with sagittal and lambdoidal crests sharply edged. Where its range overlaps that of *T. georgianus* in the Mt Isa area, *T. troughtoni* is larger, but becomes smaller towards the southern end of its range. *T. georgianus* usually has a shorter forearm (67.9 mm; 61.7–73.1 mm), smaller outer canine width (4.17 mm; 3.95–4.46 mm), and relatively weak sagittal and lambdoidal crests. The two species are very similar and have been found sharing roosts in the Mt Isa district.

● **ROOST HABITS** Troughton's sheathtail bats are cave-dwelling. They generally roost in shallow caves or the twilight zone of larger ones, frequently near narrow crevices into which they retreat when alarmed. They roost in natural caves, rock crevices, boulder piles and abandoned mines. There is little difference between microclimate conditions inside or outside the roost. Most roost caves are occupied by fewer than 20 individuals although one colony contained 100 bats. Each bat uses several caves and they have been observed to move 12 km to alternate roosts. They are known to give birth in their normal twilight zone roosts but have also been observed to use dark and humid caves as maternity sites. Individuals are well spaced at the roost, only rarely are two to three bats seen in close contact. One male was observed to vigorously defend his personal roost area from other bats attempting to alight nearby.

● **HABITAT** Wet and dry sclerophyll forests, open woodland, mulga shrublands, spinifex-covered hills, and grasslands, where there are rocky areas, caves or mines.

● **DIET AND FORAGING** A radio-tracked individual at Chillagoe hunted aerial insects in an area about 2 km from its roost cave. Starting 30 minutes after sunset it foraged continuously for 5 hours, rested for 3 hours in a group of boulders then foraged briefly again before returning to its cave at dawn.

| MEASUREMENTS | | Wt | Fa | Ear | Tibia | 3 met | Tail | HB | OCW | Skull |
|---|---|---|---|---|---|---|---|---|---|---|
| | MEAN | 32.2 | 72.3 | 23.8 | 31.4 | 62.5 | 34.1 | 85.3 | 4.34 | 24.1 |
| | MIN | 24.3 | 67.2 | 21.4 | 29.8 | 57.4 | 28.4 | 79.4 | 3.95 | 24.0 |
| | MAX | 51.0 | 75.9 | 27.1 | 33.4 | 65.0 | 38.0 | 93.3 | 4.68 | 24.3 |
| | NO | 1380 | 109 | 9 | 17 | 8 | 17 | 17 | 92 | 4 |

Chimimba & Kitchener 1991; Jolly 1990; Reardon & Thomson 2002; A. Young.

BRUCE THOMSON

allowing their body temperature to drop.

● **REPRODUCTION** Testes remain abdominal for most of the year but are scrotal for a few months in summer. Sperm is produced in summer and autumn and stored until spring in the epididymides, which remain permanently in the scrotum. Mating occurs in late August and early September, and females give birth to single young between late November and early December after a 3-month gestation. The newborn young are large, one-quarter of the mother's weight, fully furred and have their eyes open. Young bats cling to their mother continuously during lactation until they reach about 50% of her weight at 3–4 weeks old. At this age they are apparently independent and capable of flight. They achieve adult size at 3 months of age. Females become reproductively mature at 9 months. In males, spermatogenesis starts at 9 months old but they do not mate until 21 months old. Their annual survival rate has been estimated to be about 60%, but mature males have a substantially lower survival rate than adult females.

Their diet has not been examined but like the common sheathtail bat they are presumed to feed mainly on beetles. At the southern extremes of their range, there is a marked seasonal variation in body weight due to fat deposits. They are heaviest in April and lightest in September. In mid-winter they conserve energy during the day by

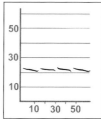

**REFERENCES** Chimimba & Kitchener 1991; Jolly 1990; Jolly, in Strahan 1995; Jolly & Blackshaw 1987; Reardon & Thomson 2002.

# Appendix: Latest state of play

## Bats added to the list

Due to the lack of published information I have attempted to scrape together any field data and distribution records I could find to help people identify these taxa in the field. Eventually we will have scientific names to use and hopefully the data we have collected in the meantime will be valuable and not a mixture of several different forms lumped together.

Work by Harry Parnaby has shown that the species we currently recognise as *Nyctophilus timoriensis* in Australia should be separated into **four different species**: the **western long-eared bat**, *Nyctophilus major*; the **central long-eared bat**, *Nyctophilus* **species 1**; the **south-eastern long-eared bat**, *Nyctophilus* **species 2**; and the **Tasmanian long-eared bat**, *Nyctophilus sherrini*. The true *N. timoriensis* does not occur in Australia. I have included separate species accounts for each of these recognisable forms.

Harry Parnaby has also shown that the two subspecies of *Nyctophilus bifax* are not closely related and are to be elevated to full species. They now become the **eastern long-eared bat**, *Nyctophilus bifax*, of eastern Australia and the **northern long-eared bat**, *Nyctophilus daedalus*, of north-western Australia.

The undescribed **central-eastern broad-nosed bat**, *Scotorepens* **species**, has also been included. There has been little information published about it but it is important to know it exists, especially if you are trying to identify *Scotorepens* in south-east Queensland and northern New South Wales.

In 2000 a new subspecies, ***Miniopterus schreibersii* bassanii**, was described from the south-east of South Australia and south-west Victoria (Cardinal & Christidis 2000). There are now three described subspecies, including *M. s. oceanensis* on the east coast and *M. s. orianae* in the Top End and Kimberley.

Recent research has shown that the genus *Miniopterus* is so different from other bats that it has been placed in a new family of its own—the family Miniopteridae (Hutcheon & Kirsch 2004). Other work has shown that the true *Miniopterus schreibersii* of Europe does not occur in Australia (Appleton et al. 2004; Tian et al. 2004). The problem is that we do not know what to call the Australian species of *schreibersii*. It has been referred to in the literature as *M. oceanensis* by Tian et al. (2004) but the name *orianae* actually should have precedence over *oceanensis* as it is the oldest available name (B. Appleton pers. com.). For this reason I have used the name ***Miniopterus orianae*** although this has not yet been formally published.

The status of the **three subspecies** is still under debate and they are likely to be elevated to full species. In the meantime to avoid confusion I have included species accounts for each of the subspecies while we await the final decision.

## Bats removed from the list

The Torresian flying-fox was described as ***Pteropus banikrisi*** by Richards and Hall (2002). However, re-examination of the specimens by Helgen (2004) found that the specimens used in the description were all juvenile *Pteropus alecto* and the species has been determined to be invalid.

The large-eared flying-fox, ***Pteropus macrotis***, is found in New Guinea and was reported to occur in Torres Strait by Hall and Richards (1991) and Hall (in Strahan 1995). Helgen (2004) examined the specimens referred to as this species and found that they belong to *Pteropus scapulatus*. It is quite possible that this species does occur in the Torres Strait as recent photos are known, but as yet no specimens have been collected to confirm its presence.

The Torresian tube-nosed bat, **Nyctimene cephalotes**, has been reported from Moa Island in Torres Strait and Cape York by Richards (in Strahan 1995), and Hall and Richards (2000). The problem here is that there are no good features for identification of *Nyctimene*. *Nyctimene robinsoni* has always been considered to be restricted to Australia but genetic work by Donnellan et al. (1995) showed that *N. robinsoni* commonly occurs in New Guinea but under a range of different names. There are no descriptions in the literature that provide characteristics to distinguish *N. robinsoni* from *N. cephalotes*. The measurements published for these specimens (forearm length, weight and tail length) fall within the range of *Nyctimene robinsoni*. Helgen and Oliver (2004) working in the Trans-Fly region of New Guinea examined many *Nyctimene cephalotes* in that area and concluded that they were most likely to be *N. robinsoni*. The addition of this species to our Australian fauna will have to await a taxonomic revision of Australian and New Guinea *Nyctimene*.

Two species have been removed from the molossid list due to combining several forms. The southern and western freetail bats have been combined, all now being called the southern freetail bat, **Mormopterus species 4** (they may prove to be sub-specifically different). The little northern freetail bat from the Top End and the little western freetail bats are now all **Mormopterus cobourgiana**. The little northern freetail bat from eastern Cape York and the eastern freetail bat have been combined to form **Mormopterus ridei**. The taxonomy of the genus *Mormopterus* is still in progress and we are likely to see more changes here. Even the genus name will be changed as the true *Mormopterus* do not occur in Australia (T. Reardon pers. com.).

## Changes in circumstance

Troughton's sheathtail bat, **Taphozous troughtoni**, was a species described in 1952 from several large specimens collected in the Mt Isa region of Queensland. The species was then ignored and included as *T. georgianus* until a morphological revision by Chimimba and Kitchener (1991) again identified it. Recent genetic examination by Reardon and Thomson (2002) has shown not only that this is a valid species but that it is widespread and common throughout most of Queensland. The two species occur together at Mt Isa and northern Queensland.

## Name changes

The **Arnhem leaf-nosed bat, Hipposideros inornatus**, has been elevated to full species status. It was formerly considered a subspecies of *Hipposideros diadema*. There are several reasons for this change. Firstly I have handled and examined large numbers of both *H. inornatus* and *H. diadema reginae* in the field and consider them to be distinctly different in appearance and behaviour. Secondly, there are several precedents in the literature. McKean (1970) in his description of the species considered calling it a new species. In a partial revision of *H. diadema*, Kitchener et al. (1992) noted that the subspecies *inornatus* and *demissus* (from the Solomon Islands) were not closely enough related to other *H. diadema* to warrant inclusion in the revision. Flannery (1995b) accepted this finding to elevate both *H. demissus* and *H. inornatus* to full species status.

The name of the **orange leaf-nosed bat** has been researched by Armstrong (2006) and we now have consensus with both the species and the genus names changed to ***Rhinonicteris aurantia***.

The **Christmas Island flying-fox** was originally named *Pteropus natalis* by Thomas (1887). Andersen (1912) included *P. natalis* within the *P. melanotus* group of species but considered it to be the most aberrant member of the group. Chasen (1940) placed it as a subspecies of *P. melanotus* with little justification. Tidemann (1985) considered this unlikely to be correct and James et al. (2006) recommended reverting to the original name ***Pteropus natalis***.

Reardon (1999) considered that the name *Nyctinomus* for the **white-striped freetail bat** was invalid and he recommended reinstating the name *Tadarida*. However, more recently his taxonomic revision of the family Molossidae has shown that the genus *Tadarida* does not occur in Australia (T. Reardon pers. com.). The name ***Austronomus australis***, a name originally used by Troughton (1941), will now be used for this species.

Terry Reardon (pers. com.) has also reinstated the name ***Micronomus norfolkensis*** for the east-coast freetail bat, another name established by Troughton (1944).

Unfortunately, in the first edition of this book sections of the species accounts for the two forms of *Rhinolophus philippinensis* were swapped. I have re-examined all the material on *Rhinolophus philippinensis* in the Queensland Museum and have sorted out the confusion. There are definitely two recognisably distinct sympatric forms.

Interestingly a molecular study by Cooper et al. (1998) (using allozyme electrophoresis and mitochondrial DNA) of both forms of *R. philippinensis* and the sympatric *R. megaphyllus* found virtually no genetic differences between them. It is a bit of a mystery why this has happened and it has stalled the taxonomic revision of these bats. The study also showed that the Queensland forms of *R. philippinensis* are different to *R. philippinensis* in New Guinea and Borneo as well as being distinctly different to the eight other regional *Rhinolophus* species examined.

As the Australian forms are not *R. philippinensis*, the only available name is *robertsi*, the name of the subspecies described by Tate (1952) from specimens collected near Cooktown. The type specimens from near Cooktown clearly belong to the large, widespread form

**LEFT** The dusky leaf-nosed bat, *Hipposideros ater*, typically roosts by hanging from its toes.

BRUCE THOMSON

of this species. I am proposing that we use the name **_Rhinolophus robertsi_** for this species. I also consider that the intermediate form is morphologically distinct enough to be considered a separate species and the fact that they occur sympatrically strengthens this assessment. I have referred to it as **_Rhinolophus_ species** in this book.

Strangely, the Cooper et al. (1998) study also found that specimens of _R. megaphyllus_ from southern Australia were genetically distinctly different to the northern specimens. They are superficially identical throughout their range but have been previously described as two subspecies, _R. megaphyllus megaphyllus_ in the south and _R. m. inguifer_ in the north. The dividing line falls somewhere in south-eastern Queensland but further work is needed before this is better defined and I will leave this problem for the next edition.

In the first edition of this book I unfortunately spelt the name of the **inland forest bat** as '_findlaysoni_' when everyone knows it should be spelt '**_Vespadelus finlaysoni_**' without the 'd'.

In the first edition I was unhappy with a taxonomic paper (Kitchener et al. 1995) that split _Myotis_ into three species in Australia and I recommended retaining the original name _Myotis adversus_ until the situation was resolved. Fortunately a clarification of the species boundaries of _Myotis_ by Cooper et al. (2001) has shown that there is only one species of _Myotis_ in Australia and it is a different species from the Indonesian _M. adversus_. They allocated the name **_Myotis macropus_** to the Australian species.

As in the first edition I have retained the generic name of _Phoniscus_ instead of _Kerivoula_ for the **golden-tipped bat, _Phoniscus papuensis_**. I have had some experience with catching species of both _Phoniscus_ and _Kerivoula_ in Australia, south-east Asia and Africa. In my opinion they are really quite distinctly different. The genus _Phoniscus_ is distinguished from _Kerivoula_ by having a longitudinal groove on the front of the canine, and by the reduced size of the third lower incisor compared to the second. Although some authors consider _Phoniscus_ to be a subgenus of _Kerivoula_, most authors in south-east Asia (where there are many species) and New Guinea use the genus name _Phoniscus_.

# Glossary

**Adit**  A horizontal tunnel in a mine.

**Anterior**  Forward end; nearest the nose of the bat.

**Avon**  A dome-shaped depression in the ceiling of a cave that often traps warm rising air.

**Baculum**  A bone in the penis of many species of bats. Bacula are often a characteristic shape and may be used for species identification.

**Blastocyst**  An early embryonic stage comprising of fewer than a hundred cells.

**Calcar**  (or calcaneum) A spur of cartilage that extends from the ankle and supports the outer edge of the tail membrane.

**Canines**  The longest and most distinctly pointed teeth.

**Carnivorous**  Eating vertebrate prey, mammals, birds, reptiles and amphibians (usually does not include fish; see Piscivorous).

**Cauliflorous**  Producing flowers on older, thickened branches, trunk or base of roots.

**Digit**  The supporting bones of the bat's wing, equivalent to human fingers and numbered from one to five, the clawed thumb being number one and the digit closest to the body being number five.

**Diurnal**  Active by day.

**Dorsal**  Towards or on the back of the bat.

**Dorsoventrally compressed**  Flattened from the top and bottom.

**Endemic**  Unique to the place being discussed, in this case Australia.

**Epididymis**  A convoluted tube attached to the testes. It is used for storing sperm. (plural epididymides)

**Extralimital**  Occupying an area outside the area being considered, in this case Australia.

**Flyway**  An area or passageway habitually used by bats for travel.

**Glans penis**  The part of the penis that lies under the foreskin.

**Gleaning**  A foraging method of plucking food items, usually insects, off surfaces, such as tree trunks, leaves or the ground.

**Habitat**  An area providing the physical and biological requirements of a species.

**Incisors**  The teeth between the canines at the front of the mouth. They are usually simple, sometimes forked and may be minute.

**Insectivorous**  Eating insects and other arthropods.

**Lactating**  Producing milk from the breasts.

**Laterally compressed**  Flattened from the sides.

**Mantle**  A patch of fur, of different colour to the rest of the body, on the nape of the neck and/or shoulders.

**Metacarpal**  The long bone closest to the wrist in each finger.

**Mist net**  A fine meshed net set vertically between poles to catch bats or birds.

**Molars**  The rear teeth, large and complex in shape with a pattern of ridges and grooves for grinding food.

**Nectarivorous**  Nectar eating.

**Nocturnal**  Active by night.

**Nose-leaf**  Growths of skin or fleshy lobes located on the top of the muzzle to aid in echolocation.

**Nulliparous**  Has never given birth. Could apply to a pregnant or non-pregnant sub-adult.

**Outer canine width (OCW)** The maximum measurement of the outer distance between the canines measured at the gum-line.

**Phalanx** The shorter bones in the wings and feet, analogous to fingers and toes. (plural phalanges)

**Piscivorous** Fish eating.

**Pit trap** A large bucket sunk flush into the ground to trap ground-dwelling animals when they fall in.

**Premolars** Teeth lying between the molars and the canines. Shape may vary from complex to very simple.

**Pubic teats** Two accessory nipples located in the pubic region. They do not secrete milk but provide an attachment point for the young. Found in rhinolophids, hipposiderids and megadermatids.

**Scrotum** Sacs of skin on either side of the penis that accommodate the testes. Testes alternate between being abdominal or scrotal depending on reproductive condition.

**Tail membrane** A flight membrane that stretches between the legs in some bats. It may incorporate the tail or be reduced to small flaps of skin along the insides of the legs. Also called interfemoral membrane or uropatagium.

**Taxonomic revision** A re-evaluation of the number of species within a genus or family.

**Testes** The male sex glands that manufacture sperm.

**Throat pouch** A circular pouch of skin on the throat. Mostly restricted to males and reduced to a rudimentary circular ridge in females. Found in molossids and emballonurids. Also called a gular pouch.

**Torpor** A method for reducing energy loss by lowering body temperature. Torpid bats are inactive, appear to be asleep, take some time to arouse and are usually cool to touch. Bats may use torpor on a daily basis or for extended periods of time (hibernation).

**Tragus** A small fleshy projection located anteriorly inside the ear. These are often of a characteristic size and shape.

**Ventral** Towards or on the underside (belly) of the bat.

**Wing pouch** A flap of skin extending from the forearm to the fifth finger forming a pocket near the wrist. Found in emballonurids. Also called a radio-metacarpal pouch.

# Bibliography

Adams, M., Reardon, T.R., Baverstock, P.R. & Watts, C.H.S. 1988, 'Electrophoretic resolution of species boundaries in Australian Microchiroptera. IV. The Molossidae (Chiroptera)', *Aust. J. Biol. Science*, vol. 41, pp. 315–26.

Adams, M.D., Law, B.S. & French, K.O. 2005, 'Effect of lights on activity levels of forest bats: increasing the efficiency of surveys and species identification', *Wildl. Res.*, vol. 32, pp. 173–82.

Aitken, P.F. 1975, 'Two new bat records for South Australia, with a field key and checklist to bats of the state', *South Aust. Nat.*, vol. 50, pp. 9–15.

Alison, F.R. 1989, 'Molossidae', in D.W. Walton & B.J. Richardson (eds), *Fauna of Australia. Volume 1B: Mammalia*, Australian Government Publishing Service, Canberra, ch. 43.

Andersen, K. 1912, *Catalogue of the Chiroptera in the collection of the British Museum, Volume 1. Megachiroptera*, 2nd edn, British Museum of Natural History, London.

Anderson, J., Law, B. & Tidemann, C. 2006, 'Stream use by the large-footed myotis *Myotis macropus* in relation to environmental variables in northern New South Wales', *Aust. Mammal.*, vol. 28, pp. 15–26.

Andrews, C.W. 1900, 'Mammals', in *A monograph of Christmas Island (Indian Ocean)*, British Museum of Natural History, London, pp. 22–37.

Appleton, B.R., McKenzie, J.A. & Christidis, L. 2004, 'Molecular systematics and biogeography of the bent-wing bat complex *Miniopterus schreibersii* (Kuhl, 1817) (Chiroptera: Vespertilionidae)', *Molecular Phylogenetics Evol.*, vol. 31, pp. 431–9.

Armstrong, K.N. 2002a, 'The distribution and roost habitat of the orange leaf-nosed bat, *Rhinonicteris aurantius*, in the Pilbara region of Western Australia', *Wildl. Res.*, vol. 28, pp. 95–104.

Armstrong, K.N. 2002b, 'Morphological divergence among populations of *Rhinonicteris aurantius* (Chiroptera: Hipposideridae) in northern Australia', *Aust. J. Zool.*, 50, pp. 649–69.

Armstrong, K.N. 2006a, 'Phylogeographic structure in *Rhinonicteris aurantia* (Chiroptera: Hipposideridae): implications for conservation', *Acta Chiropterologica*, vol. 8, pp. 63–81.

Armstrong, K.N. 2006b, 'Resolving the correct nomenclature of the orange leaf-nosed bat *Rhinonicteris aurantia* (Gray 1845) (Hipposideridae)', *Aust. Mammal.*, vol. 28, pp. 125–30.

Armstrong, K.N. & Anstee, S.D. 2000, 'The ghost bat in the Pilbara: 100 years on', *Aust. Mammal.*, vol. 22, pp. 93–101.

Bailey, W.J. & Haythornthwaite, S. 1998, 'Risks of calling by the field cricket *Teleogryllus oceanicus*; potential predation by Australian long-eared bats', *J. Zool., Lond.*, vol. 244, pp. 505–13.

Barclay, R.M.R., Chruszcz, B.J. & Rhodes, M. 2000, 'Foraging behaviour of the large-footed myotis, *Myotis moluccarum* (Chiroptera: Vespertilionidae) in south-eastern Queensland', *Aust. J. Zool.*, vol. 48, pp. 385–92.

Bartels, W., Law, B.S. & Geiser, F. 1998, 'Daily torpor and energetics in a tropical mammal, the northern blossom-bat *Macroglossus minimus* (Megachiroptera)', *J. Comp. Physiol. B*, vol. 168, pp. 233–9.

Baudinette, R.V., Churchill, S.K., Christian, K.A., Nelson, J.E. & Hudson, P.J. 2000, 'Energy, water balance and the roost microclimate in three Australian cave-dwelling bats (Microchiroptera)', *J. Comp. Physiol. B*, vol. 170, pp. 439–46.

Baudinette, R.V., Wells, R.T., Sanderson, K.J. & Clark, B. 1994, 'Microclimatic conditions in maternity caves of the bent-wing bat, *Miniopterus schreibersii*: an attempted restoration of a former maternity site', *Wildl. Res.*, vol. 21, pp. 607–19.

Begg, R.L. & McKean, J.L. 1982, 'Cave dwelling in the molossid bat, *Tadarida jobensis colonicus*', *N.T. Nat.*, vol. 5, p. 12.

Birt, P., Hall, L.S. & Smith, G.C. 1997, 'Ecomorphology of the tongues of Australian Megachiroptera (Chiroptera: Pteropodidae)', *Aust. J. Zool.*, vol. 45, pp. 369–84.

Birt, P. & Markus, N. 1999, 'Notes on the temporary displacement of *Pteropus alecto* and *P. poliocephalus* by *P. scapulatus* within a daytime campsite', *Aust. Mammal.*, vol. 21, pp. 107–10.

Boles, W.E. 1999, 'Avian prey of the Australian Ghost Bat *Macroderma gigas* (Microchiroptera: Megadermatidae): prey characteristics and damage from predation', *Australian Zoologist*, vol. 31, pp. 82–91.

Bonaccorso, F.J. 1998, *Bats of New Guinea*, Conservation International, Tropical Field Guide Series 2, Washington DC.

Bonaccorso, F.J. & McNab, B.K. 1997, 'Plasticity of Energetics in Blossom Bats (Pteropodidae): Impact on Distribution', *J. Mammal.*, vol. 78, pp. 1073–88.

Bonaccorso, F.J. & McNab, B.K. 2003, 'Standard energetics of leaf-nosed bats (Hipposideridae): its relationship to intermittent- and protracted-foraging tactics in bats and birds', *J. Comp. Physiol. B*, vol. 173, pp. 43–53.

Breed, A.C., Field, H.E., Epstein, J.H. & Daszak, P. 2006, 'Emerging henipaviruses and flying-foxes—Conservation and management perspectives', *Biol. Cons.*, vol. 131, pp. 211–20.

Brigham, R.M., Francis, R.L. & Hamdorf, S. 1997, 'Microhabitat use by two species of *Nyctophilus* bats: a test of ecomorphology theory', *Aust. J. Zool.*, vol. 45, pp. 553–60.

Brown, P.E. & Berry, R.D. 1983, 'Echolocation behaviour in a "flycatcher" bat, *Hipposideros diadema*', *J. Acoust. Soc. Amer.*, vol. 74, pp. 32–3.

Bullen, R.D. & McKenzie, N.L. 2001, 'Bat airframe design: flight performance, stability and control in relation to foraging ecology', *Aust. J. Zool.*, vol. 49, pp. 235–61.

Bullen, R.D. & McKenzie, N.L. 2002a, 'Differentiating Western Australian *Nyctophilus* (Chiroptera: Vespertilionidae) echolocation calls', *Aust. Mammal.*, vol. 23, pp. 89–93.

Bullen, R.D. & McKenzie, N.L. 2002b, 'Scaling bat wingbeat frequency and amplitude', *J. Exper. Biol.*, vol. 205, pp. 2615–26.

Bullen, R.D. & McKenzie, N.L. 2004, 'Bat flight-muscle mass: implications for foraging strategy', *Aust. J. Zool.*, vol. 52, pp. 605–22.

Bullen, R.D. & McKenzie, N.L. 2005, 'Seasonal range variation of *Tadarida australis* (Chiroptera: Molossidae) in Western Australia: the impact of enthalpy', *Aust. J. Zool.*, vol. 53, pp. 145–56.

Caddle, C.R. 1998, 'Tree roost selection by the large-footed myotis (*Myotis macropus*) in Victoria', unpublished Honours thesis, Department of Zoology, Melbourne University.

Calaby, J.H. 1966, 'Mammals of the upper Richmond and Clarence Rivers, New South Wales', *CSIRO Div. Wildl. Res. Tech. Paper no. 10*, pp. 1–55.

Campbell, B. 2001, 'Aspects of roost selection by microchiropteran bats in Bundjalung National Park, north-eastern NSW', *Aust. Bat. Soc. Newsl.*, vol. 17, pp. 16–33.

Campbell, S., Lumsden, L.F., Kirkwood, R. & Coulson, G. 2005, 'Day roost selection by female little forest bats (*Vespadelus vulturnus*) within remnant woodland on Phillip Island, Victoria', *Wildl. Res.*, vol. 32, pp. 183–91.

Cardinal, B.R. & Christidis, L. 2000, 'Mitochondrial DNA and morphology reveal three geographically distinct lineages of the Large bentwing bat (*Miniopterus schreibersii*) in Australia', *Aust. J. Zool.*, vol. 48, pp. 1–19.

Chasen, F.N. 1940, 'A handlist of Malaysian mammals: A systematic list of the mammals of the Malay Peninsular, Sumatra, Borneo and Java, including the adjacent small mammals', *Bull. Raffles Mus., Singapore*, vol. 15, pp. 1–207.

Chimimba, C.T. & Kitchener, D.J. 1987, 'Breeding in the Australian Yellow-bellied Sheath-tailed bat, *Saccolaimus flaviventris* (Peters, 1867) (Chiroptera: Emballonuridae)', *Rec. West. Aust. Mus.*, vol. 13, pp. 241–8.

Chimimba, C.T. & Kitchener, D.J. 1991, 'A systematic revision of Australian Emballonuridae (Mammalia: Chiroptera)', *Rec. West. Aust. Mus.*, vol. 15, pp. 203–65.

Churchill, S. 1987, 'Observations on breeding behaviour in cave dwelling *Taphozous*', *Macroderma*, vol. 3, pp. 36–8.

Churchill, S. 1998, *Australian Bats*, Reed New Holland, Sydney.

Churchill, S., Draper, R. & Marais, E. 1997, 'Cave utilization by Namibian bats: Population, microclimate and roost selection', *South African J. Wildl. Res.*, vol. 27, pp. 44–50.

Churchill, S.K. 1991, 'Distribution, abundance and roost selection of the Orange Horseshoe-bat, *Rhinonycteris aurantius*, a tropical cave-dweller', *Wildl. Res.*, vol. 18, pp. 343–53.

Churchill, S.K. 1994, 'Diet, prey selection and foraging behaviour of the Orange Horseshoe-bat, *Rhinonycteris aurantius*', *Wildl. Res.*, vol. 21, pp. 115–30.

Churchill, S.K. 1995, 'Reproductive ecology of the Orange Horseshoe-bat, *Rhinonycteris aurantius* (Hipposideridae: Chiroptera), a tropical cave-dweller', *Wildl. Res.*, vol. 22, pp. 687–98.

Churchill, S.K., Hall, L.S. & Helman, P.M. 1984, 'Observations on long-eared bats (Vespertilionidae: *Nyctophilus*) from Northern Australia', *Aust. Mammal.*, vol. 7, pp. 17–28.

Churchill, S.K. & Helman, P.M. 1990, 'Distribution, population and status of the Ghost Bat, *Macroderma gigas* (Chiroptera: Megadermatidae), in central and South Australia', *Aust. Mammal.*, vol. 13, pp. 149–56.

Churchill, S.K., Helman, P.M. & Hall, L.S. 1988, 'Distribution, population and status of the Orange Horseshoe-bat, *Rhinonycteris aurantius* (Chiroptera: Hipposideridae)', *Aust. Mammal.*, vol. 11, pp. 27–33.

Churchill, S.K. & Zborowski, P.J. 1987, 'A bat survey of Bako National Park, Sarawak, Malaysia', *Sarawak Mus. J.*, vol. 37, pp. 171–9.

Clague, C. 2000, 'Tube-nosed Insectivorous bat', *Nature Aust.*, autumn, pp. 22–3.

Clague, C.I., Coles, R.B., Whybird, O.J., Spencer, H.J. & Flemons, P. 1999, 'The occurrence and distribution of the tube-nosed Insectivorous bat (*Murina florium*) in Australia', *Proc. Linnaean Soc. New South Wales*, vol. 121, pp. 175–91.

Coburn, D.K. & Geiser, F. 1998, 'Seasonal changes in energetics and torpor patterns in the sub-tropical blossom-bat *Syconycteris australis* (Megachiroptera)', *Oecologica*, vol. 113, pp. 467–73.

Codd, J.R., Sanderson, K.J. & Branford, A.J. 2003, 'Roosting activity budget of the southern bent-wing bat (*Miniopterus schreibersii bassanii*)', *Aust. J. Zool.*, vol. 51, pp. 307–16.

Coles, R.B. 2002, 'Acoustic dimorphism in *Rhinolophus philippinensis*', *Aust. Bat Soc. Newsl.*, vol. 18, p. 31.

Coles, R.B. & Lumsden, L. 1993, 'Report on the survey of bats in the Heathlands area of Cape York Peninsula', Royal Geographical Society of Queensland in *Cape York Peninsula Scientific Expedition Wet Season 1992 Report*, vol. 2, pp. 247–59.

Compton, A. & Johnson, P.M. 1983, 'Observations of the Sheath-tailed bat, *Taphozous saccolaimus* Temminck (Chiroptera: Emballonuridae), in the Townsville region of Queensland', *Aust. Mammal.*, vol. 6, pp. 83–7.

Conole, L.E. 2000, 'Acoustic differentiation of Australian populations of large bentwing bats *Miniopterus schreibersii* (Kuhl, 1817)', *Aust. Zool.*, vol. 31, pp. 443–6.

Cooper, S.J.B., Day, P.R., Reardon, T.B. & Schulz, M. 2001, 'Assessment of species boundaries in Australian *Myotis* (Chiroptera: Vespertilionidae) using mitochondrial DNA', *J. Mammal.*, vol. 82, pp. 328–38.

Cooper, S.J.B., Reardon, T.B. & Skilins, J. 1998, 'Molecular systematics of Australian rhinolophid bats (Chiroptera: Rhinolophidae)', *Aust. J. Zool.*, vol. 46, pp. 203–20.

Corben, C. 2002, 'Getting good calls from captured bats', *Aust. Bat Soc. Newsl., Aust. Bat Res. News.*, vol. 18, pp. 19–23.

Corben, C. 2003, 'How Anabat works', *Aust. Bat Res. News.*, vol. 20, pp. 19–23.

Crichton, E.G. & Krutzsch, P.H. 1987, 'Reproductive biology of the female Little mastiff bat, *Mormopterus planiceps* (Chiroptera: Molossidae) in southeast Australia', *Amer. J. Anat.*, vol. 178, pp. 369–86.

Daniel, M.J. 1975, 'First record of an Australian Fruit bat (Megachiroptera: Pteropodidae) reaching New Zealand', *New Zeal. J., Zool.*, vol. 2, pp. 227–31.

de Lestang, A. 1929, 'A bat colony (*Chaerephon plicatus colonicus*) in north Queensland', *Aust. Zool.*, vol. 6, pp. 106–7.

de Oliveira, M.C. 1998, 'Echolocation calls of seventeen species of microchiropterans from South-east Queensland, including pulse design terminology', *Aust. Zool.*, vol. 31, pp. 55–61.

de Oliveira, M.C. & Pavey, C.R. 1995, 'In search of *Hipposideros semoni* at St Mary's State Forest, south-east Queensland', *Aust. Bat Soc. Newsl.*, vol. 4, pp. 46–8.

de Oliveira, M.C. & Schulz, M. 1997, 'Echolocation and roost selection in Semon's leaf-nosed bat *Hipposideros semoni*', *Mem. Qld. Mus.*, vol. 41, p. 158.

de Oliveira, M.C., Smith, G.C. & Hogan, L.D. 1999, 'Current limitations in the use of bat detectors to assess the impact of logging—a pilot study in south-east Queensland', *Aust. Zool.*, vol. 31, pp. 110–17.

Dixon, J.M. & Huxley, L. 1989, 'Observations on a maternity colony of Gould's Wattled bat *Chalinolobus gouldii* (Chiroptera: Vespertilionidae)', *Mammalia*, vol. 53, pp. 395–414.

Dixon, K.J. & Rose, R.W. 2003, 'Thermal energetics of *Nyctophilus geoffroyi* (Chiroptera: Vespertilionidae) at the southern limits of its distribution', *Aust. J. Zool.*, vol. 51, pp. 43–50.

Dobson, G.E. 1876, 'A monograph of the group *Molossi*', *Proc. Zool. Soc. Lond.*, vol. 1876, pp. 701–35.

Dominelli, S. 2000, 'Distribution, roost requirements and foraging behaviour of the greater long-eared bat (*Nyctophilus timoriensis*) and the little pied bat (*Chalinolobus picatus*) in the Bookmark Biosphere Reserve', unpublished report for The Bookmark Biosphere Trust, Adelaide.

Donnellan, S.C., Reardon, T.B. & Flannery, T.F. 1995, 'Electrophoretic resolution of species boundaries in tube-nosed bats (Chiroptera: Pteropodidae) in Australia and Papua New Guinea', *Aust. Mammal.*, vol. 18, pp. 61–70.

Douglas, A.M. 1967, 'The natural history of the Ghost bat, *Macroderma gigas* (Microchiroptera, Megadermatidae), in Western Australia', *West. Aust. Nat.*, vol. 10, pp. 125–38.

Duffy, A.M., Lumsden, L.F., Caddle, C.R., Chick, R.R. & Newell, G.R. 2000, 'The efficacy of Anabat ultrasonic detectors and harp traps for surveying microchiropterans in south-eastern Australia', *Acta Chiropterologica*, vol. 2, pp. 127–44.

Duncan, A., Baker, G.B. & Montgomery, N. (eds) 1999, *The Action Plan for Australian Bats*, Environment Australia, Canberra.

Dwyer, P.D. 1963, 'The breeding biology of *Miniopterus schreibersii blepotis* (Temminck) (Chiroptera) in north-eastern New South Wales', *Aust. J. Zool.*, vol. 11, pp. 219–40.

Dwyer, P.D. 1965, 'Flight patterns of some eastern Australian bats', *Vic. Nat.*, vol. 82, pp. 36–41.

Dwyer, P.D. 1966a, 'Observations on the Eastern Horse-shoe Bat in north-eastern New South Wales', *Helictite*, vol. 4, pp. 73–82.

Dwyer, P.D. 1966b, 'Observations on *Chalinolobus dwyeri* (Chiroptera: Vespertilionid) in Australia', *J. Mammal.*, vol. 47, pp. 716–18.

Dwyer, P.D. 1966c, 'The population pattern of *Miniopterus schreibersii* (Chiroptera) in north-eastern New South Wales', *Aust. J. Zool.*, vol. 14, pp. 1073–137.

Dwyer, P.D. 1968, 'The biology, origin and adaption of *Miniopterus australis* (Chiroptera) in New South Wales', *Aust. J. Zool.*, vol. 16, pp. 49–68.

Dwyer, P.D. 1970a, 'Foraging behaviour of the Australian Large-footed Myotis', *Mammalia*, vol. 34, pp. 76–80.

Dwyer, P.D. 1970b, 'Social organisation in the bat *Myotis adversus*', *Science*, vol. 168, pp. 1006–8.

Dwyer, P.D. 1975, 'Notes on *Dobsonia moluccensis* (Chiroptera) in the New Guinea highlands', *Mammalia*, vol. 39, pp. 113–18.

Eby, P. 1991, 'Seasonal movements of Grey-headed flying-foxes, *Pteropus poliocephalus* (Chiroptera: Pteropodidae), from two maternity camps in northern New South Wales', *Wildl. Res.*, vol. 18, pp. 547–59.

Eby, P. & Lunney, D. (eds) 2002, *Managing the Grey-headed flying-fox as a threatened species in NSW*, Royal Zoological Society of New South Wales, Mosman.

Ellis, M. 1989, 'Extensions to the known range of Gould's long-eared bat *Nyctophilus gouldi* Tomes, 1858 (Chiroptera: Vespertilionidae) in New South Wales', *Aust. Zool.*, vol. 25, pp. 79–82.

Ellis, M. 2001, 'Extension to the known range of the Eastern cave bat *Vespadelus troughtoni* (Kitchener, Jones and Caputi 1987) into the Brigalow Belt South Bioregion in New South Wales', *Aust. Bat Soc. Newsl.*, vol. 16, pp. 39–41.

Ellis, M. & Turbill, C. 2002, 'The box-ironbark forests of central–western New South Wales are a distinct stronghold for *Nyctophilus timoriensis* (south-eastern form)', *Aust. Bat Soc. Newsl.*, vol. 18, p. 22.

Flannery, T.F. 1995a, *Mammals of the South-west Pacific and Moluccan Islands*, Reed Books and the Australian Museum, Sydney.

Flannery, T.F. 1995b, *Mammals of New Guinea*, Reed Books and the Australian Museum, Sydney.

Fullard, J.H., Koehler, C., Surlykke, A. & McKenzie, N.L. 1991, 'Echolocation ecology and flight morphology of insectivorous bats (Chiroptera) in south-western Australia', *Aust. J. Zool.*, vol. 39, pp. 45–56.

Garnett, S., Whybird, O. & Spencer, H. 1999, 'The conservation status of the Spectacled flying-fox *Pteropus conspicillatus* in Australia', *Aust. Zool.*, vol. 31, pp. 38–54.

Gee, D. 1999, 'Range extension of the Gould's long-eared bat, *Nyctophilus gouldi*', *Aust. Bat Soc. Newsl.*, vol. 13, pp. 25–6.

Geiser, F. & Brigham, R.M. 2000, 'Torpor, thermal biology, and energetics in Australian long-eared bats (*Nyctophilus*)', *J. Comp. Physiol. B*, vol. 170, pp. 153–62.

Geiser, F. & Coburn, D.K. 1999, 'Field metabolic rates and water uptake in the blossom-bat *Syconycteris australis* (Megachiroptera)', *J. Comp. Physiol. B*, vol. 169, pp. 133–8.

Geiser, F., Coburn, D.K. & Kortner, G. 1996, 'Thermoregulation, energy metabolism, and torpor in blossom-bats, *Syconycteris australis* (Megachiroptera)', *J. Zool., Lond.*, vol. 239, pp. 583–90.

Geiser, F., Kortner, G. & Law, B. 2001, 'Daily torpor in a pregnant common blossom-bat (*Syconycteris australis*: Megachiroptera)', *Aust. Mammal.*, vol. 23, pp. 53–6.

Geiser, F., Law, B. & Kortner, G. 2005, 'Daily torpor in relation to photoperiod in a subtropical blossom-bat, *Syconycteris australis* (Megachiroptera)', *J. Therm. Biol.*, vol. 30, pp. 574–9.

Grant, J.D.A. 1991, 'Prey location by two Australian Long-eared bats, *Nyctophilus gouldi* and *N. geoffroyi*', *Aust. J. Zool.*, vol. 39, pp. 45–56.

Hall, L. & Pettigrew, J. 1995, 'The bat with the stereo nose', *Aust. Nat. Hist.*, autumn vol., pp. 26–8.

Hall, L.S. 1970, 'A collection of the bat *Chalinolobus morio* (Gray) from the Nullarbor Plain, Western Australia', *Helictite*, vol. 8, pp. 51–7.

Hall, L.S. 1987, 'Identification, distribution and taxonomy of Australian flying-foxes (Chiroptera: Pteropodidae)', *Aust. Mammal.*, vol. 10, pp. 75–9.

Hall, L.S. 1989, 'Rhinolophidae', in D.W. Walton & B.J. Richardson (eds), *Fauna of Australia. Volume 1B: Mammalia*, Australian Government Publishing Service, Canberra, ch. 40.

Hall, L.S. & Gordon, G. 1982, 'The throat pouch of the Yellow-bellied sheath-tailed bat, *Taphozous flaviventris*', *Mammalia*, vol. 46, pp. 247–52.

Hall, L.S. & Richards, G.C. 1972, 'Notes on *Tadarida australis* (Chiroptera: Molossidae)', *Aust. Mammal.*, vol. 1, pp. 46–7.

Hall, L.S. & Richards, G.C. 1979, *Bats of Eastern Australia*, Queensland Museum Booklet No. 12, Brisbane.

Hall, L.S. & Richards, G.C. 1991, 'Flying-fox camps', *Wildl. Aust.*, vol. 28, pp. 19–22.

Hall, L.S. & Richards, G.C. 2000, *Flying-foxes: Fruit and Blossom Bats of Australia*, University of New South Wales Press, Sydney.

Hall, L.S., Young, R.A. & Spate, A.P. 1975, 'Roost selection of the Eastern Horseshoe bat, *Rhinolophus megaphyllus*', *Proc. 10th Biennial Conf. Aust. Speleol Fed.*, pp. 47–56.

Helgen, K.M. 2004, 'On the identity of flying-foxes, genus *Pteropus* (Mammalia: Chiroptera), from islands in the Torres Strait, Australia', *Zootaxa*, vol. 780, pp. 1–14.

Helgen, K.M. & Oliver, P.M. 2004, 'A review of the mammal fauna of the TransFly Ecoregion', unpublished report to WWF South Pacific Region.

Helman, P. & Churchill, S. 1986, 'Bat capture techniques and their use in surveys', *Macroderma*, vol. 2, pp. 32–53.

Herr, A. 1998, 'Aspects of the ecology of insectivorous forest-dwelling bats (Microchiroptera) in the western slopes of the Australian alps', unpublished PhD thesis, Charles Sturt University.

Herr, A. & Klomp, N.I. 1999, 'Preliminary investigation of roosting habitat preferences of the large forest bat *Vespadelus darlingtoni* (Chiroptera, Vespertilionidae)', *Pacific Cons. Biol.*, vol. 5, pp. 208–13.

Hill, J.E. 1963, 'A revision of the genus *Hipposideros*', *Bull. British Mus. (Nat. Hist.) Zool.*, series 11, pp. 1–129.

Hill, J.E. 1965, 'Asiatic bats of the genera *Kerivoula* and *Phoniscus* (Vespertilionidae), with a note on *Kerivoula aerosa* Tomes', *Mammalia*, vol. 29, pp. 524–56.

Hill, J.E. & Pratt, T.K. 1981, 'A record of *Nyctophilus timoriensis* (Geoffroy, 1806) (Chiroptera: Vespertilionidae) from New Guinea', *Mammalia*, vol. 45, pp. 264–6.

Hill, J.E. & Smith, J.D. 1984, *Bats: a Natural History*, British Museum of Natural History, London.

Holsworth, W.N. 1986, 'Homing ability of the little mastiff-bat *Mormopterus planiceps*', *Macroderma*, vol. 2, pp. 54–8.

Hood, C.S. & Smith, J.D. 1989, 'Sperm storage in a tropical nectar-feeding bat, *Macroglossus minimus* (Pteropodidae)', *J. Mammal.*, vol. 70, pp. 404–6.

Hosken, D.J. 1996, 'Roost selection by the Lesser long-eared bat, *Nyctophilus geoffroyi*, and the Greater long-eared bat, *N. major* (Chiroptera: Vespertilionidae) in *Banksia* woodlands', *J. Roy. Soc. West. Aust.*, vol. 79, pp. 211–16.

Hosken, D.J. 1997a, 'Thermal biology and metabolism of the Greater Long-eared Bat, *Nyctophilus major* (Chiroptera: Vespertilionidae)', *Aust. J. Zool.*, vol. 45, pp. 145–56.

Hosken, D.J. 1997b, 'Reproduction and the female reproductive cycle of *Nyctophilus geoffroyi* and *N. major* (Chiroptera: Vespertilionidae) from south-western Australia', *Aust. J. Zool.*, vol. 45, pp. 489–504.

Hosken, D.J. 1997c, 'Sperm Competition in Bats', *Proc. Roy. Soc. Lond.*, vol. 264, pp. 385–92.

Hosken, D.J. 1997d, 'Thermal biology and metabolism of the Greater long-eared bat, *Nyctophilus major* (Chiroptera: Vespertilionidae)', *Aust. J. Zool.*, vol. 45, pp. 145–56.

Hosken, D.J. 1997e, 'Seasonal changes in testis mass and epididymal volume in the Greater long-eared bat, *Nyctophilus timoriensis* (*major*), from the Goldfields region of Western Australia', *Aust. Mammal.*, vol. 20, pp. 121–2.

Hosken, D.J. 1998a, 'Sperm fertility and skewed paternity during sperm competition in the Australian long-eared bat *Nyctophilus geoffroyi* (Chiroptera: Vespertilionidae)', *J. Zool. Lond.*, vol. 245, pp. 93–100.

Hosken, D.J. 1998b, 'Testes mass in megachiropterans bats varies in accordance with sperm competition theory', *Behav. Ecol. Sociobiol.*, vol. 44, pp. 169–77.

Hosken, D.J., Bailey, W.J., O'Shea, J.E. & Roberts, J.D. 1994, 'Localisation of insect calls by the bat *Nyctophilus geoffroyi* (Chiroptera: Vespertilionidae): a laboratory study', *Aust. J. Zool.*, vol. 42, pp. 177–84.

Hosken, D.J., Blackberry, M.A., Stewart, T.B. & Stucki, A.F. 1998, 'The male reproductive cycle of three species of Australian vespertilionid bat', *J. Zool. Lond.*, vol. 245, pp. 261–70.

Hosken, D.J. & O'Shea, J.E. 1994, '*Falsistrellus mackenziei* at Jandakot', *West. Aust. Nat.*, vol. 19(4), p. 351.

Hosken, D.J., O'Shea, J.E. & Blackberry, M.A. 1996, 'Blood plasma concentrations of progesterone, sperm storage, and sperm viability and fertility in Gould's wattled bat (*Chalinolobus gouldii*)', *J. Reprod. Fert.*, vol. 108, pp. 171–7.

Hosken, D.J. & Withers, P.C. 1997, 'Temperature regulation and metabolism of an Australian bat, *Chalinolobus gouldii* (Chiroptera: Vespertilionidae) when euthermic and torpid', *J. Comp. Physiol. B*, vol. 167, pp. 71–80.

Hosken, D.J. & Withers, P.C. 1999, 'Metabolic physiology of euthermic and torpid lesser long eared bats, *Nyctophilus geoffroyi* (Chiroptera: Vespertilionidae)', *J. Mammal.*, vol. 80, pp. 42–52.

Hoye, G. 1985, 'Observations on bats of Cape Hillsborough National Park, Queensland', *Macroderma*, vol. 1(2), pp. 48–51.

Hutcheon, J.M. & Kirsch, J.A. 2004, 'Camping in a different tree: results of molecular systematic studies of bats using DNA–DNA hybridization', *J. Mammal. Evol.*, vol. 11, pp. 17–47.

Ingleby, S. & Colgan, D. 2003, 'Electrophoretic studies of the systematic and biogeographic relationships of the Fijian bat genera *Pteropus, Pteralopex, Chaerephon* and *Notopteris*', *Aust. Mammal.*, vol. 25, pp. 13–29.

James, D.J. 2005, 'Christmas Island Pipistrelle *Pipistrellus murrayi*: An interim assessment of conservation status and threats', report to Parks Australia North, Christmas Island, Australian Government Department of the Environment and Heritage.

James, D.J., Dale, G.J., Retallick, K. & Orchard, K. 2006, 'Christmas Island Flying-fox *Pteropus natalis* Thomas 1887: An assessment of conservation status and threats', report to Department of Finance and Administration, Department of Environment and Heritage.

Jansen, L. 1987, 'The occurrence of *Myotis adversus* confirmed on the River Murray in South Australia', *Macroderma*, vol. 3, pp. 14–15.

Jenkins, P.D. & Hill, J.E. 1981, 'The status of *Hipposideros galeritus* Cantor, 1846 and *Hipposideros cervinus* (Gould 1854) (Chiroptera: Hipposideridae)', *Bull. British Mus. (Nat. Hist.) Zool.*, vol. 41, pp. 279–94.

Johnson, D.L. 1964, 'Mammals of the Arnhemland Expedition', in R.L. Specht (ed.), *Records of the American–Australian Expedition to Arnhemland, 4. Zoology*, Melbourne University Press, Melbourne, pp. 427–515.

Jolly, S. 1988, 'Five colonies of the Orange horseshoe bat, *Rhinonycteris aurantius*, in the Northern Territory', *Aust. Wildl. Res.*, vol. 14, pp. 41–9.

Jolly, S. 1990, 'The Biology of the Common Sheath-tail Bat, *Taphozous georgianus* (Chiroptera: Emballonuridae), in Central Queensland', *Aust. J. Zool.*, vol. 38, pp. 65–77.

Jolly, S.E. & Blackshaw, A.W. 1987, 'Prolonged epididymal sperm storage, and temporal dissociation of testicular and accessory gland activity in the common sheath-tail bat, *Taphozous georgianus*, of tropical Australia', *J. Reprod. Fert.*, vol. 81, pp. 205–11.

Kincade, T.J., Jones, S.M. & Richardson, A.M.M. 2000, 'Evidence for a shift in timing of reproductive events in Tasmanian bats', *Aust. Bat Soc. Newsl.*, vol. 15, p. 32.

Kingston, T., Jones, G., Zubaid, A. & Kunz, T.H. 1999, 'Echolocation signal design in Kerivoulinae and Murininae (Chiroptera: Vespertilionidae) from Malaysia', *J. Zool. Soc. Lond.*, vol. 249, pp. 359–74.

Kingston, T. & Rossiter, S.J. 2004, 'Harmonic-hopping in Wallacea's bats', *Nature* (London), vol. 429, pp. 654–7.

Kitchener, D.J. 1973, 'Reproduction in the Common sheathtail bat, *Taphozous georgianus* (Thomas) (Microchiroptera: Emballonuridae) in Western Australia', *Aust. J. Zool.*, vol. 21, pp. 375–89.

Kitchener, D.J. 1975, 'Reproduction in female Gould's wattled bat, *Chalinolobus gouldii* (Gray) (Vespertilionidae) in Western Australia', *Aust. J. Zool.*, vol. 23, pp. 29–42.

Kitchener, D.J. 1976a, 'Further observations on the Common Sheath-tailed bat, *Taphozous georgianus* Thomas, 1915, in Western Australia, with notes on the gular pouch', *Rec. West. Aust. Mus.*, vol. 4, pp. 335–47.

Kitchener, D.J. 1976b, '*Eptesicus douglasi*, a new Vespertilionid bat from the Kimberley, Western Australia', *Rec. of the West. Aust. Mus.*, vol. 4, pp. 295–301.

Kitchener, D.J. 1978, 'Mammals of the Ord River area, Kimberley, Western Australia', *Rec. of the West. Aust. Mus.*, vol. 6, pp. 189–219.

Kitchener, D.J. 1980, '*Taphozous hilli sp. nova.* (Chiroptera: Emballonuridae), a new sheath-tailed bat from Western Australia and Northern Territory', *Rec. West. Aust. Mus.*, vol. 8, pp. 161–9.

Kitchener, D.J., Adams, M. & Boeadi 1994, 'Morphological and genetic relationships among populations of *Scotorepens sanborni* (Chiroptera: Vespertilionidae) from Papua New Guinea, Australia and Indonesia', *Aust. Mammal.*, vol. 17, pp. 31–42.

Kitchener, D.J. & Caputi, N. 1985, 'Systematic revision of Australian *Scoteanax* and *Scotorepens* (Microchiroptera: Vespertilionidae), with remarks on relationships to other Nycticeiini', *Rec. West. Aust. Mus.*, vol. 12, pp. 85–146.

Kitchener, D.J., Caputi, N. & Jones, B. 1986, 'Revision of Australo-Papuan *Pipistrellus* and *Falsistrellus* (Microchiroptera: Vespertilionidae)', *Rec. West. Aust. Mus.*, vol. 12, pp. 435–95.

Kitchener, D.J., Cooper, N. & Maryanto, I. 1995, 'The *Myotis adversus* (Chiroptera: Vespertilionidae) species complex in Eastern Indonesia, Australia, Papua New Guinea and the Solomon Islands', *Rec. West. Aust. Mus.*, vol. 17, pp. 191–212.

Kitchener, D.J. & Coster, P. 1981, 'Reproduction in female *Chalinolobus morio* (Gray) (Vespertilionidae) in south-western Australia', *Aust. J. Zool.*, vol. 29, pp. 305–20.

Kitchener, D.J., How, R.A., Cooper, N.K. & Suyanto, A. 1992, '*Hipposideros diadema* (Chiroptera Hipposideridae) in the Lesser Sunda Islands, Indonesia: taxonomy and geographic morphological variation', *Rec. West. Aust. Mus.*, vol. 16, pp. 1–60.

Kitchener, D.J. & Hudson, C.J. 1982, 'Reproduction in the female White-striped Mastiff bat, *Tadarida australis* (Gray) (Molossidae)', *Aust. J. Zool.*, vol. 30, pp. 1–22.

Kitchener, D.J., Jones, B. & Caputi, N. 1987, 'Revision of Australian *Eptesicus* (Microchiroptera: Vespertilionidae)', *Rec. West. Aust. Mus.*, vol. 13, pp. 427–500.

Kitchener, D.J., Keller, L.E., Chapman, A., McKenzie, N.L., Start, A.N. & Kenneally, K.F. 1981, 'Observations on mammals of the Mitchell Plateau area, Kimberley, Western Australia', in *Biol. Survey Mitchell Plateau Admiralty Gulf*, Western Australian Museum Publication, Perth.

Koopman, K.F. 1984, 'Taxonomic and distributional notes on tropical Australian bats', *Amer. Mus. Novit.*, vol. 2778, pp. 1–48.

Kristo, F. 1987, 'White-striped mastiff bat, *Tadarida australis*, (Molossidae) feeding on the ground', *Macroderma*, vol. 3, pp. 32–3.

Krutzsch, P.H. & Crichton, E.G. 1987, 'Reproductive biology of the male Little mastiff bat, *Mormopterus planiceps* (Chiroptera: Molossidae), in southeast Australia', *Amer. J. Anat.*, vol. 178, pp. 352–68.

Krutzsch, P.H., Young, R.A. & Crichton, E.G. 1992, 'Observations on the reproductive biology and anatomy of *Rhinolophus megaphyllus* (Chiroptera: Rhinolophidae) in eastern Australia', *Aust. J. Zool.*, vol. 40, pp. 533–49.

Kulzer, E., Nelson, J.E., McKean, J.L. & Mohres, F.P. 1984, 'Prey catching behaviour and echolocation in the Australian Ghost Bat, *Macroderma gigas* (Microchiroptera: Megadermatidae)', *Aust. Mammal.*, vol. 7, pp. 37–50.

Kunz, T.H. & Kurta, A. 1988, 'Capture methods and holding devices', in *Ecological and Behavioural Methods for the Study of Bats*, T.H. Kunz (ed.), Smithsonian Institution Press, Washington, pp. 1–29.

Kutt, A.S. 2003, 'Two north-western Queensland records of Gould's Long-eared bat *Nyctophilus gouldi* (Chiroptera: Vespertilionidae) and evidence of cave roosting', *Aust. Zool.*, vol. 32, pp. 480–1.

Kutt, A.S. 2004, 'Clarification of the distribution of the Long-eared horseshoe bat *Rhinolophus philippinensis* complex in Australia', *Aust. Zool.*, vol. 32, pp. 629–31.

Kutt, A.S. & Schulz, M. 2000, 'Distribution and habitat of the flute-nosed bat *Murina florium* (Chiroptera: Vespertilionidae) in the wet tropics of north-eastern Queensland', *Aust. Zool.*, vol. 31, pp. 458–67.

Law, B.S. 1992, 'Physiological factors affecting pollen use by Queensland blossom bats (*Syconycteris australis*)', *Funct. Ecol.*, vol. 6, pp. 257–64.

Law, B.S. 1993, 'Roosting and foraging ecology of the Queensland blossom bat (*Syconycteris australis*) in north-eastern New South Wales: flexibility in response to seasonal variation', *Wildl. Res.*, vol. 20, pp. 419–31.

Law, B.S. 1994, '*Banksia* nectar and pollen: Dietary items affecting the abundance of the common blossom bat, *Syconycteris australis*, in south-eastern Australia', *Aust. J. Ecol.*, vol. 19, pp. 425–34.

Law, B.S. 1995, 'The effect of energy supplementation on the local abundance of the common blossom bat, *Syconycteris australis*, in south-eastern Australia', *Oikos*, vol. 72, pp. 42–50.

Law, B.S. 1997, 'The lunar cycle influences time of roost departure in the Common Blossom Bat, *Syconycteris australis*', *Aust. Mammal.*, vol. 20, pp. 21–4.

Law, B.S. 2001, 'The diet of the common blossom bat, (*Syconycteris australis*) in upland tropical rainforest and the importance of riparian areas', *Wildl. Res.*, vol. 28, pp. 619–26.

Law, B.S. & Anderson, J. 1999, 'A survey for the Southern Myotis *Myotis macropus* (Vespertilionidae) and other bat species in river red gum *Eucalyptus camaldulensis* forests of the Murray River, New South Wales', *Aust. Zool.*, vol. 31, pp. 166–74.

Law, B.S. & Anderson, J. 2000, 'Roost preferences and foraging ranges of the eastern forest bat *Vespadelus pumilus* under two disturbance histories in northern New South Wales, Australia', *Austral. Ecol.*, vol. 25, pp. 352–67.

Law, B.S., Anderson, J. & Chidel, M. 1998, 'A bat survey in State Forests on the south-west slopes region of New South Wales with suggestions of improvements for future surveys', *Aust. Zool.*, vol. 30, pp. 467–79.

Law, B.S., Anderson, J. & Chidel, M. 1999, 'Bat communities in a fragmented forest landscape on the south-west slopes of New South Wales, Australia', *Biol. Cons.*, vol. 88, pp. 333–45.

Law, B.S. & Chidel, M. 2000, 'Roosts of a male and female Little Forest Bat *Vespadelus vulturnus* in northern New South Wales', *Aust. Bat Soc. Newsl.*, vol. 15, pp. 27–9.

Law, B.S. & Chidel, M. 2002, 'Tracks and riparian zones facilitate the use of Australian regrowth forest by insectivorous bats', *J. Appl. Ecol.*, vol. 39, pp. 605–17.

Law, B.S. & Chidel, M. 2004, 'Roosting and foraging ecology of the golden-tipped bat (*Kerivoula papuensis*) on the south coast of New South Wales', *Wildl. Res.*, vol. 31, pp. 73–82.

Law, B.S. & Chidel, M. 2006, 'Eucalypt plantings on farms: Use by insectivorous bats in south-eastern Australia', *Biol. Cons.*, vol. 133, pp. 236–49.

Law, B.S., Chidel, M., Britton, A. & Fawcett, A. 2004, 'Monitoring Australia's largest roost of eastern horseshoe bats', *Aust. Bat Soc. Newsl.*, vol. 22, p. 41.

Law, B.S., Chidel, M. & Mong, A. 2005, 'Life under a sandstone overhang: the ecology of the eastern cave bat *Vespadelus troughtoni* in northern New South Wales', *Aust. Mammal.*, vol. 27, pp. 137–45.

Law, B.S., Chidel, M. & Towerton, A. 2001, 'A maternity roost of the Southern Myotis *Myotis macropus* in a rural landscape', *Aust. Bat Soc. Newsl.*, vol. 17, pp. 13–15.

Law, B.S., Chidel, M. & Turner, G. 2000, 'The use of wildlife of paddock trees in farmland', *Pacific Cons. Biol.*, vol. 6, pp. 130–43.

Law, B.S. & Lean, M. 1999, 'Common blossom bats *Syconycteris australis* as pollinators in fragmented Australian tropical rainforest', *Biol. Cons.*, vol. 91, pp. 201–12.

Law, B.S., Reinhold, L. & Pennay, M. 2002, 'Geographic variation in the echolocation calls of *Vespadelus* spp. (Vespertilionidae) from New South Wales and Queensland, Australia', *Acta Chiropterologica*, vol. 4, pp. 201–15.

Law, B.S. & Urquhart, C. 2000, 'Diet of the large-footed Myotis *Myotis macropus* at a forest stream roost in northern New South Wales', *Aust. Mammal.*, vol. 22, pp. 121–4.

Little, L. & Hall, L.S. 1996, 'Preliminary observations on the bats of Cape Melville National Park', *Aust. Bat Soc. Newsl.*, vol. 7, p. 62.

Lloyd, A., Law, B. & Goldingay, R. 2006, 'Bat activity on riparian zones and upper slopes in Australian timber production forests and the effectiveness of riparian buffers', *Biol. Cons.*, vol. 129, pp. 207–20.

Lloyd, S., Hall, L.S. & Bradley, A.J. 1999, 'Reproductive strategies of a warm temperate Vespertilionid, the large-footed myotis, *Myotis moluccarum* (Microchiroptera: Vespertilionidae)', *Aust. J. Zool.*, vol. 47, pp. 261–74.

Lowry, J.B. 1989, 'Green-leaf fractionation by fruit bats: is this feeding behaviour a unique nutritional strategy for herbivores?', *Aust. Wildl. Res.*, vol. 16, pp. 203–6.

Lumsden, L. 1994, 'The distribution, habitat and conservation status of the Greater Long-eared bat *Nyctophilus timoriensis* in Victoria', *Vic. Nat.*, vol. 111, pp. 4–9.

Lumsden, L. 1999, 'Does the white-striped freetail bat, *Tadarida australis*, migrate north for the winter?', *Aust. Bat Res. News.*, vol. 12, pp. 24–6.

Lumsden, L. 2004, 'The ecology and conservation of insectivorous bats in rural landscapes', unpublished PhD thesis, Deakin University.

Lumsden, L., Bennett, A. & Silins, J. 2002, 'Location of roosts of the lesser long-eared bat *Nyctophilus geoffroyi* and Gould's wattled bat *Chalinolobus gouldii* in a fragmented landscape in south-eastern Australia', *Biol. Cons.*, vol. 106, pp. 237–49.

Lumsden, L., Bennett, A., Silins, J. & Krasna, S. 1994, 'Fauna in a remnant vegetation-farmland mosaic: movements, roosts and foraging ecology of bats', report to the Australian Nature Conservation Agency 'Save the Bush' Program.

Lumsden, L. & Cherry, K. 1997, 'Report on a preliminary investigation of the Christmas Island Pipistrelle, *Pipistrellus murrayi*, in June-July 1994', a report to Parks Australia North, Christmas Island, Arthur Rylah Institute for Environmental Research, Heidelberg.

Lumsden, L. & Churchill, S. 1999, 'A survey of bats from the Ord River Irrigation Area Stage 2 Project', a report to Kinhill Pty Ltd, Arthur Rylah Institute for Environmental Research, Heidelberg.

Lumsden, L., Churchill, S. & Schulz, M. 2005, 'Bat survey of the Ord River Stage 2, M2 Area, Western Australia', report for the Western Australian Department of Industry and Resources, pp. 1–187.

Lumsden, L. & Coles, R. 1993, 'Fast fliers of the night', *Wildl. Aust.*, autumn, pp. 21–3.

Lumsden, L.F. & Bennett, A.F. 1995, 'Bats of a semi-arid environment in South-eastern Australia: Biogeography, Ecology and Conservation', *Wildl. Res.*, vol. 22, pp. 217–40.

Lumsden, L.F. & Bennett, A.F. 1996, 'Roost site selection of the lesser long-eared bat *Nyctophilus geoffroyi* and Gould's wattled bat *Chalinolobus gouldii* in a fragmented rural landscape in northern Victoria', *Aust. Bat Soc. Newsl.*, vol. 7, p. 56.

Lumsden, L.F. & Bennett, A.F. 2005, 'Scattered trees in rural landscapes: foraging habitat for insectivorous bats in south-eastern Australia', *Biol. Cons.*, vol. 122, pp. 205–22.

Lumsden, L.F., Johnstone, P.D. & Temby, I.D. 1993, 'A roosting colony of the Northern Mastiff-bat *Chaerephon jobensis* at Derby, Western Australia', *Aust. Bat Soc. Newsl.*, vol. 2, pp. 13–15.

Lunney, D. & Barker, J. 1986, 'The occurrence of *Phoniscus papuensis* (Dobson) (Chiroptera: Vespertilionidae) on the south coast of New South Wales', *Aust. Mammal.*, vol. 9, pp. 57–8.

Lunney, D. & Barker, J. 1987, 'Mammals of the coastal forest near Bega, New South Wales, annotated checklist', *Aust. Zool.*, vol. 23, pp. 41–9.

Lunney, D., Barker, J., Leary, T., Priddel, D., Wheeler, R., O'Connell, M. & Law, B. 1995, 'Roost selection by the North Queensland long-eared bat, *Nyctophilus bifax*, in littoral rainforest in the Iluka World Heritage Area, New South Wales', *Aust. J. Ecol.*, vol. 20, pp. 532–7.

Lunney, D., Barker, J. & Priddel, D. 1985, 'Movements and day roosts of the Chocolate wattled bat *Chalinolobus morio* (Gray) (Microchiroptera: Vespertilionidae) in a logged forest', *Aust. Mammal.*, vol. 8, pp. 313–17.

Lunney, D., Barker, J., Priddel, D. & O'Connell, M. 1988, 'Roost selection by Gould's long-eared bat, *Nyctophilus gouldi* Tomes (Chiroptera: Vespertilionidae), in logged forest on the south coast of New South Wales', *Aust. Wildl. Res.*, vol. 15, pp. 375–84.

Mackey, R.L. & Barclay, R.M.R. 1989, 'The influence of physical clutter and noise on the activity of bats over water', *Can. J. Zool.*, vol. 67, pp. 1167–70.

Maddock, T.H. & McLeod, A.N. 1974, 'Polyoestry in the little Brown bat, *Eptesicus pumilus,* in central Australia', *South Aust. Nat.*, vol. 48, pp. 50–63.

Maddock, T.H. & McLeod, A.N. 1976, 'Observations on the Little brown bat, *Eptesicus pumilus caurinus* Thomas, in the Tennant Creek area of the Northern Territory. Part one: introduction and breeding biology', *South Aust. Nat.*, vol. 50, pp. 42–50.

Markus, N. 2002, 'Behaviour of the Black flying-fox *Pteropus alecto*: II. Territoriality and courtship', *Acta Chiropterologica*, vol. 4, pp. 153–66.

Markus, N. & Hall, L.S. 2004, 'Foraging behaviour of the Black flying-fox (*Pteropus alecto*) in the urban landscape of Brisbane, Queensland', *Wildl. Res.*, vol. 31, pp. 1–11.

Martin, L., Towers, P.A., McGuckin, M.A., Little, L., Luckhoff, H. & Blackshaw, A.W. 1987, 'Reproductive biology of flying-foxes (Chiroptera: Pteropodidae)', *Aust. Mammal.*, vol. 10, pp. 115–18.

McKean, J.L. 1970, 'A new sub-species of the horseshoe bat, *Hipposideros diadema*, in Australia', *West. Aust. Nat.*, vol. 11, pp. 138–40.

McKean, J.L. & Friend, G.R. 1979, '*Taphozous kapalgensis*, a new species of Sheath-tailed bat from the Northern Territory, Australia', *Vic. Nat.*, vol. 96, pp. 239–41.

McKean, J.L., Friend, G.R. & Hertog, A.L. 1981, 'Occurrence of the sheath-tailed bat, *Taphozous saccolaimus*, in the Northern Territory', *N.T. Nat.*, vol. 1, p. 20.

McKean, J.L. & Hertog, A.L. 1979, 'Extension in range in the horseshoe bat', *N.T. Nat.*, vol. 1, p. 5.

McKenzie, N.L. & Bullen, B. 2003, 'Identifying Little Sandy Desert bat species by their echolocation calls', *Aust. Mammal.*, vol. 25, pp. 73–80.

McKenzie, N.L., Burbidge, A.A., Chapman, A. & Youngson, W.K. 1978, 'Mammals. Part III in The islands of the north-west Kimberley, Western Australia', A.A. Burbidge & N.L. McKenzie (eds), *Wildl. Res. Bull. West. Aust.*, vol. 7, pp. 1–47.

McKenzie, N.L., Chapman, A. & Youngson, W.K. 1975, 'Mammals of the Prince Regent River Reserve, North-west Kimberley, Western Australia', *Wildl. Res. Bull. West. Aust.*, vol. 3, pp. 69–74.

McKenzie, N.L., Gunnell, A.C., Yani, M. & Williams, M.R. 1995, 'Correspondence between flight morphology and foraging ecology in some Paleo-tropical bats', *Aust. J. Zool.*, vol. 43, pp. 241–57.

McKenzie, N.L. & Muir, W.P. 2000, 'Bats of the Carnarvon Basin, Western Australia', *Rec. West. Aust. Mus. Suppl.*, no. 61, pp. 467–77.

McKenzie, N.L. & Rolfe, J.K. 1986, 'Structure of bat guilds in the Kimberley mangroves, Australia', *J. Anim. Ecol.*, vol. 55, pp. 401–20.

McKenzie, N.L., Start, A.N. & Bullen, R.D. 2002, 'Foraging ecology and organisation of a desert bat fauna', *Aust. J. Zool.*, vol. 50, pp. 529–48.

Menkhorst, P. (ed.) 1995, *The Mammals of Victoria: Distribution, ecology and conservation*, Oxford University Press, Melbourne.

Menzies, J.I. 1971, 'The lobe-lipped bat (*Chalinolobus nigrogriseus* Gould) in New Guinea', *Rec. Papua New Guinea Mus.*, vol. 1, pp. 6–8.

Metcalf, B. 2002, 'Effect of roost behaviour and sampling technique on sex ratio estimates in an inland cave bat (*Vespadelus finlaysoni*) population', *Aust. Bat Res. News.*, vol. 18, p. 37.

Mickleburgh, S.P., Hutson, A.M. & Racey, P.A. 1992, *Old World Fruit Bats. An Action Plan for their Conservation*, IUCN, Gland.

Milledge, D., Parnaby, H. & Phillips, S. 1992, 'Recent records of the Hoary bat *Chalinolobus nigrogriseus* from New South Wales', *Aust. Zool.*, vol. 28, pp. 55–7.

Milledge, D.R. 1987a, 'Predation of a mist-netted Queensland Blossom-bat', *Macroderma*, vol. 3, p. 30.

Milledge, D.R. 1987b, 'Notes on the occurrence of the Queensland tube-nosed bat *Nyctimene robinsoni*, in north-eastern New South Wales', *Aust. Zool.*, vol. 3, pp. 29–30.

Milne, D. & Burwell, C. (unpubl.) 'Diet of Top End bats', unpublished report, Parks and Wildlife Commission of the Northern Territory.

Milne, D.J. 2002, *Key to the bat calls of the Top End of the Northern Territory*, Technical Report No. 71, Parks and Wildlife Commission of the Northern Territory.

Milne, D.J., Armstrong, M., Fisher, A., Flores, T. & Pavey, C.R. 2005, 'Structure and environmental relationships of insectivorous bat assemblages in tropical Australian savannas', *Austral. Ecol.*, vol. 30, pp. 906–19.

Milne, D.J., Fisher, A. & Pavey, C.R. 2006, 'Models of the habitat associations and distributions of insectivorous bats of the Top End of the Northern Territory, Australia', *Biol. Cons.*, vol. 130, pp. 370–85.

Milne, D.J., Fisher, A., Rainey, I. & Pavey, C.R. 2005, 'Temporal patterns of bats in the Top End of the Northern Territory, Australia', *J. Mammal.*, vol. 86, pp. 909–20.

Milne, D.J., Jackling, F.C. & Appleton, B.R. 2008, 'A large range extension for the critically endangered Bare-rumped sheathtail bat *Saccolaimus saccolaimus* (chiroptera: Emballonuridae) including genetic analysis, notes on field identification and description of echolocation call', *Wildl. Res.* (in press).

Milne, D.J. & Nash, K.L. 2003, 'Range extension for the white-striped freetail bat *Tadarida australis* in the Northern Territory, from Anabat recordings', *N.T. Nat.*, vol. 17, pp. 46–9.

Milne, D.J., Reardon, T.B. & Watt, F. 2003, 'New Records for the Arnhem sheathtail bat *Taphozous kapalgensis* (Chiroptera: Emballonuridae) from voucher specimens and Anabat recordings', *Aust. Zool.*, vol. 32, pp. 439–45.

Murphy, S. 2002, 'Observations of the "critically endangered" bare-rumped sheathtail bat *Saccolaimus saccolaimus* Temminck (Chiroptera: Emballonuridae) on Cape York Peninsula, Queensland', *Aust. Mammal.*, vol. 23, pp. 185–7.

Nelson, J.E. 1964, 'Notes on *Syconycteris australis*, Peters, 1867 (Megachiroptera)', *Mammalia*, vol. 28, pp. 429–32.

Nelson, J.E. 1965a, 'Movements of Australian flying foxes (Pteropodidae: Megachiroptera)', *Aust. J. Zool.*, vol. 13, pp. 53–73.

Nelson, J.E. 1965b, 'Behaviour of Australian Pteropodidae (Megachiroptera)', *Anim. Behaviour*, vol. 13, pp. 544–57.

Nelson, J.E. 1989, 'Megadermatidae', in D.W. Walton & B.J. Richardson (eds), *Fauna of Australia. Volume 1B: Mammalia*, Australian Government Publishing Service, Canberra, ch. 39.

O'Brien, G.M. 1993, 'Seasonal reproduction in flying-foxes, reviewed in the context of other tropical mammals', *Reprod., Fert. Devel.*, vol. 5, pp. 499–521.

O'Brien, G.M., Curlewis, J.D. & Martin, L. 1993, 'Effect of photoperiod on the annual cycle of testis growth in a tropical mammal, the little red flying-fox, *Pteropus scapulatus*', *J. Reprod. Fert.*, vol. 98, pp. 121–7.

O'Neill, M.G. & Taylor, R.J. 1986, 'Observations on the flight patterns and foraging behaviour of Tasmanian bats', *Aust. Wildl. Res.*, vol. 13, pp. 427–32.

O'Neill, M.G. & Taylor, R.J. 1989, 'Feeding ecology of Tasmanian bat assemblages', *Aust. J. Ecol.*, vol. 14, pp. 19–31.

Palmer, C., Price, O. & Bach, C. 2000, 'Foraging ecology of the black flying-fox (*Pteropus alecto*) in the seasonal tropics of the Northern Territory, Australia', *Wildl. Res.*, vol. 27, pp. 160–78.

Palmer, C. & Woinarski, J.C.Z. 1999, 'Seasonal roosts and foraging movements of the black flying-fox (*Pteropus alecto*) in the Northern Territory; resource tracking in a landscape mosaic', *Wildl. Res.*, vol. 26, pp. 823–38.

Parnaby, H. 1976, 'Live records for Victoria of the bat *Pipistrellus tasmaniensis* (Gould 1858)', *Vic. Nat.*, vol. 93, pp. 190–3.

Parnaby, H. 1977, 'Bat survey of the Dalesford Area, Victoria', *Vic. Nat.*, vol. 94, pp. 191–7.

Parnaby, H. 1992, 'An interim guide to the identification of bats in south-eastern Australia', *Tech. Rep. Aust. Mus.*, vol. 8, pp. 1–33.

Parnaby, H. 1996, 'The common name and common misconceptions about the common bent-wing bat', *Aust. Bat Soc. Newsl.*, vol. 7, pp. 35–8.

Parnaby, H.E. 1987, 'Distribution and taxonomy of the Long-eared Bats, *Nyctophilus gouldi* Tomes, 1858 and *Nyctophilus bifax* Thomas, 1915 (Chiroptera: Vespertilionidae) in eastern Australia', *Proc. Linnaean Soc. NSW*, vol. 109, pp. 153–74.

Parnaby, H.E. 2007, 'A taxonomic review of the Australian Greater Long-eared Bat *Nyctophilus timoriensis* (Chiroptera: Vespertilionidae) and associated taxa', *Zootaxa* (in press).

Parris, K.M. & Hazell, D.L. 2005, 'Biotic effects of climate change in urban environments: the case of the grey-headed flying-fox (*Pteropus poliocephalus*) in Melbourne, Australia', *Biol. Cons.*, vol. 124, pp. 267–76.

Parry-Jones, K. & Augee, M. 1991, 'Food selection by Grey-headed flying foxes (*Pteropus poliocephalus*) occupying a summer colony site near Gosford, New South Wales', *Wildl. Res.*, vol. 18, pp. 111–24.

Parry-Jones, K.A. & Augee, M.L. 2001, 'Factors affecting the occupation of a colony site in Sydney, New South Wales by the Grey-headed flying-fox *Pteropus poliocephalus* (Pteropodidae)', *Aust. Ecol.*, vol. 26, pp. 47–55.

Pavey, C.R. 1994, 'Foraging ecology and habitat use of the Diadem Horseshoe bat in north Queensland', *Aust. Bat Soc. Newsl.*, vol. 3, p. 8.

Pavey, C.R. 1995, 'Foraging ecology of a guild of insectivorous bats (Rhinolophoidea) in eastern Australia: a test resource partitioning theory', unpublished PhD thesis, University of Qld.

Pavey, C.R. 1998a, 'Colony sizes, roost use and foraging ecology of *Hipposideros diadema reginae*, a rare bat from tropical Australia', *Pacific Cons. Biol.*, vol. 4, pp. 232–9.

Pavey, C.R. 1998b, Habitat use by the eastern horseshoe bat, *Rhinolophus megaphyllus*, in a fragmented woodland mosaic', *Wildl. Res.*, vol. 25, pp. 489–98.

Pavey, C.R. 1999, 'Foraging ecology of the two taxa of large-eared horseshoe bat, *Rhinolophus philippinensis*, on Cape York Peninsula', *Aust. Mammal.*, vol. 21, pp. 135–8.

Pavey, C.R. & Burwell, C.J. 1997, 'The diet of the Diadem leaf-nosed bat, *Hipposideros diadema*: confirmation of a morphologically-based prediction of carnivory', *J. Zool., Lond.*, vol. 243, pp. 295–303.

Pavey, C.R. & Burwell, C.J. 1998, 'Bat predation on eared-moths: a test of the allotonic frequency hypothesis', *Oikos*, vol. 81, pp. 143–51.

Pavey, C.R. & Burwell, C.J. 2000, 'Foraging strategies of three species of hipposiderid bats in tropical rainforest in north-east Australia', *Wildl. Res.*, vol. 27, pp. 283–7.

Pavey, C.R. & Burwell, C.J. 2004, 'Foraging ecology of the horseshoe bat, *Rhinolophus megaphyllus* (Rhinolophidae), in eastern Australia', *Wildl. Res.*, vol. 31, pp. 403–13.

Pavey, C.R. & Burwell, C.J. 2005, 'Cohabitation and predation by insectivorous bats on eared moths in subterranean roosts', *J. Zool., Lond.*, vol. 265, pp. 141–6.

Pennay, M. 2002, 'Fauna species profiles—bats', in Appendix 2, 'Brigalow Belt South Stage Two, Vertebrate Fauna Survey, Analysis Modelling', unpublished report, Resource and Conservation Division, Planning NSW, Sydney, pp. 24–39.

Pennay, M. 2006, 'Ecological Study Endangered Bristle-nosed bat (*Mormopterus* "species 6") survey microchiropteran bats in Gundabooka National Park', unpublished report, NSW Department of Environment and Conservation, Queanbeyan, pp. 1–24.

Pennay, M. & Freeman, J. 2005, 'Day roost of the little pied bat *Chalinolobus picatus* (Gould) (Microchiroptera: Vespertilionidae) in north inland New South Wales, Australia', *Aust. Zool.*, vol. 33, pp. 166–7.

Pennay, M., Law, B. & Reinhold, L. 2004, 'Bat calls of New South Wales: Region based guide to the echolocation calls of microchiropteran bats', report published by the NSW Department of Environment and Conservation, Hurstville.

Pettigrew, J., Baker, G., Baker-Gabb, D., Baverstock, G., Coles, R., Canole, L., Churchill, S., Fitzherbert, K., Guppy, A., Hall, L., Helman, P., Nelson, J., Priddel, D., Pulsford, I., Richards, G., Schulz, M. & Tidemann, C. 1986, 'The Australian Ghost Bat, *Macroderma gigas,* at Pine Creek, Northern Territory', *Macroderma,* vol. 2, pp. 8–19.

Phillips, W.R. & Inwards, S.J. 1985, 'The annual activity and breeding cycles of Gould's long-eared bat, *Nyctophilus gouldi* (Microchiroptera: Vespertilionidae)', *Aust. J. Zool.,* vol. 33, pp. 111–26.

Phillips, W.R., Tidemann, C.R., Inwards, S.J. & Winderlich, S. 1985, 'The Tasmanian Pipistrelle: *Pipistrellus tasmaniensis* Gould 1858: annual activity and breeding cycles', *Macroderma,* vol. 1, p. 1.

Pinson, D. 2007, *The Flying-fox manual, a new handbook for wildlife carers involved in the care of orphaned baby, and the rescue, rehabilitation and release of adult flying-foxes in Australia,* release version 1.1, published by the author and available at www.stickeebatz.com.

Prociv, P. 1983, 'Seasonal behaviour of *Pteropus scapulatus* (Chiroptera: Pteropodidae)', *Aust. Mammal.,* vol. 6, pp. 45–6.

Purchase, D. 1982, 'An Australian bat longevity record', *Aust. Bat Res. News,* vol. 18, p. 11.

Queale, L.F. 1997, 'Field identification of female little brown bats *Vespadelus* spp. (Chiroptera: Vespertilionidae) in South Australia', *Rec. Sth. Aust. Mus.,* vol. 30, pp. 29–30.

Ratcliffe, F.N. 1931, 'The flying fox (*Pteropus*) in Australia', *Council for Sci. Indust. Res. Bull.,* vol. 53, pp. 1–81.

Rautenbach, I.L. 1985, 'A new technique for the efficient use of macromist-nets', *Koedoe,* vol. 28, pp. 81–6.

Reardon, T. 1999, 'Nomenclature of *Tadarida australis* (Gray 1838)', *Aust. Bat Soc. Newsl.,* vol. 12, pp. 22–4.

Reardon, T. & Thomson, B. 2002, 'Taxonomy and conservation status of Troughton's sheathtail bat—(*Taphozous troughtoni*)', report to Natural Heritage Trust.

Reardon, T.B. 2001, 'The unusual penis morphology of the hairy-nosed freetail bat', *Aust. Bat Soc. Newsl.,* vol. 17, pp. 53–4.

Reardon, T.B. & Flavel, S.C. 1991, *A Guide to the Bats of South Australia,* The South Australian Museum and the Field Naturalists' Society of South Australia, Adelaide.

Reinhold, L. 1997, 'Taxonomy of bent-winged bats (genus *Miniopterus*) in northern Australia and New Guinea', BSc (Hons) thesis, University of Queensland.

Reinhold, L., Law, B., Ford, G. & Pennay, M. 2001, *Key to the bat calls of south-east Queensland and north-east New South Wales,* Forest Ecosystem Research and Assessment Technical paper 2001–07, Department of Natural Resources and Mines, Queensland.

Reside, A. 2004, 'Resource partitioning of two closely related insectivorous bat species (*Mormopterus* spp.) in sympatry', BSc (Hons) thesis, Dept of Zoology, University of Melbourne.

Rhodes, M. 2001, 'Roost ecology and conservation of insectivorous bats in suburban Brisbane: and assessment of natural roost habitat of the white-striped free-tail bat (*Tadarida australis*), and artificial roost habitats (bat boxes) for insectivorous bats in Brisbane', *Aust. Bat Soc. Newsl.,* vol. 16, pp. 11–18.

Rhodes, M., Wardell-Johnson, G.W., Rhodes, M.P. & Raymond, B. 2005, 'Applying network analysis to the conservation of habitat trees in urban environments: a case study from Brisbane, Australia', *Conservation Biology,* vol. 20, pp. 861–70.

Rhodes, M.P. 1995, 'Wing morphology and flight behaviour of the Golden-tipped bat, *Phoniscus papuensis* (Dobson) (Chiroptera: Vespertilionidae)', *Aust. J. Zool.*, vol. 43, pp. 657–63.

Rhodes, M.P. & Hall, L.S. 1997a, 'Bats of Fraser Island', *Aust. Zool.*, vol. 30, pp. 346–50.

Rhodes, M.P. & Hall, L.S. 1997b, 'Observations on Yellow-bellied sheath-tailed bats *Saccolaimus flaviventris* (Peters, 1867) (Chiroptera: Emballonuridae)', *Aust. Zool.*, vol. 30, pp. 351–7.

Rhodes, M.P. & Wardell-Johnson, G. 2006, 'Roost tree characteristics determine the use of the white-striped freetail bat (*Tadarida australis*, Chiroptera: Molossidae) in suburban subtropical Brisbane, Australia', *Austral. Ecol.*, vol. 31, pp. 228–39.

Richards, G. 1979, 'New information on the Little pied bat, *Chalinolobus picatus*', *Aust. Bat Res. News*, vol. 14, pp. 6–7.

Richards, G. 1986, 'Notes on the natural history of the Queensland tube-nosed bat, *Nyctimene robinsoni*', *Macroderma*, vol. 2, pp. 64–7.

Richards, G.C. 1987, 'Aspects of the ecology of Spectacled Flying-foxes, *Pteropus conspicillatus*, (Chiroptera: Pteropodidae) in Tropical Queensland', *Aust. Mammal.*, vol. 10, pp. 87–8.

Richards, G.C. 1990a, 'The Spectacled flying-fox, *Pteropus conspicillatus*, (Chiroptera: Pteropodidae) in north Queensland. 1. Roost sites and distribution patterns', *Aust. Mammal.*, vol. 13, pp. 17–24.

Richards, G.C. 1990b, 'The Spectacled flying-fox, *Pteropus conspicillatus*, (Chiroptera: Pteropodidae), in north Queensland. 2. Diet, seed dispersal and feeding ecology', *Aust. Mammal.*, vol. 13, pp. 25–31.

Richards, G.C. & Hall, L.S. 2002, 'A new flying-fox of the genus *Pteropus* (Chiroptera: Pteropodidae) from Torres Strait, Australia', *Aust. Zool.*, vol. 32, pp. 69–75.

Richards, G.C., Hall, L.S., Helman, P.M. & Churchill, S.K. 1982, 'The first discovery of the rare Tube-nosed Insectivorous Bat (*Murina*) in Australia', *Aust. Mammal.*, vol. 5, pp. 149–51.

Richardson, E.G. 1977, 'The biology and evolution of the reproductive cycle of *Miniopterus schreibersii* and *M. australis* (Chiroptera: Vespertilionidae)', *J. Zool.*, vol. 183, pp. 353–75.

Robson, S. 1986, 'A new locality for the bare-backed fruit bat *Dobsonia moluccensis* (Quoy and Gaimard 1830)', *Macroderma*, vol. 2, pp. 63–4.

Robson, S.K. 1984, '*Myotis adversus* (Chiroptera: Vespertilionidae): Australia's fish-eating bat', *Aust. Mammal.*, vol. 7, pp. 51–2.

Rounsevell, D.E., Taylor, R.J. & Hocking, G.J. 1991, 'Distribution records of native terrestrial mammals in Tasmania', *Wildl. Res.*, vol. 18, pp. 699–717.

Ryan, R.M. 1965, 'Taxonomic status of the Vespertilionid genera *Kerivoula* and *Phoniscus*', *J. Mammal.*, vol. 46, pp. 517–18.

Ryan, R.M. 1966a, 'A new and imperfectly known Australian *Chalinolobus* and the taxonomic status of African *Glauconycteris*', *J. Mammal.*, vol. 47, pp. 86–91.

Ryan, R.M. 1966b, 'Observations on the broad-nosed bat, *Scoteinus balstoni* in Victoria', *J. Zool., Lond.*, vol. 148, pp. 162–6.

Sanderson, K. 2000, 'Observations on bat roosts in the Adelaide Hills 1999–2000', *Aust. Bat Res. News.*, vol. 15, pp. 40–1.

Schulz, M. 1986, 'Vertebrate prey of the Ghost bat, *Macroderma gigas*, at Pine Creek, Northern Territory', *Macroderma*, vol. 2, pp. 59–62.

Schulz, M. 1994, 'A bat survey of the south-west coast of Tasmania—an example of remote area sampling', *Aust. Bat Soc. Newsl.*, vol. 3, pp. 9–10.

Schulz, M. 1995a, 'Notes on the eastern tube-nosed bat *Nyctimene robinsoni* from the Richmond range, north-eastern New South Wales', *Aust. Mammal.*, vol. 20, pp. 127–9.

Schulz, M. 1995b, 'Utilisation of suspended bird nests by the Golden-tipped Bat, (*Kerivoula papuensis*) in Australia', *Mammalia*, vol. 59, pp. 280–3.

Schulz, M. 1996, 'Notes on selected bat species from Mt Surgeon and Chudleigh Park Stations, north of Hughenden', *Qld Nat.*, vol. 34, pp. 48–57.

Schulz, M. 1997a, 'Bats in bird nests in Australia: a review', *Mammal Review*, vol. 27, pp. 69–76.

Schulz, M. 1997b, 'The little bentwing bat, *Miniopterus australis*, roosting in a tree hollow', *Aust. Zool.*, vol. 30, p. 329.

Schulz, M. 1998, 'Bats and other fauna in disused fairy martin *Hirundo ariel* nests', *Emu*, vol. 98, pp. 184–91.

Schulz, M. 2000a, 'Diet and foraging behaviour of the Golden-tipped bat, *Kerivoula papuensis*: A spider specialist?', *J. Mammal.*, vol. 81, pp. 948–57.

Schulz, M. 2000b, 'Roosts used by the Golden-tipped bat, *Kerivoula papuensis* (Chiroptera: Vespertilionidae)', *J. Zool., Lond.*, vol. 250, pp. 467–78.

Schulz, M. & de Oliveira, M.C. 1995, 'Microchiropteran fauna of Kroombit Tops, central Queensland, including a discussion on survey techniques', *Aust. Zool.*, vol. 30, pp. 71–7.

Schulz, M., de Oliveira, M.C. & Eyre, T. 1994, 'Notes on the Little Pied Bat *Chalinolobus picatus* in Central Queensland', *Qld Nat.*, vol. 33, pp. 35–8.

Schulz, M. & Eyre, T. 2000, 'Habitat selection by the rare golden-tipped bat *Kerivoula papuensis'*, *Aust. Mammal.*, vol. 22, pp. 23–33.

Schulz, M. & Hannah, D. 1996, 'Notes on the Tube-nosed Insect Bat, *Murina florium* (Chiroptera, Vespertilionidae) from the Atherton Tableland, north-eastern Queensland, Australia', *Mammalia*, vol. 60, pp. 312–16.

Schulz, M. & Hannah, D. 1998, 'Relative abundance, diet and roost selection of the Tube-nosed Insect Bat, *Murina florium* of the Atherton Tablelands, Australia', *Wildl. Res.*, vol. 25, pp. 261–71.

Schulz, M. & Lumsden, L. 2004, *National Recovery Plan for the Christmas Island Pipistrelle* Pipistrellus murrayi, Commonwealth of Australia, Canberra.

Schulz, M. & Menkhorst, K. 1984, 'Notes on the Lesser wart-nosed horseshoe bat (*Hipposideros stenotis*)', *Aust. Bat Res. News*, vol. 20, pp. 14–16.

Schulz, M. & Menkhorst, K. 1986, 'Roost preferences of cave-dwelling bats at Pine Creek, Northern Territory', *Macroderma*, vol. 2, pp. 2–7.

Schulz, M. & Wainer, J. 1997, 'Diet of the Golden-tipped bat *Kerivoula papuensis* (Microchiroptera) from north-eastern New South Wales, Australia', *J. Zool., Lond.*, vol. 243, pp. 653–8.

Shaw, M. 1996, 'Some mammal observations from the McIlwraith Range including a new roost for the Dusky leaf-nosed bat, *Hipposideros ater'*, *Qld Nat.*, vol. 34, pp. 35–40.

Smales, I. & Koehler, S. 2005, *Targeted survey for Greater long-eared bat* Nyctophilus timoriensis *within the long term containment facility study area, Nowingi, Victoria*, Biosis Research report for Major Projects Victoria, Project no. 4689.

Spencer, H. 2005, 'Insectivorous flying-foxes', *Aust. Bat Soc. Newsl.*, vol. 25, pp. 27–8.

Spencer, H. & Coles, R. 1996, 'So you want to buy a bat detector!', *Aust. Bat Res. News.*, vol. 6, pp. 8–13.

Spencer, H.J. & Fleming, T.H. 1989, 'Roosting and foraging behaviour of the Queensland tube-nosed bat, *Nyctimene robinsoni* (Pteropodidae): preliminary radio-tracking study', *Aust. Wildl. Res.*, vol. 16, pp. 413–20.

Spencer, H.J., Palmer, C. & Parry-Jones, K. 1991, 'Movements of fruit-bats in Eastern Australia, determined by using radio-tracking', *Wildl. Res.*, vol. 18, pp. 463–8.

Stager, K.E. & Hall, L.S. 1983, 'A cave-roosting colony of the black flying-fox (*Pteropus alecto*) in Queensland, Australia', *J. Mammal.*, vol. 64, pp. 523–5.

Strahan, R. (ed.) 1995, *Mammals of Australia*, Australian Museum and Reed Books, Sydney.

Tate, G.H.H. 1941, 'Results of the Archbold Expeditions No 40. Notes on Vespertilionid Bats', *Bull. Amer. Mus. Nat. Hist.*, vol. 78, pp. 567–97.

Tate, G.H.H. 1942, 'Results of the Archbold Expeditions No 47. Review of the Vespertilionidae Bats, with special attention to genera and species of the Archbold Collections', *Bull. Amer. Mus. Nat. Hist.*, vol. 80, pp. 221–97.

Tate, G.H.H. 1952, 'Results of the Archbold Expeditions No 66. Mammals of Cape York Peninsula, with notes on the occurrence of rainforest in Queensland', *Bull. Amer. Mus. Nat. Hist.*, vol. 98, pp. 563–616.

Taylor, R.J. & O'Neill, M.G. 1986, 'Composition of the bat (Chiroptera: Vespertilionidae) communities in Tasmanian forests', *Aust. Mammal.*, vol. 9, pp. 125–30.

Taylor, R.J. & O'Neill, M.G. 1988, 'Summer activity patterns of insectivorous bats and their prey in Tasmania', *Aust. Wildl. Res.*, vol. 15, pp. 533–9.

Taylor, R.J., O'Neill, M.G. & Reardon, T.B. 1987, 'Tasmanian bats: Identification, distribution and natural history', *Papers Proc. Roy. Soc. Tas.*, vol. 121, pp. 109–19.

Taylor, R.J. & Savva, N.M. 1988, 'Use of roost sites by four species of bats in State Forest in south-eastern Tasmania', *Aust. Wildl. Res.*, vol. 15, pp. 637–45.

Taylor, R.J. & Savva, N.M. 1990, 'Annual activity and weight cycles of bats in south-eastern Tasmania', *Aust. Wildl. Res.*, vol. 17, pp. 181–8.

Thomas, O. 1915, 'Notes on the Genus *Nyctophilus*', *Ann. Mag. Nat. Hist.*, Series 8, vol. 15, pp. 493–9.

Thomson, B., Pavey, C. & Reardon, T. 2001, 'Recovery plan for cave-dwelling bats, *Rhinolophus philippinensis*, *Hipposideros semoni* and *Taphozous troughtoni* 2001–2005', The State of Queensland, Environmental Protection Agency.

Thomson, B.G. 1982, 'Records of *Eptesicus vulturnus* (Thomas) (Vespertilionidae: Chiroptera) from the Alice Springs Area, Northern Territory', *Aust. Mammal.*, vol. 5, pp. 69–70.

Thomson, B.G. 1991, *A Field Guide to the Bats of the Northern Territory*, Conservation Commission of the Northern Territory, Darwin.

Tian, L., Liang, B., Maeda, K., Metzner, W. & Zhang, S. 2004, 'Molecular studies on the classification of *Miniopterus schreibersii* (Chiroptera: Vespertilionidae) inferred from mitochondrial cytochrome b sequences', *Folia Zool.*, vol. 53, pp. 303–11.

Tidemann, C. 1993b, 'The contentious flying-fox', *Aust. Nat. Hist.*, vol. 24, pp. 36–45.

Tidemann, C. 1999, 'Biology and management of the Grey-headed flying-fox, *Pteropus poliocephalus*', *Acta Chiropterologica*, vol. 1, pp. 151–64.

Tidemann, C. 2002, 'Sustainable management of the Grey-headed flying-fox *Pteropus poliocephalus*', in P. Eby & D. Lunney (eds), *Managing Grey-headed Flying-fox as a Threatened species in New South Wales*, Royal Zoological Society of New South Wales, Mosman, pp. 122–7.

Tidemann, C.R. 1985, 'A study of the status, habitat requirements and management of the two species of bat on Christmas Island (Indian Ocean)', unpublished report to The Australian National Parks and Wildlife Service, Canberra, April 1985.

Tidemann, C.R. 1986, 'Morphological variation in Australian and island populations of Gould's Wattled Bat, *Chalinolobus gouldii* (Gray) (Chiroptera: Vespertilionidae)', *Aust. J. Zool.*, vol. 34, pp. 503–14.

Tidemann, C.R. 1987, 'Notes on the flying-fox, *Pteropus melanotus* (Chiroptera: Pteropodidae), on Christmas Island, Indian Ocean', *Aust. Mammal.*, vol. 10, pp. 89–91.

Tidemann, C.R. 1993a, 'Reproduction in the bats *Vespadelus vulturnus*, *V. regulus* and *V. darlingtoni* (Microchiroptera: Vespertilionidae) in coastal south-eastern Australia', *Aust. J. Zool.*, vol. 41, pp. 21–35.

Tidemann, C.R. & Flavel, S.C. 1987, 'Factors affecting choice of diurnal roost site by tree-hole bats (Microchiroptera) in south-eastern Australia', *Aust. Wildl. Res.*, vol. 14, pp. 459–73.

Tidemann, C.R. & Loughland, R.A. 1993, 'A harp trap for large Megachiroptera', *Wildl. Res.*, vol. 20, pp. 607–11.

Tidemann, C.R. & Nelson, J.E. 2004, 'Long-distance movements of the grey-headed flying-fox (*Pteropus poliocephalus*)', *J. Zool., Lond.*, vol. 263, pp. 141–6.

Tidemann, C.R., Priddel, D.M., Nelson, J.E. & Pettigrew, J.D. 1985, 'Foraging behaviour of the Australian Ghost Bat, *Macroderma gigas* (Microchiroptera: Megadermatidae)', *Aust. J. Zool.*, vol. 33, pp. 705–13.

Tidemann, C.R., Vardon, M.J., Loughland, R.A. & Brocklehurst, P.J. 1999, 'Dry season camps of flying-foxes (*Pteropus* spp.) in Kakadu World Heritage Area, north Australia', *J. Zool., Lond.*, vol. 247, pp. 155–63.

Tidemann, C.R. & Woodside, D.P. 1978, 'A collapsible bat trap and a comparison of results obtained with the trap and with mist nets', *Aust. Wildl. Res.*, vol. 5(3), pp. 355–62.

Tidemann, C.R., Yorkston, H.D. & Russack, A.J. 1994, 'The diet of cats, *Felis cattus*, on Christmas Island, Indian Ocean', *Wildl. Res.*, vol. 21, pp. 279–86.

Toop, J. 1985, 'Habitat requirements, survival strategies and ecology of the Ghost bat *Macroderma gigas* Dobson (Microchiroptera, Megadermatidae) in central coastal Queensland', *Macroderma*, vol. 1, pp. 37–44.

Troughton, E. le G. 1925, 'A revision of the genera *Taphozous* and *Saccolaimus* (Chiroptera) in Australia and New Guinea, including a new species, and a note on two Malayan forms', *Rec. Aust. Mus.*, vol. 14, pp. 313–39.

Troughton, E. le G. 1937, 'Six new bats (Microchiroptera) from the Australasian region', *Aust. Zool.*, vol. 8, pp. 274–81.

Troughton, E. le G. 1941, *Furred Animals of Australia*, 1st edn, Angus & Robertson, Sydney.

Troughton, E. le G. 1944, *Furred Animals of Australia*, 2nd edn, Angus & Robertson, Sydney.

Turbill, C. & Ellis, M. 2006, 'Distribution and abundance of the south-eastern form of the Greater Long-eared bat *Nyctophilus timoriensis*', *Aust. Mammal.*, vol. 28, pp. 1–6.

Turbill, C., Law, B.S. & Geiser, F. 2003, 'Summer torpor in a free-ranging bat from sub-tropical Australia', *J. Therm. Biol.*, vol. 28, pp. 223–6.

van der Ree, R., McDonnell, M.J., Temby, I., Nelson, J. & Whittingham, E. 2006, 'The establishment and dynamics of a recently established urban camp of flying-foxes (*Pteropus poliocephalus*) outside their geographic range', *J. Zool.*, vol. 268, pp. 177–85.

Van Deusen, H.M. 1973, 'History of Semon's horseshoe bat in Australia', *North Qld Nat.*, 42, pp. 4–5.

Van Deusen, H.M. & Koopman, K.F. 1971, 'Results of the Archbold Expeditions No. 95. The genus *Chalinolobus* (Chiroptera: Vespertilionidae) Taxonomic review of *Chalinolobus picatus*, *C. nigrogriseus* and *C. rogersi*', *Amer. Mus. Novit.*, vol. 2468, pp. 1–30.

Van Dyck, S. & Strahan, R. (eds) 2008, *Mammals of Australia*, 3rd edn, Reed New Holland, Sydney.

Vardon, M.J., Brocklehurst, P.J., Woinarski, J.C.Z., Cunningham, R.B., Donnelly, C.F. & Tidemann, C.R. 2001, 'Seasonal habitat use by flying-foxes, *Pteropus alecto* and *P. scapulatus* (Megachiroptera), in monsoonal Australia', *J. Zool., Lond.*, vol. 253, pp. 523–35.

Vardon, M.J. & Tidemann, C.R. 1998, 'Reproduction, growth and maturity in the black flying-fox, *Pteropus alecto* (Megachiroptera: Pteropodidae)', *Aust. J. Zool.*, vol. 46, pp. 329–44.

Vardon, M.J. & Tidemann, C.R. 1998, 'Black flying-foxes, *Pteropus alecto*: are they different in north Australia?', *Aust. Mammal.*, vol. 20, pp. 131–3.

Vardon, M.J. & Tidemann, C.R. 1999, 'Flying-foxes, (*Pteropus alecto* and *P. scapulatus*) in the Darwin region, north Australia: patterns in camp size and structure', *Aust. J. Zool.*, vol. 47, pp. 411–23.

Vardon, M.J. & Tidemann, C.R. 2000, 'The black flying-fox (*Pteropus alecto*) in north Australia: juvenile mortality and longevity', *Aust. J. Zool.*, vol. 48, pp. 91–7.

Vestjens, W.J.M. & Hall, L.S. 1977, 'Stomach contents of forty-two species of bats from the Australasian region', *Aust. Wildl. Res.*, vol. 4, pp. 25–35.

Walton, D.W., Busby, J.R. & Woodside, D.P. 1992, 'Recorded and predicted distribution of *Phoniscus papuensis* (Dobson, 1878) in Australia', *Aust. Zool.*, vol. 28, pp. 52–5.

Walton, D.W. & Richardson, B.J. (eds) 1987, *Fauna of Australia Volume 1B. Mammalia*, Australian Government Publishing Service, Canberra.

Webber, J. 1992, 'Preliminary observations on the Northern Blossom-bat *Macroglossus minimus* in captivity', *N.T. Nat.*, vol. 13, pp. 25–9.

Whybird, O. 1998, 'Methods of sampling forest bats and bat activity above the ground', *Aust. Bat Soc. Newsl.*, vol. 11, pp. 31–5.

Williams, A.J. & Dickman, C.R. 2004, 'The ecology of insectivorous bats in the Simpson Desert, Central Australia: habitat use', *Aust. Mammal.*, vol. 26, pp. 205–14.

Williams, N.S.G., McDonnell, M.J., Phelan, G.K., Keim, L.D. & van der Ree, R. 2006, 'Range extension due to urbanisation: Increased food resources attract grey-headed flying-foxes (*Pteropus poliocephalus*) to Melbourne', *Austral. Ecol.*, vol. 31, pp. 190–8.

Wilson, P. 1985, 'Does *Dobsonia* (Chiroptera: Pteropodidae) have a fling?', *Macroderma*, vol. 1, pp. 53–5.

Wilson, P.D. 2006, 'The distribution of the Greater broad-nosed bat *Scoteanax rueppellii* (Microchiroptera: Vespertilionidae) in relation to climate and topography', *Aust. Mammal.*, vol. 28, pp. 77–85.

Winter, J. & Atherton, R. 1982, 'A new collection of the Papuan sheath-tail bat, *Taphozous mixtus*, in Australia', *Aust. Bat Res. News*, 18, pp. 9–10.

Woinarski, J. & Milne, D. 2002a, 'Arnhem sheathtail bat, *Taphozous kapalgensis*', *Threatened species of the Northern Territory*, Threatened Species Information Sheet, Parks and Wildlife Commission of the Northern Territory.

Woinarski, J. & Milne, D. 2002b, 'Arnhem leaf-nosed bat, *Hipposideros (diadema) inornata*', *Threatened species of the Northern Territory*, Threatened Species Information Sheet, Parks and Wildlife Commission of the Northern Territory.

Woinarski, J. & Milne, D. 2002c, 'Bare-rumped sheathtail bat, *Saccolaimus saccolaimus*', *Threatened species of the Northern Territory*, Threatened Species Information Sheet, Parks and Wildlife Commission of the Northern Territory.

Woodside, D. 1984, 'Gould's Long-eared Bat. The cute or the ugly?', *Aust. Nat. Hist.*, vol. 21, pp. 300–1.

Woodside, D.P. & Long, A. 1984, 'Observations on the feeding habits of the Greater broad-nosed bat, *Nycticeius rueppellii* (Chiroptera: Vespertilionidae)', *Aust. Mammal.*, vol. 7, pp. 121–9.

Woodside, D.P. & Taylor, K.J. 1985, 'Echolocation calls of fourteen bats from eastern New South Wales', *Aust. Mammal.*, vol. 8, pp. 279–97.

Worthington-Wilmer, J. & Barratt, E. 1996, 'A non-lethal method of tissue sampling for genetic studies of Chiropterans', *Bat Res. News*, vol. 37, pp. 1–3.

Worthington-Wilmer, J., Hall, L., Barratt, E. & Moritz, C. 1999, 'Genetic structuring and male-mediated gene flow in the Ghost bat (*Macroderma gigas*)', *Evolution*, vol. 53, pp. 1582–91.

Worthington-Wilmer, J., Moritz, C., Hall, L. & Toop, J. 1994, 'Extreme population structuring in the threatened Ghost bat, *Macroderma gigas*: evidence from mitochondrial DNA', *Biol. Science*, vol. 257, no. 1349, pp. 193–8.

Young, R.A. 1975, 'Ageing criteria, pelage colour polymorphism and moulting in *Rhinolophus megaphyllus* (Chiroptera) from south-eastern Queensland, Australia', *Mammalia*, vol. 39, pp. 75–111.

Young, R.A. 1979, 'Observations on parturition, litter size, and foetal development at birth in the chocolate wattled bat, *Chalinolobus morio* (Vespertilionidae)', *Vic. Nat.*, 96, pp. 90–1.

Young, R.A. 1980, 'Observations on the vulnerability of two species of wattled bats (*Chalinolobus*) to diurnal avian predators', *Vic. Nat.*, vol. 97, pp. 258–62.

Young, R.A. 2001, 'The eastern horseshoe bat, *Rhinolophus megaphyllus*, in south-east Queensland, Australia: colony demography and dynamics, activity levels, seasonal weight changes and capture–recapture analyses', *Wildl. Res.*, vol. 28, pp. 425–34.

Young, R.A. & Ford, G.I. 1998, 'Range extension of the Little Forest bat *Vespadelus vulturnus* (Chiroptera: Vespertilionidae) into a semi-arid area of central Queensland, Australia', *Aust. Zool.*, vol. 30, pp. 392–7.

Young, R.A. & Ford, G.I. 2000, 'Bat fauna of a semi-arid environment in central western Queensland, Australia', *Wildl. Res.*, vol. 27, pp. 203–15.

Young, R.A., Ford, G.I., McDonnell, P. & Mathieson, M. 1996. 'A review of information on the pied bat *Chalinolobus picatus*', *Aust. Bat Soc. Newsl.*, vol. 7, p. 63.

Youngson, W.K. & McKenzie, N.L. 1977, 'An improved bat-collecting technique', *Bull. Aust. Mammal. Soc.*, vol. 3, pp. 20–1.

# Index to common names

# Index to scientific names